THE FISH MARKET

THE FISH MARKET

Inside the Big-Money
Battle for the Ocean and
Your Dinner Plate

LEE VAN DER VOO

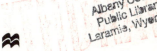
St. Martin's Press
New York

www.stmartins.com

Design by Kelly S. Too

Library of Congress Cataloging-in-Publication Data

Names: Van der Voo, Lee, author.
Title: The fish market : inside the big money battle for the ocean and your dinner plate / Lee van der Voo.
Description: New York : St. Martin's Press, 2016. | Includes bibliographical references and index.
Identifiers: LCCN 2016024624| ISBN 9781250079107 (hardcover) | ISBN 9781466891739 (e-book)
Subjects: LCSH: Fisheries—Privatization—United States. | Sustainable fisheries—United States. | Fisheries—Economic aspects—United States.
Classification: LCC SH328 .V36 2016 | DDC 333.95/60973—dc23
LC record available at https://lccn.loc.gov/2016024624

First edition: November 2016

10 9 8 7 6 5 4 3 2 1

We pressed against
The limits of the sea:
I saw there were no oceans left
For scavengers like me.
I made it to the forward deck
I blessed our remnant fleet—
And then consented to be wrecked
A thousand kisses deep.

—Leonard Cohen, "A Thousand Kisses Deep"

Now fisheries experts speculate on the possibility and the probability of literally "farming the ocean." These experts talk of huge undersea fish "ranches" where fish are herded like cattle and fenced in by curtains of air-bubbles, and of artificial water-circulation techniques being used to increase plankton productivity. It takes only a lively imagination to envision whole cities under the sea.

—From the *U.S. Department of the Interior Annual Report, 1970,* quoted in *From Abundance to Scarcity: A History of U.S. Marine Fisheries Policy* by Michael L. Weber

CONTENTS

━━━━━━

THIS BOOK IS THE PRODUCT of a lost bet. That's the truth. In winter 2011, I had just written a story for a regional magazine about salmon fishing. And I was in a bar in Portland, Oregon, a wood-paneled place downtown called Cassidy's, loudly proclaiming that I was never going to do it again. Fish stories are boring, I said. Nobody reads them. There's nothing in them but a bunch of fishermen haggling over who gets to catch what.

I was with a small group of writers, most of whom agreed by glazing over. *See what I mean?* I thought. But there was one exception. A colleague had just taken a job with the nonprofit group Ecotrust and bet me on the spot that he could get me to write another fish story. Then he started telling me that the United States was privatizing its oceans through a policy called "catch shares." And that, while the work was dovetailing with a lot of foodie-centric and eco-conscious buzzwords, it was also creating class warfare on the seas, upending fishing families and unmooring fishing towns all over the nation. His was one of a handful of groups brewing antidotes to the fallout. The more he talked, the more I knew I'd lose the bet.

I was doing a lot of food and sustainability writing at the time, so the idea of goofy policy hiding behind eco-friendly jargon wasn't exactly new. To a journalist, greenwashing was the consumer plague of the millennium, amping up while organic food shifted from back-to-the-land hippies to the mainstream. By then, organics were a $25 billion industry in the United States, one in which fair-trade and environmentally conscious brands were garnering a premium from people dining on a do-no-harm ethos. Consumers who didn't want their eggs laid by caged chickens or their beef culled from penned cows were easy marks. I was already covering an enormous number of bunk-but-presumably-green-leaning food and product schemes. And given that the seafood counter was the place inside the grocery store where people looked the most lost, it seemed like a reasonable venue for a hoodwinking.

I was lucky the wager was only beer. A few months later I was on a plane to Alaska with loose orders from an editor to go sniff around. In between, I'd managed to get a handle on what catch shares were. The quick way to describe them is to say they're like cap-and-trade for fish; they deploy caps on the amount of fish that can be caught, then dole out the rights to fish them among qualifying entities. Those who qualify can be fishermen, boats, corporations—the design varies. It takes some history in the industry to get a piece. But once those rights are awarded by the government, whoever holds that slice of the pie holds exclusive access to a corresponding percentage of fish. Those rights are privately controlled after that. By law, the government can take them back at any time. But it hasn't. Every catch share in America has remained steadily in private hands since 1992. Now the rights to catch fish are private market assets that trade hotter in places like Alaska than brick-and-mortar real estate.

Promoters of catch shares are always quick to say that they're not privatizing the fish in the ocean, just the rights to catch them. It's a small distinction that translates, in practice, to the same thing. But the delicate public relations dance that attends that particular point has been whirling for the better part of a decade in America. For good reason, I've surmised. There is a strange marriage at the heart of this policy: one between the environmental lobby and privatization interests. And the effort, though well intentioned by many within organizations like the Environmental Defense Fund, has been substantially funded by conservatives and property-rights promoters, chiefly the founders of Walmart, facts that would give anybody with enviro cred pause if they were better known.

Before I went to Alaska, I spent two days in Oregon's Rogue Valley with a man named John Enge, a fisheries expert who ran a seafood-politics blog called Alaska Cafe. He was a saint of a person who is no longer with us. He sat me at his kitchen table and patiently brain-dumped at me until I understood three things: First, the private property rights attending catch shares had locked many fishermen and even whole communities out of the oceans. Second, catch shares had created powerful landlords on water. And third, as those landlords grew more powerful, catch shares were converting fishermen from proud family-business sorts into sharecroppers who were leasing their access to the sea from wealthy and increasingly corporate power brokers.

That was in 2012. What I'd envisioned was a quick jaunt to Alaska and a handful of stories. Instead, my trip turned into a four-year reporting odyssey that ended, back in Alaska, in the bunks of a fishing boat with a couple of twenty-something dudes. In between, I learned that I do indeed get seasick. And that a careful regimen of non-drowsy Dramamine, vanilla yogurt, and green-yellow Gatorade keeps it to a no-fuss affair. I also traveled to every catch share in America to walk the docks and talk to fishermen about how catch shares had changed their world. Some were kind enough to take me fishing and show me how that world worked. For context, I spent countless days in the fluorescent-lit meetings of US fishery management councils, the regulatory bodies that control commercial fishing in America. And I talked to chefs and fishermen, seafood buyers and suppliers, conservation groups, lobbyists, and political sorts, many of whom believed very deeply in catch shares. I learned there is a decent business case for privatizing the oceans. And that, while it can conflict with the social-equity ideas that many eco-conscious eaters go in for, it may be one that consumers find quite valid.

After years of staring at it, I've come to think of this as a David-and-Goliath kind of tale. It's about the fight between seafarers—those who held out against privatization—and powerful conservationists who were willing to trade privatization for both environmental gain and the most sustainable, traceable seafood in the world. It is a story full of grizzled, off-beat characters; action and adventure on the vast oceans off America's shores; good food; and big, big money. It caused me to see fishermen as just a particularly colorful brand of organic farmer. And catch-share holdouts as the only resisters to the denationalization of a natural resource most Americans believe they still own.

But Americans don't own the fish in their oceans anymore, not really.

This book is the straight-ahead telling of why that is true and how we got here. It is framed within the tale of a single seafood brand—Gulf Wild—as its creators try to trace each individual fish from the sea to the dinner plate. Interwoven within their adventure are the fates of those left behind: small-boat fishermen, crews, and whole communities.

This story matters. Wild fish, unlike beef and chicken, will never have an easy path to the dinner plate. And managing that journey is one of the most complex tasks any policymaker can undertake. It is also phenomenally difficult for the marketplace to finagle. And it's something conservationists have rightly tried to clean up. That's why consumers ought to know, when they pay a premium for sustainable wild seafood, what it is they are really buying.

THE FISH MARKET

Bering Sea

"Monsanto on the Ocean"

PHOTO BY DAVE WAGENHEIM

Dave Wagenheim drops his knife into the head of a pollock. A little flick of the wrist, a poke from the edge of the blade, and the otoliths role out. Two tiny circular bones. The move is practiced enough that he can do it now, over and over, without much attention to how. Inscribed with growth rings, the bones are to the fish what rings of the trunk are to the tree. A biologist for a company contracted by the National Marine Fisheries Service, it's Wagenheim's job to collect the rings.

It's tedious work. And not at all helped by the unending rise and fall of the factory floor. It's no ordinary factory. Instead, he's standing at his sampling table with its measuring stick and its scale inside a 272-foot ship on the Bering Sea. The tide beneath it is sometimes so strong that the work requires a kind of balancing act with the scale at the end of his arms, making Wagenheim into some kind of stumbling maître d'.

But despite its undulations, this place is a firestorm of busy. He stops its conveyor belts only long enough to collect his sample of fish. The rest of the time those belts are rattling like a roller coaster inside the lower deck of the boat, so that the sound of their creaking is like a kind of white noise beneath all other things. Hair-netted workers line up alongside it, toiling in a constant state of motion. Although this vessel rides the most remote waters surrounding North America, it's a

surprisingly wakeful place. Three shifts a day tend a mostly auto-
mated menagerie of flash freezers and fish-gutting machines and meat
grinders.

Wagenheim is among the luckiest on board. He works only twelve
hours a day and can move around freely—the majority of everyone else
being confined to the factory, their quarters, or a few common areas.
Still, within six years, he will have a different career entirely, running the
vegan food cart Viva! Vegetarian Grill in downtown Eugene, Oregon,
where he will describe his newly flesh-free endeavor as the only way
he can participate in the food-service industry without feeling like he
is polishing a turd. But in 2008, the last year Wagenheim worked as
an at-sea biologist, he labored in what has since become lauded as
the world's largest sustainable fishery: Alaska pollock.

In short, boats like this one are where your Filet-O-Fish comes
from. Your Seafood Sensation from Subway. They are the origin of
Burger King's Extra Long Fish Sandwich and the fish fries and sandwiches at restaurant chains like Long John Silver's. Beyond the massive
amount of fast food fueled by pollock, the fish is also funneled to a
vast array of boxed fare: fish sticks, fillets, and breaded squares found
in the freezer aisles of grocery stores. It is also the impersonator of the
crab, and sends a tidy amount of roe and *kamaboko*—a kind of cured
krab with a *k*—to Japanese markets. A handful of potions convert
what's left to fish meals and oils, too.

Which is why the first fish to fall out of the holding tank and onto
the conveyor belt belong to Wagenheim. He steps up to fill his basket,
waving off the workers in the headphones and rubber gloves that man
the stations along the belt. He eyes the gap between the belt and the
holding tank. Sometimes things get stuck in there. Sea lions, for example. Halibut the size of German shepherds. Salmon. All are occasional
collateral damage in the pollock industry, the mammals the main reason marine biologists were put on these boats in the first place.

He weighs the fish. Sexes them. Writes it all down on the neat government forms provided. "Pollock. Species number 201. Haul number 487. Sex M. Length 42 [centimeters]. Weight .64 [kilograms]." He readies the otoliths to be peered at through a microscope in some distant laboratory. Five pairs from each basket. No more than twenty-five a day.

Right now, these notes by Wagenheim and his counterparts, scientific sheriffs riding the seas from Dutch Harbor to the Bering Strait, keep this industry on its leash. And the leash is part of what gives pollock its certification as environmentally sustainable. Biologists on board, counting the harvest, carefully measuring all the things that pollock boats kill by accident. Such data helps the government set the bar on how much pollock this industry can catch to avoid fishing the species, and others, into extinction. It's a lot. Two and a half billion pounds of pollock, give or take a few million, have been captured on these waters annually for the past two decades. It's the weight of the world's largest aircraft carrier with a blue whale riding on the deck. By the industry's estimate, it feeds billions.

The success these boats—and an entourage of smaller ones—have at feeding so many people, and so cheaply, while mostly curtailing collateral damage, accounts in part for the ubiquitous markets pollock's champions have built. Though pollock boats kill, at last check, 260,000 salmon a year and an annual average of about 470,000 pounds of halibut, this accidental catch is a tiny fraction of the pollock haul. The ongoing effort to bring science and invention to bear on avoiding such waste—it is illegal to trawl for salmon or halibut, so they are thrown back dead—has produced everything from real-time mapping of non-target fish to nets with escape hatches and trapdoors to help them get away.

Such efforts combine with the size of the catch to make pollock attractive to high-volume buyers eager for sustainable bragging rights. Alaska pollock is certified sustainable by the Marine Stewardship Council, a London-based certifying agency that balances the health of the pollock with its impact on surrounding aquatic life—for a price. Everyone who handles pollock, on these trawl boats and elsewhere, is certified to a chain of custody so that no imposters creep in. There are also audits and scientific assessments and third-party overseers. The task of satisfying them is not so easy.

But beyond the selling point of the ecolabel, there's another thing that makes pollock the denizen of the fish stick, the fast-food menu, and, more recently, the sustainable sushi scene: this is factory fishing. Pollock arrives at buyers' doorstep looking not at all like fish, but freakishly like dimensional lumber. On board trawlers while at sea, or on land later, pollock is pressed and frozen into blocks. These so-called fillet blocks are made to standard size so that they are easily fed to the next series of food-processing conveyors belts, making them ready protein fodder for just about anything. Half-moons of *kamaboko*. Cubes and rectangles for sandwiches. Tubes for fake crab legs and fish sticks. Or recut into fillets, then breaded and striped with grill-tread.

Wagenheim likes a lot about the job of minding this catch from the factory floor. He likes timing the lowering and the raising of the trawl nets, browsing the captain's logs, and standing on two legs above that vast swath of water between the United States and Russia. But he sees the contradictions between pollock's sustainable image and its reality. From his vantage of all there is to see in this industry, he sees things he could not have imagined from the foot of the backlit menu at a McDonald's or the freezer aisle of a Kroger. In that way, the ship is beyond most people's imaginings.

Most don't assume that their fish is caught by a ship the size of a Home Depot, a football field's length from bow to stern. Or envision its several decks and dozens of factory workers, its bunk beds or its massive galley kitchen, or the numerous and sometimes questionably performing toilets. Harder still to associate what happens on the deck with that ubiquitous blue label: the Marine Stewardship Council's insignia check arching over a fisheye.

It's a symbol that gives no hint of the huge net lowered into the water, the ropes as thick as baseballs, or the winch that hauls it, the hook alone larger than a man's head. It doesn't suggest a net that unfurls across the sea and drops, somewhere west of Alaska, and rises again full to the width of a manufactured home and twice the length, bulging with fish, the whole deck creaking and rattling with the effort to contain the weight, anywhere from seventy to two hundred tons.

When people look at the fish sticks in the freezer aisle and see the sustainable label, many are more likely to think of that Gorton's Fisherman on the box—the man with the trim beard, the yellow slicker, the wooden captain's wheel—rather than the people of enormous strength whose job it is to tend a factory trawler's net. Those men don't stand at wooden wheels scanning the sea in the open air. They are instead alternately hulks and quiet tailors, at one moment dropping ton after ton of fish into a holding tank below deck and squatting in piles of mesh in the next, sewing, patching, mending. They have to be watchful, ready to run if the net's cables break, the awful tinning snap of those loose whips scattering them. The cables can wreck a man, and killed one in the eleven years ending in 2012, during which accidents on these boats maimed more than four hundred people.

Other things about this industry are not so intuitive. For example, that most of the workers who sign contracts for tours aboard these ships, five months being the average, work two shifts a day, seven days a week, and do things as rote as stacking boxes inside a freezer, one after another. A large number of the people who sign up are hired from impoverished places, these jobs being a saving grace for many of them. But they are helpless to leave without severe financial penalties. And those penalties are often so steep that people desperate for land, people who simply can't hack it, have been known to feed their fingers to the factory's machines on purpose to escape.

What is most difficult to envision amid all those freezer boxes and all that fast food, however, is that when it's all over, the billions of pounds of pollock captured from American waters every year belong to a small number of people. It's not just that the proceeds of the catch belong to those who own the boats, that's a given. This is America, after all. Boat owners earn their share of the roughly $250 million in annual revenue. But what they also own are the rights to the fish. Alaska pollock is a privatized fishery. And they are its keepers.

———

How THIS HAPPENED is a long story. But the brief truth of it is that it began as an effort to recapture the bounty of American oceans from foreign-owned trawl boats and ended with an exclusive list of who could fish pollock.

It's a story that dates back a few decades, to the seventies, when Americans didn't have much of a hand in what happened off their westernmost shore. The United States didn't have big boats to harvest pollock then. Up until that time, it was regarded as a kind of seafood surplus instead, a deep-sea oddball that Americans hadn't yet found a use for or a way to catch. That changed when foreign trawlers came to the Bering Sea to capture it for themselves. Recognizing pollock fishing could be their own bountiful market, fishing industry and political leaders aligned behind the Magnuson-Stevens Act, the seafood equivalent of the Farm Bill. In 1976, when it passed, it kicked the foreign boats out. It claimed the two hundred miles off the coastal United States for Americans, then laid down the rules for fishing there. The law became, in effect, a kind of Constitution of the sea.

Within a couple of decades, however, the plan for managing pollock fishing shifted from keeping foreign boats out to controlling the massive domestic fleet that took over. Through the eighties and nineties, so many boats took to pollock that the Bering Sea had become the scene of an aquatic gold rush. The government, worried about the potential for overfishing, legislated how the boats could fish. But when it cut the fishing season to just two months a year, there were clashes on the water and squabbles over the haul.

The solution that emerged in 1998 remains today: the Alaska Fisheries Act Pollock Cooperatives. It was a long name for saying that $90 million was spent buying boats out of the water. And that after the government thinned the herd, it handed the rights to fish the pollock to the boats that remained, and thus to their owners. The industry paid for $70 million of the cost of its exclusive access to pollock over time. Taxpayers bore the rest, fated to buy their fish sticks from the same pack of newly minted millionaires who would henceforth control the resource.

This arrangement of gifting the rights to fish to boats or people or to the private companies that control them has a lot of names. In America it gained the most momentum in the Obama administration under the moniker "catch sharing," a polite-sounding term that implied things got shared when what they really got was privatized. Elsewhere catch-share policies have been known by a suite of other names, mostly letters—ITQs, IFQs, sometimes TURFs, or just "rights-based fishing." They had been tried abroad, but pollock was only the third time they were tried in the United States. Today, what the pollock cooperative has left the country with is 102 boats owned by 132 entities that are allowed to fish a multimillion-dollar natural resource exclusively. While some boats are small, the largest share of the pollock is caught by just sixteen factory-sized ships owned by six companies, five of them based in Seattle. In its best year, revenue from this fish soared to $385 million, with the boats that fished that year earning an average of $3.4 million.

Though pollock was corralled into US territory as a public resource, the public enjoys no commercial access to this fish on the Bering Sea today and no significant financial benefit from its capture, aside from low-cost access to fish sticks and fast food. A great many people will say that's enough. This has always been an industrial, deep-sea fishery, one impossible to fish with the small boats helmed by fishermen from nearby Bering Sea islands. And there is no disputing that the pollock cooperative feeds people all over the world at a price most can afford. But there are also critics of the system, who argue that it benefits an elite class of owners and differs from other industries in which a natural resource is extracted from a public place for a price. The timber, ranching, mining, wind, and solar industries, to give a few obvious examples, all pay lease fees for the use of natural resources and land in America. Rent, basically, for using a thing everyone agrees belongs to everybody. The pollock cooperative does not.

And this is where we have arrived in American seafood: at this union of privatization and conservation.

Though conceived as an economic device, today conservationists regard catch shares as more of an environmental tool than anything else. In the seas these groups envision, excess boats can be thinned, ownership rights bestowed, and those rights are assumed to translate into good stewardship of the oceans and fish. The idea is not so much that catch shares are a new religion. It's that money motivates people. And if you give fishermen a piece of the ocean, they will take care of the ocean or they will lose their money.

There are other selling points. Preassigning catch, as catch shares do, can eliminate many of the safety issues that attend fishing. And, as pollock illustrates, it also steadies the seafood supply in a way that builds markets from nothing and makes seafood vastly more valuable over time. Supply begets demand and begets jobs, too. And so the fish stick rose to power.

But much the same way the pollock catch share locked foreign competitors out, it locked other people out, including some neighboring islands where economies are sputtering, even as factory fishing makes life more complicated there. Such exclusion is a problem that continues, even while catch shares became the national model for sustainable seafood. And it's why Pat Pletnikoff, the mayor of the Bering

Sea town of St. George on St. George Island, is not so fond of privatization.

————

PLETNIKOFF FEARED TRAWL boats would be the new barons of the sea when he first began sidling up to these ships on the hunt for halibut. His island has a lot of experience with oligarchies. St. George is almost the farthest west place in America, an island so scoured by wind that trees don't grow there, nor vegetables. Yet centuries ago, Aleut natives traversed hundreds of frigid sea miles to visit St. George, coveted as it was for its fur seal hunting and its fishing.

That yearning was contagious enough that St. George has since been occupied by two governments and numerous corporations and can now claim an unseemly history of forced labor, kidnapping, and war. Russian and American corporations once jockeyed for the island's seal pelts so steadily that today most of the people who remain here are descendants of slaves, captured in Siberia and the Aleutian Islands and put to work by those same companies. The US government took control of St. George in 1910 and technically freed its people. But slavery begat servitude to the US Bureau of Fisheries while other jobs were scarce. It stayed that way until government-sponsored seal clubbing peppered the nightly news in the 1980s. Shortly thereafter, the federal Fur Seal Act ended seal clubbing, and the island's economy.

The government left St. George then. When it did it gave the community $8 million in reparations and told its people to build a fishing community. The $8 million didn't cut it, and the fishing era never came. Instead, St. George now sits in the middle of the most productive seafood waters in America with very little involvement in the seafood industry.

Pollock processed aboard the factory trawlers is ferried past St. George to Dutch Harbor instead, a twenty-four-hour trip away by boat, then flown to wherever pollock is processed into foodstuff and eaten. Much of that pollock makes the cross-country trip to Gorton's Seafood in Gloucester, Massachusetts, where it is sliced and coated with breading and shipped to retail stores or to McDonald's. It's a journey that's so dialed in to the global food trade that if one were to eat a Filet-O-Fish sandwich back in Alaska, say in Anchorage, the fish inside has already crossed the continental United States twice.

Which accounts for why, when Pletnikoff sees the trawlers pass St. George every few days, driving past its rocky coastline on their slow march from Dutch Harbor to the fishing grounds and back, a certain bitterness takes hold. That so few boats and their owners control a bounty that could be a lifeline for his town—it chafes him.

St. George has struggled mightily since the fur seal market ended. There are very few jobs. Not a single business license. Only ten people have access to commercial fishing. Because there is only half a harbor to bridge the gap between the island and the nearby bounty of the sea—a well-meaning effort to jump-start the fishing industry that was never fully funded—only a few small boats port there. The larger trawl vessels that otherwise dominate the sea cannot stop, as they sometimes do on neighboring St. Paul Island, and leave a few dollars.

"Every year the industry takes about $2 billion in gains out of this fish resource on the Bering Sea. Not one plug nickel sticks to St. George," Pletnikoff says.

The pollock industry does set aside 10 percent to benefit nearby Alaska native communities, as do other Bering Sea fisheries, and St. George is among the beneficiaries, at least on paper. But St. George hasn't emerged a winner in the local competition for the funds. It used to receive about $100,000 a year, which Pletnikoff spent on fuel to fire up the town's diesel-powered electric plant. Now the money doesn't come anymore. And Pletnikoff hasn't been successful in lobbying state authorities and Congress, the president and the Coast Guard, the state of Alaska, nonprofits, and other agencies for help to complete St. George's harbor so that more of its residents can fish halibut for a living, a fish the community's small boats can handle.

And now that fish is imperiled, partly by trawlers for both pollock and another sustainably certified fishery for groundfish.

What he had hoped for was something else. In the tight steel cabin of the fifty-foot troller the *Taty Z*, Pletnikoff navigates the boat at a careful distance—a mile or so—away from a trawler. He invites his youngest crewman, an eighteen-year-old, to ride shotgun. Perched in the leather seat on the boat's starboard side, the sun shining on the water, Pletnikoff steers the boat through the sea's rocky waves while the kid looks on.

"There are no signs saying 'Fish Halibut Here,'" Pletnikoff tells him. He points to the tight lines stacking up on the face of the depth sounder. "There. See the steep drop there?" The kid peers at the screen on the left of the throttle, one of a handful of electronics ringing the wooden dash. It shows the edge of the Zhemchug Canyon, with depths of about twelve hundred or fifteen hundred feet on one side and more than twenty-four hundred feet on the other. It's a place where the ocean currents break and change and where driving can be tough.

Pletnikoff guides the *Taty Z* along the rim, the tight stacks of lines falling into the center of his chart plotter, gently sloping to one side, flat on the other. There are halibut along these ridges and walls. But they don't just hang around. They're migratory fish, with a sprawling range from north of Alaska to California. Different times of year they can be found on the shelf in the Bering Sea. But when it's colder they go south. Pletnikoff believes that if young people can learn how the fish live in this kind of terrain, how they migrate at certain depths and at certain times of the year, they can make a living on the island. Put down their iPads and get out of their parents' houses.

He gives up the captain's seat and lets the kid drive, watching to be sure the nearby trawler is a safe distance away, where its wake won't toss the *Taty Z* or tangle or cut its fishing lines when they turn those lines loose. Though the *Taty Z* rides low and looks heavy with the galley on half the deck, it has a mean thrust. Pletnikoff knows such things will hold a young man's attention. Maybe the fishing will follow.

Soon they see it: halibut territory. A blend of ridge and rock. Pletnikoff sends the kid back to the deck. He takes over the driving, slowly now, while the crewmen drop long lines of baited hooks, each rope eighteen hundred feet, the hooks spaced at intervals the length of a man.

There used to be a sixty-mile radius around St. George and its neighbor, St. Paul, but the invisible ring that protected the area from fishing was dismantled through some combination of political and industry pressure years ago. Those protections covered the Zhemchug Canyon, which is both wider and deeper than the Grand Canyon, and its neighbor the Pribilof Canyon. Two of the five canyons in the eastern Bering Sea, they are considered two of the largest underwater canyons in the world. And they are critical habitat for fish. People with lengthy histories on this water regard them as a kind of ecological fountain from which fish flow in near-mythic abundance and feed the surrounding ecosystem, including the ecosystems of the islands.

Those who live near the canyons, like Pletnikoff, say the ocean has changed greatly since trawl boats came. And environmental groups like Greenpeace have sought to make the canyons off limits to trawling.

Though the pollock still return in enough abundance for the fishing to continue, meeting the threshold for a sustainable fishery, the industrial-scale capture of this fish that's low in the region's food chain may be shifting most everything else. There have been steep declines in the populations of the pollock's top predators—from whales and sea lions to several species of seal, including the fur seals that used to be the mainstay of the island. Where its shores serve as rookeries for seal rearing, Pletnikoff has stood and watched young fur seals die of starvation while older seals struggle to find food nearby. Seabirds, their killing by sonar cables mostly unaddressed by the trawl industry, are also dwindling. And now halibut are also in decline.

Scientists have yet to determine why, blaming everything from past overfishing to climate change, but trawlers for pollock, cod, sole, and flounder are at least partly to blame. Together in some years, the boats accidentally kill more than double the amount of halibut caught by the hook-and-line fishers who catch and sell it as a main source of income.

All of this sends morale plummeting on the island. Though St. George still boasts 210 species of birds, and reindeer and Arctic fox still roam the grasslands, the human population is falling fast. Families seeking hopeful futures for children, or for themselves, or just eager to escape the difficulty of life in such a remote and declining place, have trickled so steadily off the island that only eighty people remain and only five children attend the public school. That's five fewer than the number St. George needs to receive educational funding from the state of Alaska. If the school closes, Pletnikoff believes it could be the end of St. George.

"It's so sad to see this community die," he says.

To hear him speak of it is gut-wrenching. As the push for ocean sustainability in America and abroad now drives a worldwide push for catch shares, fewer, bigger boats do more of the fishing. Small-boat fishers who once made homes in coastal towns are much rarer. And in places, they are being stripped of their access to the sea, and of the cultures that once tethered them to it.

"I never thought there was anything wrong with a family-owned farm," Pletnikoff says. "There was a certain amount of pride. Fisheries were always that way. They were a mom-and-pop operation. Every child in the family became a fisherman and loved it. Nowadays it is nothing like that. It is Monsanto on the ocean."

Monsanto on the ocean. It is hard to know, when we look for that blue label, that big business is a part of what we are getting. But so it is.

Pletnikoff doesn't fish anymore. In 2009 he retired from fishing, an old man. And one year after that, catch shares became national policy in America. As they took hold across the nation, fishermen everywhere began to scrap for their place on the ocean. While they did, they began to align into two neat columns: winners and losers.

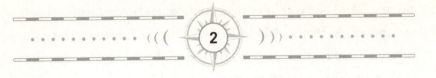

Gulf Wild

*How to Make Money in Seafood
Just by Watching TV*

to explain why De La Cruz—a work-a-day sort with no particular hunger for fine things—took a second mortgage on his home and bet it all on derelict boats and grouper permits.

But that's exactly what he did. Egged on in part by watching catch shares come to *Deadliest Catch* on TV, De La Cruz even cajoled his best friend, Matt Joswig, to join him in buying their piece of the sea. Caught up in their own daydreams—mostly De La Cruz's—and a state in which real money had been moving around the economy in clumps like Monopoly paper, each had sucked $250,000 in equity out of his home before De La Cruz went on the manic errand of spending it. The aim was to control as much grouper as they could before catch shares, which looked to be headed to law in the Gulf of Mexico, took hold.

Now, in a few short minutes, the duo would either be rich men or facing foreclosure. De La Cruz looked at Joswig, his friend of thirty years, who was sitting beside him in a similar state of unease. Already a powerhouse in business, Joswig would be okay, though considerably less wealthy, if things went bad. He was running a successful concrete company with 110 people on the payroll. For De La Cruz, things were different.

"I was like holy crap," De La Cruz said later. "I'm going to lose everything if this doesn't go down the right way." He imagined a brisk, uncomfortable fall. And while he had been an upstart in life before and hadn't much minded, he didn't really care to do it again.

He was like a lot of fishermen this way: a salt-of-the-earth sort who sprang up from the docks. He was nine years old when he first went fishing for money, hawking finfish to commercial fishermen as bait. He loved standing next to those guys, hearing their wild tales of the ocean, imagining the great wonder of the sea far west of the dock his little-kid feet seemed permanently stuck on. This curiosity he had for all things underwater—it was a condition that never died.

The spot where he'd gotten his foothold, called Madeira Bay, is

Jason De La Cruz had no clue about what was happening on the Bering Sea. On October 22, 2009, he was just a guy gripped with fear in the dizzily carpeted conference room of a Holiday Inn in Texas.

At the front of the room was a U-shaped table ringed with microphones. And seated at the table was a little-known federal council of seafood moguls, fishermen, and government types who were about to decide the regulatory fate of a fish called grouper. The room was packed. Starring in fried fish sandwiches and grilled pilafs from the Carolinas to Texas, the speckled, pouting grouper drew a crowd.

The Southern seafood favorite was a fish De La Cruz had speared in the depths of the Gulf of Mexico, eaten, sold, and, most recently, gambled fiercely on. It was the gambling that provoked the fear. He and his best friend had just bet $500,000 on this fish. Now, in a few short minutes, depending on the vote at the U-shaped table, he would prove either a genius or an idiot.

Up until two years before, when the grouper bet began, De La Cruz was a boat mechanic. A regular small-business guy from Largo, Florida, he was somebody who could earn $3,000 on a job and feel like life was good. He didn't come from money. His main motivation in business, to those around him, seemed only to impress the old-timers he ate breakfast with once a week, a group that included an uncle and his uncle's friends, businessmen and hot rod fanatics both. So it's hard still a hub of seafood sales. The shimmering fingers of water that run through the city of Madeira Beach, Florida, are anchored by John's Pass Village, with a pink, barnlike restaurant called Bubba Gump Shrimp at one end—a monstrous building that sprouts a wooden boardwalk on pilings—and blues bands, ice cream, fish tacos, and shrimp on the other.

The underside of this boardwalk is where De La Cruz will end up. But it's also close to where he started, selling his bait fish outside the industrial rectangle of a building that once housed John's Pass Seafood. In the 1980s, this was the largest seafood unloading facility in the region. To a kid with a fishing pole, it was a gateway to a world that seemed to fit him. He cut bait and fixed rigs for tourists through his tweens for a weathered, white-haired captain on the *Daytona Cat*. Fishing was only briefly overshadowed by girls and a job in a salvage yard. Then in 1999 he took up spearfishing with a harpoon and everything changed. By then he was in his mid-twenties. And while he built his business repairing boats, he caught so many fish in his free time in a wetsuit that as the years passed he had to get a commercial fishing permit and start selling them just to justify the amount of time he spent underwater.

He couldn't really explain it—the way the floor of the sea called to him, the way hunting with his hands and harpoon was all he wanted to do. Joswig was along for the ride even then. The friendship that began on dirt bikes and aged into drinking and fishing under bridges graduated, ultimately, to the once-fantasy universe of boats. As De La Cruz speared grouper in the sea, hunting between the crevices of rock and in the low, dark places of the seafloor he came to know well, Joswig was on the other end of the oxygen hose, spotting another guy in the four-man squads they'd started running.

Because a diver with a harpoon occupies the lowest rung of the pecking order in commercial fishing, De La Cruz remained a runt, though you would hardly think it to look at him. Burly and topping six feet, he is also a breathless and sure talker—so sharp-witted and infectiously enthusiastic he's not an easy man to miss. Most fishermen—the grizzled ones with the trawl nets and the long-lining gear—make fun of people like him. A spearfisherman is not a great hunter of the sea. He is a man of opportunity. And in fishing, men of opportunity, those who can tell you where the fish lived before they live in your cooler, often fall prey to the heartier carnivores. De La Cruz became a commercial fisherman, nonetheless, and occupied the cozy bottom of the fishing industry for almost a decade.

His eye for opportunity would be tested when, after a makeover in the grouper industry began—one designed to lock in environmental gain—he realized quickly that he either could risk his business to fight it or play ball. It was a choice that was dividing the fishing industry throughout Madeira Beach. And at first he wasn't sure what he would do.

The scarcity of grouper was hardly a surprise. Every popular fish in America has been nearly fished out of existence. It's practically a rule. And while "overfishing" is, in many ways, a bureaucratic word for a lack of regulation for people who are mostly trying to follow the rules, the fact is that of the 230 species of fish the government had assessed off American shores in 2007, 47 of them were being pummeled and another 45 looked to be headed that way. If not for regulators like the ones at the U-shaped table, a great many fish would cease to exist in the wild this way, just as buffalo were nearly wiped off America's Great Plains. The Atlantic salmon can be counted among the casualties. Though few people know it, it exists in such scarcity in nature it is a species born, plumped, and ported to the grocery store courtesy of tank farms.

The seventeen people at the U-shaped table tasked with overseeing grouper's rebirth make up one of eight regulatory councils in the United States. A fishermen's Congress of sorts, these councils preside over the oceans in sprawling, days-long meetings. The meetings follow an annual hotel circuit, like swap meets, to try to account for a geographically broad and sometimes nomadic constituency. They are famously boring. Among federal appointees, fishery councils and their committee members are the most notorious for on-duty napping—economists snoozing on scientists, scientists dozing on the money people. But their work is serious and careful, stretching through years of glacially paced reporting and data sifting. It follows a democratic formula in which fishermen, environmentalists, seafood buyers, charter boat companies, and others divide into trade groups and fight until somebody wins. Very often it's the group with the most money.

Nonetheless, the councils take public testimony on everything from every corner of the seafood industry. Sometimes the talking alone can take days. At the end, they make the rules of the sea. And when they do, the stakes are uncommonly high. There is $5.5 billion in seafood sitting off the coasts of America. What to do with grouper, and its apparently hastening decline, was the next multimillion-dollar question.

Rescue missions for grouper had been tried before the meeting in the Holiday Inn. The first intervention came in the form of size limits on the fish fishermen could catch. Then in 1992, when few other things stood in the way of catching grouper besides the cost of a boat and a fishing permit, there was a moratorium on new permits. It was a moderate display of austerity, accompanied by great bellyaching from fishermen anyway.

Fish traps were banned a few years later, to yet more bellyaching. As the prognosis for grouper worsened, the moratorium on new permits held steady. Then came marine reserves. Then bycatch reporting. None of it worked very well.

So around 2007 people started talking about something called an IFQ system. It was a bland acronym for the even blander term "individual fishing quota," a type of catch share. But what it meant was anything but dull. It was the bureaucratic equivalent of smashing a rulebook that took hundreds of years to make and reassembling it into something radically new. It meant privatizing the rights to catch grouper in the Gulf of Mexico. Regulators would cap the number of fish that could be caught, but the right to fish them would be doled out, like property, to the people who had historically fished them.

Not everyone would come out ahead. But to those fishermen who could own the rights to grouper, the win was big. They could trade or sell those rights like chunks of real estate. And if they had enough to start with they could buy more, then run huge seafood operations without the season ever closing.

De La Cruz didn't know a damned thing about any of it at first. All he knew was that in 2007 his business was growing—his once-weekly spearfishing trip stretching two or three days at a time. And he wanted to be able to catch grouper. It was the fish the market wanted, demanded.

He watched from the sidelines, initially bewildered by the first months of fierce arguing. The grouper catch share had heavy-hitting detractors, people who feared they'd be cut off from the sea. People who had fished since forever and owned fish houses on Madeira Bay took to microphones in meetings and used words like "un-American." And whether you were for it or against it, most people thought it was insanity that the government wanted to give away the fish in the ocean. It was the equivalent of handing the national forests over to the timber companies or the mines to the miners.

But a few environmental groups were sold on catch shares. Their leaders believed that something this sweeping had to be done to American seafood. The Environmental Defense Fund, one of the largest and most powerful conservation groups in America, was a chief supporter. "A lot of EDF's successful work over the years had been focused on looking for economic leverage points, hence the interest of EDF in getting into carbon offsets and looking at tradable carbon units," said Doug Hopkins, the attorney who would lead the organization's oceans policy in its early days. The market incentives he mentioned had caused polluters to start doing things like investing in wind farms. With that kind of success, it was natural instinct, he said, to bring the same ideas to the sea.

The theory that such ideas could work was derived from economic research, spawned by a tiny camp within academia that concerns itself with money and fish. Since the fifties, that camp has been bemoaning a lack of private property rights on the seas, reasoning that fishermen would take better care of those waters if they had a stake in them. Where those rights were deployed through catch shares—in places like Canada, the Netherlands, Iceland, and New Zealand—economically they worked. And there was some evidence to suggest they could work ecologically as well.

Though EDF hadn't been involved in the earliest catch shares in America, the organization's leaders liked some of what they saw. Sustainable wild seafood was a benefit. And they wanted people in America to be able to keep eating grouper without fishing it into the same dire state as the Atlantic salmon.

With the environmental lobby on board, there were just a few cranky fishermen left to complain. Representatives from groups like the Ocean Conservancy and EDF came to Florida, hoping fishermen would support the move to privatize. People with sea-salt hair and sun-creased faces screamed at them instead. De La Cruz and Joswig, determined to survive the transition, ultimately did not.

"As we stood there and watched and watched and watched, we came to the conclusion that there wasn't a lot of other options," De La Cruz said later. New regulations, stiff ones, were coming whether fishermen liked them or not. The more he looked at the catch share, the more he believed it was the only option that would let him stay in grouper, add value by making it environmentally sustainable, and give him the potential to grow if he worked hard. "Maybe I saw this on the front side and some people didn't. I guess I lucked out and got the picture," he said.

Getting the picture was a good start. But it was watching TV that convinced him to gamble the $500,000.

That's because, when he wasn't fishing or fixing other people's boats—now a sliver of the time—De La Cruz was absolutely glued to *Deadliest Catch*.

When the show premiered in 2005, it was the first of the reality TV genre to star fishermen on the open sea. This was like free bait for the seafaring set. Filmed in the Alaskan crab industry, the first season of the show took place in conditions so intense few fishermen can even imagine them. Rugged though their jobs may be, De La Cruz and his fishing buddies fished in tolerably cold water, often on calm seas and in T-shirt, sometimes boxer-short, temperatures. Cast members on *Deadliest Catch*, by contrast, fish on the frigid and unforgiving Bering Sea, a place where dark waves practically compete to swallow a person and temperatures on the water can fall to minus forty-nine degrees. An innocent slip into that water kills a person fast. And because Alaskan crab faced the same dwindling harvests that De La Cruz and everyone else in the Gulf faced with grouper, the same controls that had failed the grouper were being tried there, too. Crabbers in Alaska were fishing 14 million pounds of crab in brutal, sleepless, one-week seasons designed to limit overfishing. It was, doubtlessly, the roughest, meanest form of fishing known to man. And it was working about as well for the crab as it had for grouper, which is to say not at all.

Small wonder then that by the second half of the first season, six fishermen were dead. It was exactly this death toll, plus the furious, careless race for the crab, that prompted regulators in the North Pacific to convene around their own U-shaped table and convert that fishery to a catch share at the end of the first year *Deadliest Catch* aired.

As his favorite TV show unfolded in a thrilling stream of Tuesdays, De La Cruz saw that what happened in crab next was about to happen to his beloved grouper. Already popular abroad, catch shares were fast on their way to becoming national policy. Their first domestic wave roared through the United States in the 1990s. It converted Alaskan halibut and pollock, a small bass fishery on the East Coast, and the industrial clam fishing off the coast of New Jersey—the fishery that supplies most cans of clam chowder and juice, chopped clams, and clam strips in America.

A little more than a decade later, the second wave was under way. By the time De La Cruz heard the letters IFQ, catch shares had taken hold of sablefish on the West Coast and red snapper on the west side of the Gulf. They were also on deck for a bunch of New England fish, cod included. And they were retooling Alaskan crab right there on the television.

So by the third season of *Deadliest Catch*, De La Cruz was noticing something funny; fishermen had stopped talking so much about the new system, about how they were being "rationalized" or reorganized into a catch share. But the dynamics of the fishing had clearly changed. They were no longer patching up shattered arms during weeklong seasons and cheering when fifteen crabs crawled into their pots. Instead, the crabbers still fishing were catching eighty or ninety crabs at a time. And while *Deadliest Catch* didn't focus much on the former cast members, or where they ended up, the high points for those who stayed were clear: more crab over longer, safer seasons, and more money for those who remained to catch them.

For the fishermen who ended up owning a piece of the ocean, their lives were enriched enough for De La Cruz to notice. People weren't dying in batches of six anymore. Crab fishermen could go out and fish in safer weather. And a few quick pokes around the Internet showed that the prices for many rationalized fish, crab included, were on the rise as the supplies steadied enough to create demand.

These were things that set De La Cruz's tongue wagging. He started telling them to anyone who would listen. Mostly, that turned out to be Joswig. If the two of them embraced what was surely coming, he said, they could be on the winning side of the grouper game.

"He basically pulled my bitch card," said De La Cruz. "He said, 'You don't have a hair in your ass if you don't do this now.'"

So he did.

But while De La Cruz got the concepts, he had no idea what he was supposed to do. So he started reading more on the Internet and talking with the environmental advocates in Florida, a few he had gotten to know and trusted at Ocean Conservancy and EDF. They were eager to work with him, and with anybody else who wanted to understand how to fish sustainably and build a good business doing it. They helped him see that his share of the sea would be awarded based on the years that he fished. And that was a problem, because De La Cruz bought his commercial fishing permit in 2005. But the fishing rights to grouper were going to be awarded based on his fishing history since 2003. There were two whole years he didn't have a history for. But he learned that he could create it by buying up other guys' permits.

Finding permits was not tricky. He found them on Craigslist, or by sifting through a database of permit owners at the National Marine Fisheries Service and cold calling their owners. That was simple. But verifying each fisherman's tale of how much fish he caught on these permits—that was harder. And these were the numbers that mattered. When the council made its move at the U-shaped table, everything De La Cruz had learned told him it was the guys who caught the most pounds over time who would win.

Sifting through paperwork became like a second job. In the cases where a permit had more than one owner, which was common, De La Cruz had to track the prior owners to get a signed release for their part in the permit's history. It was like crossing the bureaucratic equivalent of the Arctic, sending off signed forms in the mail and then waiting, sometimes for more than a month, for anything to come back again.

This is how De La Cruz came to be sitting in the living room of a guy named Walter Buda, a man in his seventies who played piano and told him stories about a boat that sank fifteen years ago, pulling out the yellow newspaper clippings and leafing through them with his wife and De La Cruz. De La Cruz was there for hours. It took most of the first hour just to explain why he had come, the rest to hear a few tunes on the piano and leaf through the newspaper clippings.

Later, when people complained that De La Cruz had been on a path to outwit everybody, he reminded them that he had been willing to do this sort of thing. To sit with Walter Buda and look at newspaper clippings and talk about boats that sank long ago. And to do the paper-work instead of being a chicken about it.

It helped that the economy was such that anybody could get their hands on a second mortgage. The first permit De La Cruz found was only worth about $4,000. Not a problem. It was a relatively modest investment. He started to have questions, though, as the debt tally pitched steeply upward. The second permit he bought cost $60,000. And he soon found himself with a third partner, too, a boat broker who knew where the deals were, but who was a more cunning sort with a thicker checkbook.

The boat broker quickly pointed De La Cruz to a community of old trap fishermen in the Everglades, Cuban guys with grouper permits who had huge catch histories but hadn't fished since trap fishing was banned. He bought another four permits there, writing checks that made the Cuban guys—and himself—question his sanity. They were smart, though. They made him take their old, barely seaworthy boats with him.

By the time it was done, De La Cruz had four of five boats he didn't even want. He also had thirteen permits. He drove from Cedar Key, Florida, a working-class town north of Madeira Beach, north to Sopchoppy in the middle of nowhere, and south all the way to Ever-glades City to get them. In a single deal—the one he made after Walter Buda's catch history was confirmed—he spent $140,000.

"Keep in mind, the day I wrote that check, that was the largest check I'd ever written in my life. It's not like I have a lot of money," he said. "It was the time frame of life where money wasn't real."

He was still, in his words, "scared shitless."

Yet until he was waiting on the dizzy carpet, the proverbial decision gavel hovering midair, the full force of that fear didn't hit him. When it did, he felt faint, his body shivering. Joswig would later say De La Cruz looked cool, unruffled. But what he felt was like a man who might be on the edge of losing everything he'd ever worked for. The fear ripped through him like something viral. He started sweating like a guy on a treadmill.

"No guts, no glory," De La Cruz is fond of saying. He says this often, like a kind of verbal shrug. But in those last few minutes, he was clearly out of guts.

Then the deal went down. And it went down just as he thought. Two hundred and fifty thousand pounds of grouper were his that day. His with a couple of partners. Now all he had to do was build a business out of them. And to be the test case for whether guys like him—the ultimate little guy—could really make good through catch shares.

Kodiak, Alaska

A Big Squeeze, an Ugly Divorce

O F COURSE IT ALL LOOKED great on television. By the time Tom Miller actually sees it, he's in a bar in Costa Rica, pointing at himself on the screen. On the TV in the bar, the second season of *Deadliest Catch* is under way, unfurling in the same scenes that had given Jason De La Cruz a vision for how to survive the transition to catch shares. Filmed right after the crab industry converted, the show captured Miller during the 2005 snow crab season, fishing west of Alaska on the meanest sea in America.

Camouflaged behind a briar patch of blond beard, there he is. He's sliding around on the deck of a boat called the *Time Bandit*, a 113-foot pot boat dodging icebergs on the Bering Sea. He looks like a badass, wearing orange Grundéns—a fisherman's signature jumpsuit—and a green rain hat over a mop of insulating hair. He's chopping ice off the deck while nasty seas roll the boat like a Tilt-A-Whirl. The ropes are frozen solid; the crab pots are freezing too. And at one point Miller turns to the camera, smiles, and says, "It's pretty much a hopeless job," in the same energetic drawl in which Miller delivers most everything.

When it is verified that he is, in fact, the guy on the TV, Miller drinks for free that night, bolstering his celebrity in the way that free drinks do. It's a perfect end to his more than twenty years in crabbing, as good a ceremony as any. While the figures on the screen proclaim he earned $750 a day at season's end, Miller's ultimate fate looks less like a financial windfall than a straight-up fall. In reality, Miller is nearing the end of his crabbing career. He's one of dozens of crewmen to be squeezed out of the industry when catch shares took hold. And the sunset of his time crabbing is a clear example of how catch shares tied the fate of workers and towns to a new era of ocean owners and to the bizarre politics at the U-shaped tables run by America's fishery management councils.

Seven years later, Miller is sitting on his own boat in St. Paul Harbor on the northeast side of Kodiak Island when he describes what happened. He's kneeling, actually, in a black sweatshirt and paint-splattered pants, on the docks by Kodiak's downtown at Pillar Mountain's base. Little shops and fishing boats galore—mostly steel and fiberglass, painted in whites and blues—ring the bay. The place looks like a postcard with a handful of grizzled fishermen thrown at it. Miller's got a beer by his side and a couple friends on the boat, a vessel he uses to fish with his brother. The tools are scattered, the day's work half ceded to a happy hour in the five o'clock Alaska sun. His hair is short now. No more beard. And he's wearing glasses, something impossible to do aboard the *Time Bandit*, where the subzero climate would have melded the metal frames to face.

He folds his arms over his chest and talks about the day his crabbing pay dropped 76 percent, his enormous voice—part laid-back surfer, part upbeat patter—scratching its way across the harbor to ride with the birds and the breeze on the Kodiak water.

After the catch share took hold, the owners of the *Time Bandit*, in a brief financial pickle, sold their share of the crab, called "quota" in the catch-share universe, and then had to rent it back again to keep fishing. Just like that, Miller went from making 7 percent of the boat's total earnings to about the same percentage of the boat's new cut: 20 percent. It was the day his tour on the *Time Bandit* ended. He'd been crabbing for a rough two decades.

"The guys that owned the *Time Bandit* called me and said, 'By the way we sold the quota, you're supposed to be at work tomorrow.' And I'm like, 'So now I'm going to make $6,000 king crabbing instead of my usual $25,000?'... I never talked to them again. After eight years, it was a really ugly divorce. We used to be tight." He rocks on his heels, and explains how this is normal now. Especially in Kodiak.

Catch shares have been hard on this little town. Nestled into a rugged, almost roadless landscape on Kodiak Island, it's made up of mostly Coast Guard base and fishing docks. Fewer than fourteen thousand people live in the region, most somehow tied to the sea. When the catch-share program arrived, courtesy of a rider in a spending bill—called the Bering Sea Aleutian Islands Crab Rationalization, or Crab Ratz for short—it aimed to thin the number of boats catching too few crab and a problem of a lot of dead little ones.

Four kinds of the nation's most lucrative crabs were being overfished. And there was another good reason to reboot crab fishing. Beside the problem of too many boats and too few crabs, *Deadliest Catch* is aptly named—fishing crab is a killer. That isn't just because the Bering Sea is nearly 800,000 square miles of subzero seascape in winter, or because winter storms can pitch waves tall enough to coat a boat in ice. It's because, prior to catch shares, crabbing was managed through what were called fishing derbies, in which the primary conservation tool for the crab was a cap on catch.

In simple terms, that meant that the business of who got what was a dust-up that played out at sea. Thus every time a crabbing season opened, and for ever-shortening lengths of time, fishermen rushed to the water like seafaring cowboys, no matter the weather, gunning to catch more crab than the next guy. Most boats fished so hard that crab seasons for some species were as short as three days. The fishing was correspondingly rough. Boats piled ambitiously high with pots capsized and people drowned. The fishermen themselves worked nonstop, batty with sleeplessness, to catch all they could, compounding risk and injury and the number of people who slipped overboard.

The statistics from this era are grim. There were seventy-three fatalities on Alaska crab boats through the 1990s, compared with only one in the six years after the catch share took hold. That was argument enough to end the Derby Days, as the management style was called. There were others, still. Beside the hideous amount of accidental catch of young crab, the derbies were landing gobs of crab—tens of millions of pounds a year—on the docks at once, where they would pile up in heaps while processors tried to keep up. It made it tough to schedule delivery to market. And there wasn't any time to deliver crab live and keep them fresh for pricier sales.

As these Derby Days swept the country—from Alaska to California, around the Gulf of Mexico and up the Atlantic Coast—they controlled all kinds of seafood in what was then the primary plan for federal fisheries. In the ten years between 1992 and 2002, they were a major factor in the more than seven hundred deaths among commercial fishermen nationwide. And they were responsible for mountains of unprocessed fish being handled rough or just frozen, so that a lot of US seafood products were simply garbage. Fish that might have made gorgeous fillets were frozen into bricks. It sometimes took days just for that to happen, compromising quality even among frozen products. Such lousy products brought with them predictably lousy prices. So too did the snubbing of the supply-and-demand rule. All that made it so fishermen only had to fish harder.

Catch shares, when they hit the United States, were ushered in as a fix. The idea was to convert the disorganized, unsafe, and unseemly mess of domestic seafood into dependable, profitable industries. By preassigning the catch, regulators could keep fishermen safer by slowing them down, giving them longer seasons and more time to plan around bad weather. And they could steady the supply of fish, making it possible for restaurants and markets to give consumers an opportunity to fall in love with fish, fostering demand and higher prices. Fishermen could earn a better living. And though there are ways to preassign catch that don't create property rights, conservationists who would foster the development of many of the nation's catch shares after crab hoped that giving fishermen their own piece of ocean ownership, and thus a stake in oceans' futures, would inspire the well-being of entire species and the seas.

It took six years to make it happen in crab. Six long years of lobbying. Those years made it plain that many people in Kodiak weren't keen on privatizing anything. When it looked like the greatest share of the crab might go to boat owners, some of the crewmen flew to Washington, DC, and dressed up in rat costumes to make their opposition plain, chanting "No Crab Ratz."

The planned loss of boats was a much lesser worry. Most everyone thought there were too many boats. The folks at the U-shaped table—the North Pacific Fishery Management Council—used a federal loan to buy twenty-three boats out of the water, or about 9 percent of the boats in the industry. And being bought out of business was certainly better than being kicked out—basically those who took the offer were getting paid to retire. Nobody realized how much those boats would matter. They argued chiefly about whether the exclusive right to catch crab would go to the owners of the boats that remained or be shared with their workers.

After six years of arguing about it, the rules for the crab catch share set aside only 3 percent of the crab quota, as the access rights were called, for the crew who worked the boats. The other 97 percent went to boat owners. Then nine stocks of crab were divvied up. They were the good kind. Moneymakers. Tanner crab from the east and west of the Bering Sea, snow crab, and three kinds of king crab, all a bounty crawling the seafloor from Bristol Bay to the Pribilofs and the Aleutian chain. Unscrupulous bottom feeders though they are, eating everything from worms to clams, tiny animals, and dead stuff, they convert all of it into low-fat, delicious protein, hence the moneymaking. King crabs can bulk to a whopping twenty-four pounds, making their long chubby legs especially desirable. When the catch share hit, these crabs were worth a combined $125 million a year.

A bunch of new rules tethered delivery of the crab to the region's processors—requiring fishermen to deliver to established sellers to keep the market from going haywire. But what was missing were rules requiring the new owners of the access rights to the crab to actually fish it or even ride the boats. So predictably, they started staying home. It happened so fast that within the first year of the program, nearly two-thirds of crab boats were gone, 15 percent bought out, the rest parked as an era of ocean landlords took hold or the owners downsized. The new landlords of the sea began renting their access at rents that quickly hit 70 percent of what anybody could earn catching it.

Miller puts his hands in his lap, his feet still in rubber boots, two buckets of long lines behind him, and jokes about how he will someday marry for quota. In a moment of lucidity, however, when the laughter stops, after he and his friends have run through a list of eligible bachelorettes, he makes a pointed remark about the new owners of the industry. "These guys have gotten so far removed," he says. "Before, they had boats. They had crews to worry about. They were here at the grocery store, the fuel dock. And now these guys are like, 'So long as I get a check, I don't give a fuck what's going on with the fisheries, the health of the fishery, the boat, if the guys are safe, whatever, because I'm not there. I just get a check. I have no liability anymore.'"

There are some not-so-polite nicknames for ocean landlords in Kodiak now. Miller and his friends rattle them off: Q-Lords. Mailbox fishermen. Slipper Skippers. Or the special name for those who inherit: Lucky Sperm.

Miller says he's glad he's out. Being a renter in the new crab economy wasn't what he signed up for.

Admittedly, at first he didn't know what he signed up for. Raised in Anchorage, Miller was a college kid when he came to Kodiak to mountain bike, but his real ambition was to see the world. He camped on Near Island—a thumb of land across the bay—for nearly a month, his sights set on traveling to New Zealand. From his rough lodgings in an old tent under battered camouflage tarps, he rode his bike to the harbor looking for work, hawking for jobs on the boats. He was lured only in part by financial need. The rest was curiosity.

He satisfied both. His first job was as a bait guy on a crab boat, a gig he took with no idea what he was into. Days later he was riding forty-foot waves, violently seasick, with his head in a pile of stinking bait cod. By the time he'd figured out what the job was, he was two days without sleep. He survived the next eight, though, made $9,000, then went to New Zealand. It was all he wanted—to travel, to see the world, to chase the good times. He was eighteen and never made it back to college. By the time the Discovery Channel's *Deadliest Catch* made him primetime, he was deeply entrenched in this life at sea and in the travel in between. Like a lot of fishermen, he split his time between fisheries to make his living, his particular menu being salmon, crab, and halibut. Before the crab fell out.

Had the guys in the bar leaned in and listened closely to *Deadliest Catch*, they would have heard this tale, or inklings of it. A low-toned voice swept over the second season describing how some of the first season's captains hadn't come back again, aced out by "rationalization." But excepting this fact, crabbing looked, on TV, mostly the same after catch shares as it did before: like a death-defying journey on a seafaring roller coaster in which the prize was a big pile of money.

The cameras never did quite capture all the people who lost their jobs, or the rapid consolidation Miller says is driving the extinction of guys like him. So the only thing that seemed different was that the third of boats that were left catching crab were suddenly catching mountains of the stuff and everyone was saying that catch shares made it happen.

In that second season of *Deadliest Catch*, when viewers meet him on the screen, even Miller is discovering this. It's the first year of the crab catch share. He's 415 miles northwest of far-flung Dutch Harbor, and the *Time Bandit* is the only boat edging closer to the icepack rather than away from it. Captain Andy Hillstrand believes that snow crab like the calm space where the two temperatures—ice and water—meet. For the crew on the deck, the atmosphere is anything but calm. The wind chill is fifteen degrees below zero. It's 2:00 a.m. And they have been working for eighteen hours. It is so cold that even the boat's windows are frozen. And while Captain Andy can't see much, can't spot the buoys he's hunting, he is talking about how sometimes people fall overboard and quickly freeze to death, appearing not to notice the waves now crashing over the rail, washing his own crewmen backward.

Such is the choreography of reality TV. The music is maudlin—fiddles or synthesizers, hard to say—doomsday plucking playing to a backdrop of severe weather. Soon, the *Time Bandit* is skirting a large strip of floe ice. It's bobbing on the waves in huge chunks while Captain Andy works to find the edge, and to avoid the smaller pieces that are freezing together. The ice is moving faster than expected, he says—as fast as twenty-five miles a day—and from the cameras on the boat you can see the chunks as big as railcars. The *Time Bandit* is sixteen miles from its gear, moving like a slow shark, steering around the ice that most other captains are avoiding altogether.

By the time the sun is up an episode later, ten thousand pounds of ice have built up on the boat. Miller is wielding a long sturdy pole like a jousting ice fighter. He's still in the orange Grundéns, the green rain hat, a rope now cinched around his waist to contain the parts of these suits that inevitably end up caught on things. To see him through a camera's lens, he is somehow slower. Even fighting the ice one bold strike after another, he is a watered-down version of the actual Miller, a person who radiates so much energy that even sitting he appears to be in a kind of perpetual motion. Normally, Miller talks like bullets with a voice as big as the ocean. He is subdued on this vessel, though. Probably, he is in the first stages of hypothermia.

He keeps swinging at the ice. And soon the gamble pays off, one massive pot after another winch-pulled over the rail. The crews steady the pots—huge metal cages nearly as tall as Miller and probably twice as heavy—and release the crab, cheering as if they're at a party. Mountains of squirming crab—big ones—spill out onto the deck.

By the time it's all over, the music has picked up, the guitar is all rock and shredding. And Miller is no longer slipping around the deck to an especially depressing country-and-western soundtrack. Now he's winning like a guy about to stage dive. And when the boat finally hits port on St. Paul Island, it is Miller who looks happiest hustling the crab off the boat, somehow still smiling when he announces to the camera, "It feels like it's about 100 below out," though the temperature is actually a balmy zero. He earned $12,000 in sixteen days.

Right before he got aced out, things were good.

There's no denying that the crab catch share worked in some ways. That it stabilized the species and the market for crab helps account for why the overall value of crab doubled to $250 million by 2013. This is exactly the kind of thing federal regulators go gaga for: increasing the value of the nation's natural resources. But there is a cost. Opportunities for work are scarcer now in Kodiak. Catch shares have pared 757 jobs from crab fishing overall—more than 1,350 when combined with the boat buyback—mostly in the first year. Many crab landlords have sold their boats but kept their access rights, renting them to the younger generation. Nobody sets the prices. It's just captain undercutting captain at whatever price their boat and crew can work for.

A drive through Kodiak's marinas makes these changes plain. Huge vessels are collecting barnacles in these waters—boats that haven't moved since catch shares. The *Saga*, for example, a $1.3 million boat that didn't qualify for crab quota—it didn't fish during the qualifying years—spent a rough six years in Kodiak's St. Herman Harbor, rust and moss climbing the starboard side and stern, before it was purchased by up-and-comers and made a comeback on *Deadliest Catch*. A few slips away, the *Lady Kodiak* sat in similar disrepair for years as well, having also not fished since the rationalization. This boat didn't miss the qualifying years. Its owner shifted to leasing and parked it. One of Kodiak's wealthiest crab owners on paper, he's since retired and is more visible these days as the keeper of a renowned collection of muscle cars.

That much of the former crab industry vanished as fast as it did had consequences in more places than on the water. Within a year, an economist estimated that tiny Kodiak was taking a $1 million to $1.6 million annual hit in lost wages, and potentially more in retail spending to marine suppliers and boat mechanics, the main sources of income in the town. Those losses trickled down to retail shops and service businesses, too. Mayor Pat Branson says nonprofits and schools have struggled while people who used to be major contributors left town. People who benefitted from the extraction of Alaska's resources used to be part of the community. Now:

"We've just had people that have benefitted . . . who no longer have to live here," says Branson. The realignment of the town's economy has taken a painful emotional toll. It's not quite as bad as the *Exxon Valdez* oil spill, she says. But it's close.

As these landlords stockpile ocean assets and quit fishing, the way in which they are locking workers away from the opportunity to build their own seafood businesses signifies more than a cultural shift. It's a trend that allows ocean access to become its own commodity, apart from the fishing. And the deep consolidation that attends it combines with ballooning rental markets and a pattern of leaving fishermen behind to serve as a precursor to the investment speculation that would start to open the door to the seas to Wall Street in a few years.

It's trends like these like that created blowback later, when a coalition of senators from four states—Oregon, Massachusetts, Alaska, and California—dispatched a letter in 2011 highlighting problems like those in Kodiak, and called on the National Oceanic and Atmospheric Administration to help protect fishermen and their towns. What had happened in Kodiak had happened before. There were similar outcomes from catch shares implemented in the nineties for Alaskan halibut and for clams and wreckfish on the Atlantic. And in the new millennium, as catch shares started overtaking the nation's seafood, they were provoking deep consolidation of fishing jobs and boats on the Pacific, in New England, and in the Gulf of Mexico.

Later that year, House Republicans led a bipartisan effort to cut funding for new catch shares on the East Coast and a coalition from New England and Florida urged President Obama to reconsider federal policy that called for catch-share consideration in every fishery. Neither legislative effort worked. But they were among early signs that catch shares would be more than just the conservation fix that the best-intentioned conservationists imagined. They would be other things too. Retirement plans. Rental properties. Investment vehicles. Things some legislators felt ran counter to their noblest goals, the goals of keeping fishermen safe, of making them good stewards of the ocean, and of helping them build businesses on which the rest of society could depend for food.

Miller tried to change all that in Kodiak. Before he gave up crabbing, he says, he made a run at democracy, flying around the North Pacific to meetings at the U-shaped table to tell his story again and again. "Me and my brother must have dropped $30,000 in four years going to every council meeting to have it all fall on deaf ears of basically, 'Well, okay, yeah, we really feel sorry for you, but too fucking bad. Do you have a lobbyist? Do you have a million dollars? Come back and talk to us later,'" he says.

Then he laughs, rocks back on his heels again.

He says it was easy to see why his story wasn't enough. Lobbyists had the natural advantage at the U-shaped table, the costs of attending being costs that lots of people like him couldn't shoulder. The long hotel stays. The food and airfare. And trying to build a rapport with council members who'd had years to get to know the lobbyists—their time and money in greater reserve, they are regular attendees—seemed hopeless.

Stories like his are typical. The people at the table, while chosen for their expertise, often have a stake in the game: heads of trade groups, seafood company moguls, attorneys for one or the other, and, lately, environmental groups. In other words, people with clear objectives, mixed in with a few representatives of the states.

While that might look like a typical federal committee, one with stakeholder input, it's not. It's a holdover from a time when federal regulators first took control of managing the seas from the states, so that rules that normally govern federal advisory committees don't apply to the eight fishery management councils around the nation. The workers who staff the councils are outside the reach of the Freedom of Information Act. The lobbyists who inevitably turn up—the same people required to register when they lobby other federal officials—don't have to register to lobby the councils, or disclose how much money they spend influencing seafood policy. And federal auditors found in 2013 that the track record for compliance with federal conflict-of-interest rules is spotty among the people at the U-shaped tables, with more than 27 percent fudging their financial disclosures, even while they oversee the harvest of 9.8 billion pounds of seafood worth $5.5 billion.

"These are big-money lobbyists against a couple dirty fishermen. There's eighty lobbyists and they're all on their BlackBerrys deciding how they're going to cut their next pie out of the deal. If I had $2 billion, I could hire a bunch of people to be very organized too. And that's what you're dealing with. I mean, it's big money all the way around," says Miller.

For a while, crewmen like him agitated for a larger share of Bering Sea crab and fought to get back what they lost. Then they stopped. Nobody turns up at those meetings anymore, worrying about the crab crews. Nobody talks much about crab at all. The politics have moved on to remake the next fisheries.

Gulf Wild

Conservationists Reboot Fishing

THERE IS, PERHAPS, NO BETTER poster child for privatized fishing than Buddy Guindon, sitting at a restaurant table in oil-rich Galveston, Texas. He leans forward and points to a jagged scar across his face, concealed by a thatch of beard. He pulls the hair aside, a mix of whites and grays. Pulls the mustache wide too. There it is, a mean line in the skin running from one side of his face to the other. He describes it as evidence of what the Derby Days were doing, not just to people, but to the seas in the nineties.

His story takes place years before he teamed up with Jason De La Cruz. Years before anybody thought to build the seafood brand Gulf Wild, and right around the time the first catch shares were coming to America, in places thousands of miles away.

The incident that led to the scar underscored how screwed up fishing really was.

Much later it would also make Guindon—born Keith, though few would know it—a model spokesman for catch shares.

Guindon was thirty-four, maybe thirty-five, and already wearing the bramble of beard that would become a signature, though not so disorderly as the look implied. Though he had traded his Marine Blue Dress for jeans and T-shirts by then, and his main ride was a pickup truck, he was a disciplined guy. And a family guy, too. Three sons at home—the youngest a toddler, the oldest twelve—he was consumed by the pressures of breadwinning. And breadwinning for Guindon was a fish on a hook, one after another, on and on until the bills were paid. He had tried other work. Enough to know he did not like it. When his wife quit her job to tend their brood while he was seafaring, he found himself all in on fishing. And with fish stocks crashing on the Gulf of Mexico, that was a scary thing to be.

So it was that in 1992 he was fishing hard, and perhaps in a situation that he should not have been. That day aboard the *Falcon*, he was straight out of Dallas, eighteen hours from shore, in water six hundred to twelve hundred feet deep. He was, if fish puns are allowed, completely out of his depth. His usual occupation was bandit fishing closer to home, a more genteel type of fishing in which a handful of reels hang vertically off a boat. And his usual fare was another fish entirely: the sweet-tasting red snapper, a bug-eyed beauty caught typically in not so much water—sometimes at a few hundred feet but usually more like sixty. The day of the incident, however, Guindon was in deeper seas after that speckled grouch the grouper. And part of the problem was that he had no idea what he was doing.

Guindon had only owned the *Falcon* for two years, and how he got there was a little like chasing falling dominos. After a decade of scientific handwringing over the red snapper, a reef fish that was—not unlike the grouper—fished out, regulatory redress had already run the course through the usual things, known as "effort controls." These were tools that limited behavior on the sea instead of capping the catch. They included things like limiting the size of the fish one could catch and banning certain types of gear like fish traps. In 1990, in an attempt to save the red snapper, the seasons started getting shorter, like they had in crab in Alaska. Guindon jumped through the regulatory hoops with the rest of his fishing buddies. But when he arrived at shorter seasons, he had a problem. Shorter seasons meant a January opening, converting Guindon's mostly summer, drifting-in-the-wet-hot occupation into a blustery ride on six- to eight-foot waves. He didn't have the boat for it.

The choice to buy the *Falcon* then was easy in that he hardly had one. He could either pony up for a boat that could do the job, meet his death in a smaller boat like a fool, or stay on land and go broke and let his kids eat hotdogs while he looked for other work. The opportunity of the *Falcon* at least made things simple. It was practically sitting in his backyard—or in a nearby harbor. Built for Falcon Seafoods in Tarpon Springs, Florida, the steel forty-footer had been brought to Texas by an ambitious but slightly delusional seafood buyer who had already lost most of his investment trying to run it. The man had piled $50,000 in hardware on the boat. It had a canopy for rough weather and shade, and a sharp, deep nose for pushing the waves apart. Guindon had to do some cartwheels for the bank to get it, pretending he'd paid deposits he didn't have, then borrowed a bunch of money from his father to make the deal go down.

His timing, however, was impressively bad. Red snapper fishing all but shuttered a year later when the shortened season for the portly red fish was truncated yet again, this time from eight months to just seventy-five days. The Derby Days for red snapper had begun. And while Guindon would still fish those derbies like a madman—sometimes catching thousands of pounds before he even had the time to gut and ice them, the fish piling on the deck for hours—he was basically out of work the other 312 days a year.

His whole financial life riding on the *Falcon*, he did what he had to. He took the small profit he made in his last season fishing snapper and bought a used longline spool, a metal contraption that looks like a giant bobbin in a cage, and plopped it on the back of the *Falcon* so that he could go longlining. Tilefish and yellowedge grouper, in fact. Behemoths. And not something he had done before. But this is what the derbies were doing. They were pushing fishermen from one fish to another, so that the derbies were not so much controlling the bloodbath on the seas as they were shifting it from fish to fish, like a kind of roving hit mob. They were also pushing fishermen to try things that they didn't quite know how to do. It was how so many of them were getting hurt.

Guindon had hardly fished with long lines before. His only other experience was with a few feet of trotlines on a lake. Now the spool on the back of the *Falcon* carried six miles of line. In sharp contrast with the trotlines, its breaking strength weighed as much as two tightrope-walking gorillas—about seven or eight hundred pounds. It was made from a single plastic fiber, a melted polymer that's been stuffed through a hole. At different grades and weights, it varies from sturdy wisps to thick whips, and wraps around a hydraulic spool that reels it in and out without someone having to turn a crank or haul their arms into spaghetti.

This particular monofilament—mono, for short—was razor thin. It laid around him that day in one-mile sets of baited hooks that he and his crew deployed like seafloor fish carrots. Guindon's ability to wrangle it was about parallel to his know-how in running trips like this—not good, in other words—so that he was floundering around the ocean on the hunt for a fish he hadn't chased before.

The rest went down like this: John Best, the youthful deckhand, is sitting with a bucket of bait between his legs. And Guindon is working over the starboard side in a little path behind the cabin, steering the boat by the wheel and running the hydraulics that turn the spool on the back of the boat. His grouchy but endearing first mate Jim Carithers is behind him. Carithers had been the best man at Guindon's wedding. And Carithers is taking the fish off the hooks as they come up the middle of the boat from stern to bow. When the empty line arrives, Guindon takes the clips off it, metal wingdings that look like oversized diaper pins holding hook to filament. The job sounds like doing a lot of things: driving, hydraulics, pulling clips. But for anyone who has done it, it is more monotony than motion.

"Longlining is like factory work," Guindon says. "You just do the same thing over and over and over and over." Which is why this particular brand of fishing is such hell on the hands and wrists, and why, over the life of such fishermen, pain crawls from the hands to the shoulders, marking time until it works its way across the back and down to the hips and knees. Now in his sixties, Guindon says he wakes up in the morning not sure which part hurts most. He says this tongue in cheek, in his way of dryly dropping jokes until it's not quite clear where the jokes end.

This day in 1992, however, is no joke. Though Guindon is in his physical prime, he's in a mood. He is behind his mental game hunting this fish, and minute by minute his temperament vacillates between euphoria at catching a few and doom at hauling long stretches of empty hooks.

He is more accustomed to winning.

It is this swath of sea that has been Guindon's church from early days, his worship a drive into sun-soaked water with the aid of a compass and a few well-placed windows. There was no GPS back then. High-growing coral was a thing you found by accident and never made the mistake of finding again. But in some ways the fishing was easy. The oil rigs that stood in the Galveston Channel, looming over the boats like scolding aunts, marched into the sea for 150 miles plus, so that a fisherman could practically eyeball his way to the fishing grounds and the deep, cold water around the reefs.

As a snapper fisherman, this is the place that Guindon prays to, carefully cultivating his fishing spots with the aid of buoys and the arcane Loran-C, the radio navigation system that was birthed by the military and adopted by fishers before GPS and waypoints made it so boats could drive and practically park themselves.

But now the spool is turning, the monofilament is coming in. Fish are coming off the hooks. Hooks are coming off the line. The two-man crew is icing the fish, baiting the hooks. Relief.

But empty lines next bring worry. Worry about whether he can keep his house. Feed his kids. Clothe them. Make it so his wife's sacrifice in quitting her job will be worth it. Then the mono gets stuck, gets caught somehow. Guindon starts turning the boat in a circle, trying to shake it loose. He turns into the port side, letting the line drift under the boat. Then he turns starboard, letting the line pull, trying to find the angle of the knot and set it free.

Frustration plays its ugly role. He's anxious to reel it in and find fish on the line. If he cannot make it work with grouper, he cannot make it in fishing. So he keeps turning the boat. He makes a full circle but the knot won't budge. Happens, fishermen will tell you. But he wasn't a longline fisherman, he didn't know. So he didn't shut the spool off. And then he did the thing more experience would have prevented: he leaned over the rail. The last thing he saw was that the knot had pulled tight, so tight it was either going to snap or break the molding off the boat.

He pulled his head back.

But not fast enough.

When the mono snapped, it pierced the skin on the right side of his nose, dug deep, and scraped down, cutting his upper lip in two. It took less than a second. When it bridged his mouth, sunk into his lower lip, then turned to cross his chin like a figure skater, the clock was still frozen. His hand flew to his face. Something bad had happened but he could not tell what. When he turned to his crew, and blood poured out of him like rain, they could hardly bear to look. Skin dangled from his mouth and jaw like loose meat.

He asked for a towel. Someone passed it. He could see that his crewmen were white. He pressed the towel in until the blood slowed, until the stinging turned to numbness, then staggered into the *Falcon*'s cabin to the mirror over the sink. "I looked in the mirror and thought, 'You'd better get your shit together because these guys ain't gonna help you.'" Guindon's lips were cut badly and his cheek was cut too. He was eighteen hours from the dock. On the bright side, he saw that he would live. He just had to put his face back on.

At the time, he didn't know that you could glue a man back together. He'd never been injured like this fishing for snapper. So he went for a roll of duct tape behind the mirror instead, tearing it into strips. His upper lip was ground up bad. He pieced it together first, held it still with his fingers, then taped it, and wrapped the roll around his head to hold it still. His mustache was so ensnared the tape would have to be cut away later. It was not the most pressing concern.

"Eighteen hours from the dock, whatever position that shit was in when it stuck back together, that's where it was going to be," he said. He still wanted to be good looking. So he did his best.

From a first-aid kit under the sink, he found a wad of gauze and stuck a bunch of it behind the remains of his lower lip and cheek, where he found deep holes. He thought he had lost a few teeth but found that they were there, even though he could not feel them. He pulled his lower lip together so the flaps along his chin closed, then taped those, winding the roll around his head so that later, a doctor would have to tear the tape out of the hair on the back of his head too.

About half an hour passed before he'd finished. He had started thinking about his gear already, but by then the crew had wheeled the boat around and headed for land. Both Best and Carithers were standing at the wheel, looking out the front window, as if driving required four hands. Neither could turn around.

Guindon climbed into the bunk behind them and pressed a towel to his face. From underneath, he watched the radar as the boat edged closer to home. He tried to joke, but couldn't talk much. When he did, the other two men got their color back. It seemed to take them longer than it took him.

He didn't make it home. But he made it to the hospital, where he was stitched up by an on-call oncologist who complimented him on his taping skills. She gave him needles and thread and lidocaine that he would fortunately never have to use. She told him firmly that he should not go back to sea. Too much bacteria.

Indeed, it would take three weeks before he could do much without the wound breaking open. And because his boys were young and rowdy and his own home was a hazard of potential collisions and rico-chets, he went to live with a mother-in-law who was not at all fond of him, looking, by his own description, like a monster. "My head was swollen up, like, huge. Especially the left side of my face was maybe two, three times the size it was supposed to be, and that made it go up my forehead, ear, neck. It was gross looking."

Still, when he walked out of the hospital, his wife rushing toward him, all he could think of was that gear in the water. Three thousand dollars sitting in the sea.

"It was how I made my living and I couldn't afford to replace it," he said. He had borrowed all he could, for all he had. And though his stitched wound was like the crook of a rock ripe for barnacles, he was still the only one that knew how to haul his gear, however badly. So he went from the hospital to the *Falcon*, climbed back into the bunk, and fell deep asleep while the crew charted the return course. When they found the buoys, the lines, and the clips, Guindon stepped out on the deck and hauled another eighty pounds of fish with the gear. Later, they sold it with the eight hundred pounds in the hold, caught before the medical detour. It was worth $3.50 a pound. The crew got fifty cents of each. Guindon got the rest for the ice and the fuel and the bait, for the boat's costs, and for the breadwinning. Luck on his side finally, no bacteria made a nest of his face.

It went on like this for years, though, with longlining on the side. Guindon kept fishing. He fished until the pennies added up and he bought a fish house so he could become a seafood buyer. Then he bought another. More boats. When catch shares became the talk of the industry, there was a vote. He voted no. It was another change in a series of changes, most of which had turned out to be bad for him. When it passed, he panicked and prepared for the worst. He sold one of the two fish houses and a boat and got his bills under control. It wasn't until the reorganization was over, and catch shares were in place, that he realized he'd come away owning access to a rough 5 percent of the red snapper in the Gulf of Mexico—his share based on his historic catches. He was one of the largest red snapper owners in America.

He says this, still, with a kind of surprise. He is sitting in the sunny café in Galveston, his son a table behind him, his fish on the menu and his family running his now-bustling fish house, Katie's Seafood Market, a few blocks away. The only evidence of the old days, beside the signature beard and the cap, the long hair and the jeans, is the scar. "You can see that my lip ain't right," he says, pointing. But now, things are better.

"About three months into the system I realized, wow. What a difference in life." Red snapper started fetching $4.50 or $5.00 a pound, a 29 to 42 percent increase over the pre–catch-share price, when buyers clued in on the steady supply and consumer demand followed. Captains stopped running out at the same time and stopped competing for fishing bottom. Instead they worked to keep the supply steady so that the price would hold. And there was no more fishing thousands of pounds of fish before they gutted and iced them. Instead, they started chilling the fish in a mix of ice and seawater right away, then gutting them cold. "All those things that we used to compete against each other on, that was kind of gone. We started sharing." They shared crew, flushing out the undesirables. No more picking guys up at the Salvation Army and training the good ones, only to watch them get poached once they'd sobered up long enough to learn the job.

The crewmen who were left knew what they'd get paid. And everybody knew how much they could catch. They could make plans in life—no more boom and bust. Guindon had a fourth son by then, and this one he had the privilege of helping raise. He was home more. He had a business he could plan around the rest of his life, rather than the reverse.

"It was horrible to be gone so much," he says. Now he is not. He can fish when he wants, if he wants, and these days he also has a legion of people, many of them family, who fish for him. That son at the next table, that boy will never have to fish in bad weather. He will never go to sea to do a thing he doesn't know how to do.

Guindon didn't ask for a catch share. Didn't stump for it, didn't vote for it. But by 2008, when the Environmental Defense Fund asked him to join a fishing organization to protect the system he and others had embraced, he showed up in a room of seafaring loners, people who would go from being his competitors to his colleagues, to figure out how to hang onto it. Someone cut a check for five hundred dollars and put it on the podium, seeding the group's funding. Peer pressure burned through the rest. They elected a board of directors, with Guindon among them.

Later, De La Cruz would come along, and they would envision their own seafood brand. And Guindon would go from being that Texas fisherman with the thicket of beard over the scar to being a kind of poster boy for the success of catch shares. He would say then that he spent a lot of time doing things for the benefit of people other than himself. That he could make a good living just leasing his red snapper to young captains—but for what? He wanted more. Something better. He wanted to conserve the bounty of the sea. And after catch shares changed his life and his industry, he would be damned, just damned, if he didn't make it happen.

Inside Passage, Alaska

Sharecroppers of the Sea

It's 2:00 a.m. and crewman Kasper Harvey is leaning over the rail. The *Viking Spirit*, a fifty-seven-foot steel combination boat, is ten hours out of Sitka while the sea kicks at it starboard. Harvey braces himself with his leg, the bait shed behind him a backdrop of rope, miles of it, coiled on tracks. It's October. Which means the shed has just replaced a summer deck; an aluminum canopy plopped over the top. Now this boat is longline fishing for sablefish, a sharecroppers' gig on a rough sea.

If ever there was a place to fast-forward on catch-share policy and peer two decades into the future, this is it. As the second generation of fishermen to fish this catch share, the captain and crew of the *Viking Spirit* are renters in a marketplace now as engrained as the fishing itself. Though regulators tried to squash it, what happened instead is well illuminated this evening. It's a stunning example of how firmly ocean landlords can hold their foot in the door once they are made.

Harvey works by tungsten light in the night, a long line of rope rising from the water through the bait-shed door, machines pulling it along beside him. Hook after hook of sablefish come with it. And Harvey is hitting each with a gaffe—a kind of metal hook—lifting them onboard and into a hauling chute. One by one, the fish slip along this metal slide and into a nearby dump box, which measures their weight by volume before it drops them into a cargo hold below. Most boats call this simply "the hold." On this boat they call it the slaughterhouse.

It's a good morning, if you can call it morning. The rain is coming in sideways, it's cold and dark, and the deck is drenched, but the fish are coming aboard one after another, and huge. Wrapped in a raincoat and two-tone, suspendered oilskins, Harvey hooks fish after fish by the gills and drops them quick. Underneath his jacket, the back of his sweatshirt reads: THE BEATINGS WILL CONTINUE UNTIL MORALE IMPROVES! It is perhaps the best summary of longline fishing that can be had in a few words.

This is not a light-duty job. It is unceasingly repetitive, which accounts for why Harvey, though only twenty-eight, wakes up in the morning with his hands clamped closed and pain screaming up to his elbows, an ailment fishermen refer to as "the claw." That longlining is attended by brutal weather, long runs of sleepless fishing, and a frequently empty stomach are also not in its favor. Add that every odd fish weighs probably twelve pounds, and the job weeds out the meek and the weak-armed pretty quickly. Making this trip a particular hassle, though, is the fact that the crew is short. And Bob Baldwin is asleep in the stateroom, one of two cozy rooms inside the first deck.

In this market, that's the way it goes. The biggest catch on this boat is not the fat black sablefish thrashing their way to the dump box. It's Baldwin. Baldwin owns the access to the fish now coming aboard. A soon-to-be seventy-year-old fisherman, he holds what metes out to about thirty-five thousand pounds of sablefish and halibut, plus a permit for fishing the Inside Passage of southeast Alaska. All were purchased in the days when they were had much cheaper. Now they're lucrative rental properties eyed by the likes of Captain Vern Crane, who helms this vessel and leases the access to go fish. Hence, Baldwin is the landlord on this trip. When he arrived on board at noon a couple of days ago, he turned up toting a letter-sized envelope—all the paperwork he needed to make a handshake lease with Crane legal. Per its terms, Baldwin gets 65 percent of the value of the catch on the voyage. He could be playing solitaire or drawing cartoons in the galley—doesn't matter. He doesn't have to work on this boat if he doesn't want to. And while most of the time he does anyway, tonight he went to bed at an hour reasonable people deem late and left the crew to a wet night of shorthanded work.

Such are the realities of catch shares. In Alaskan halibut and sable-fish, two fish for which prices exploded under catch shares, owners can make a fine living by leasing out their access rather than fishing it. Renters make a fine living too. But as owners hang on into their retire-ment years, the rights to go fishing have become inaccessible to all but the most industrious young people, who are the first generation to have to buy them in a market that has gone gangbusters. This explains how, in less than two decades, the leasing market has sunk deep roots into this catch share. More than half the fish caught in this program are caught by renters now. And it likely portends what's next for other fishermen around the nation: small business ventures sliding toward wage jobs.

So it is that Crane is at the comby, a red metal wheel that gathers the line and hauls it back aboard. He grabs the rope as it comes through the machine and hangs it briskly by its hooks along the gear rails, the tracklike rails that wrap around the back of the bait shed. His arms run hand over hand to keep up while the comby hauls fast. Farther toward the stern, crewman Justin Sutherland works just as quickly to make repairs, tying on new hooks with a string known as a gangion and running the still-attached but battered ones through a hook bender, a hand-operated gadget that looks like a can opener. Harvey, taking the worst of the rain through the bait-shed door, keeps on haul-ing the fish.

Knees tucked under the rail, Harvey hooks fish after fish and swings them hard over his shoulder. The sea, at least, is not fighting him much. But the fish are big and mean and angry, so when they land in the chute behind him, they whip side to side, piling up rather than moving to the dump box. If Baldwin were awake he'd be standing there, as he often does, popping the gills on each for the kinder, gentler death that keeps them freshest, and sliding them along, giving Harvey a hand. But the crew is a man short without him. And because of this, the fish are stacking up on the chute. Harvey eyes the next few hooks in the water, a floodlight overhead to help him see, and, spying nothing, twists around, legs still braced, trying to shove the pile of fish into the dump box without leaving his post.

It sort of works. A few fish go down. The rest are still piled up. The comby keeps hauling them aboard. Harvey reaches for a micro-commander over his head so he can drive the boat forward along the line. Fish start coming up fast again. Big ones. And the more there are, the more gruesome this scene gets. Harvey gaffes each one, swings it aboard. But the bulk of them are still hooked and the ropes drag them back toward the gear rails.

It's the crucifier that breaks them free. It's an appropriately ugly word for a nasty device: two metal rollers, like steel fingers raised in a peace sign, brace the heads of the fish while the rope keeps going, effectively ripping the hooks from their mouths. Most of the hooks tear through their faces, leaving lips dangling, whole jaws torn away. The fish fill up along the chute mutilated and writhing, a last-ditch effort to find water or die, blood spraying the deck. Harvey keeps turning, keeps trying to push them into the dump box with a hand behind his back. He can't keep up.

When the next run of fish arrives, Harvey hoists them one by one, swinging hard now to manage the weight. A fish hits the chute and untethers from the line, falling to the floor by his feet and fighting. It's incredible how long sablefish can live out of water. Twenty minutes later, when another slaps to the floor and the two are side by side, the first fish perks up, clearly still alive. Twenty minutes of drowning on air.

Fishing is death. It is always death—that part isn't new. But death on tiny margins is less precise and a little more gruesome, attended by the machinery that makes fishing both more efficient and more brutal. Put a crew a man down and it gets worse. Three more fish hit the crucifier and throw themselves out of the chute, their bodies leaping fiercely, every muscle charged. They roll onto the deck by Harvey's feet. There is no time to collect them.

Save for his motion and the furious motion of the fish, fishing at this hour is like sleepwalking. Though the engine roars unceasingly and the sound of the hooks being drawn back onto the boat is like the sound of three dozen forks scraping dinner plates, a kind of fishing quiet envelops the bait shed. The crew move like ghosts, talk only out of necessity. And though they probably aren't thinking about sleep— their endurance for sleeplessness is as practiced as a runner's pace— they are silent in the night while their bodies keep on. Sutherland is still mending gear on the rail. Crane is checking it, hanging it up, coiling the rope off the comby. Harvey is just gaffe, swing, gaffe, swing, the occasional shove of the catch, his left hand still driving.

This isn't exactly how things were designed to go. Since the 1995 birth of the catch share for halibut and sablefish, leasing was supposed to be a means by which older fishermen aged out, intended to mimic the days in which seasoned fishermen hired young captains to helm their vessels as they grew old. Yet as the catch-share era of fishing has taken hold, the arrangement on this boat—a stealthier and more opportunistic practice called "walking on"—is a burgeoning trend born of a legal loophole.

What that means is this: Those who bought quota after January 1995 aren't allowed to lease their fishing access out to younger crews. They are supposed to sell as they retire instead, encouraged to do so by a boots-on-deck rule that says they have to be on the vessel while their fish are caught, unless they own at least 20 percent of the boat that catches it, which Baldwin does not. The aim was noble: to ensure that those who owned the access kept some skin in the game or got out, divesting so that the access, or quota, could be had by the young. But the rule left a loophole—it didn't say the owners had to actually fish. Now an entire generation of aging fishermen are riding around Alaska longliners doing whatever while sharecropping crews catch their fish for an ever-shrinking share of the profits.

These riders are in demand. With lease rates rising fast while captains undercut one another for the work, "You just get sluttier and sluttier until you get pounds," Crane says. "I will do whatever. I want the fish. I need the work." He still owes about a third of the $650,000 he paid for the *Viking Spirit*. He says leasing quota makes the boat payment. He isn't proud of it. But if he wants to keep this boat—and he does—he says he has to.

Over the last two decades the share of profits these renters pay to landlords has skyrocketed. Once typically about 50 percent of the catch, it was pushed to 75 percent by Russian-American fishermen out of Homer, who cornered the bottom of the market by operating cheap with family crews on boats they built themselves. Now captains with more costly professional crews and boat payments, like Crane, soup up their vessels to battle low rates with plush amenities. They post ads on websites like Seattle's Dock Street Brokers and mail brightly colored fliers around every spring, soliciting landlords to walk on. They offer big-screen and satellite TVs, massive DVD collections, quality grub, and staterooms. Showers, saunas, hot tubs. Thanks to an online list of owners, finding their target market isn't hard. Nearly 70 percent of them live in Alaska. The rest are scattered around the lower Forty-Eight, making Crane's model of docking near airports a fit for the fly-in crowd.

The forty-one-year-old Petersburg native has got other selling points, too. The *Viking Spirit* has a stateroom for privacy, a bonus for landlords who don't want to sleep in the bunks with a bunch of twenty-somethings. It's also got a shower, a washer and dryer, and the must-have flat-screen

TV and DVDs. Crane's membership in a Sitka co-op gives his walk-ons better pricing for their fish. And he's a hunter, so his freezer is stocked with moose meat and venison, food some walk-ons can't get elsewhere. (There are two rifles and a pair of binoculars on this boat, and Crane's been known to shoot from the wheelhouse, then zip into an unsinkable neoprene safety suit and rope his game to his body while the crew tows him in on the hauler.) These amenities, they're all he's got, he says, because he can't beat the Russian rate. As is, his agreement to forfeit all but 35 percent to landlords like Baldwin is about the lowest lease rate offered by a non-Russian captain in Alaska.

To be clear, no one on this boat is starving, at least not longer than momentarily. Renters though they may be, these crews do earn. Crane went to college for a teaching degree before he opted to fish instead. Now that was starving. His first teaching job in a remote Alaskan village paid $29,000 a year. Health care and retirement ate most of it, so that he lived in the bush on a thousand bucks a month, a terrible sum in a place so remote that it is among the most expensive places to live in America. These days? "I can make that in a week, easily," he says. And he means the $29,000.

This is exactly what stole him from the classroom. And what keeps him leasing. Money is the chief lure for fishermen. And there's so much of it in this industry thanks to catch shares that it's easy to mask how unevenly the pie is sliced. Crane grew up fishing with his father in a wooden boat, his bunk under a tarp that covered the leaks, and he wanted that money bad. Once he left teaching behind, he made his first million by the time he was thirty. His boats got fancier until he had three of them and a few properties, too. He's about to lose quite a lot of it in a divorce. And in that way of people who make a lot of money, he's got a lot of things to pay for. But the day rate on this job is not so bad—this trip will fetch about $39,000, bringing $13,650 to the boat, $12,000 after costs, or about $7,000 for Crane and $2,000 for each of the crewmen after expenses, earned in four days.

Before catch shares, halibut was worth far less. Hauled ashore in daylong derbies and necessarily frozen in bulk, it sold for $2.99 or $3.99 a pound retail in hideous frozen bricks. Now it's behind the Whole Foods counter in steaky fillets that sell for $28.00 a pound, and is a restaurant favorite. And though many Americans have never heard of the sablefish, the halibut's aquatic neighbor, it sells for nearly as much for export to Japan. On the West Coast, it's sometimes found on menus labeled black cod. That's fishermen's slang for its resemblance to cod, its expression being similarly pouty, its belly the same round paunch. But the resemblance stops at the plate. Also called butterfish— perhaps the most apt name for the omega-rich, black-skinned fillets— sablefish can taste like butter wrapped in soy sauce. It's a favorite of many seafarers. And the oft-discarded collar is an insider's gold. Crane prefers them to the best of the shrimp and crab in Alaska and says a cooler full have appeased many a wife, including his own in the days when he still had one.

Though worlds apart for consumers, sablefish is as bound to the halibut in the sea as it is in demand: caught the same way, often at the same time, in the same waters, though at varying depths. In Alaska, both are managed in the same catch share, referred to shorthand as the IFQ, officially the Halibut and Sablefish Individual Fishing Quota program, the pounds in which are often called "Qs" by the people that wrangle them ashore. The rental market for the program bleeds over into state waters, where the *Viking Spirit* fishes on this voyage.

Grateful as he is for the work, Crane says the market can bring prickly dynamics to his boat. He admits to making jokes to his crews when the seas swell and his walk-ons start vomiting, rolling around in their bunks and groaning. He admits that he thinks: *Good. At least they're suffering, too.* It keeps morale up when everybody is miserable instead of just the people he's paying. Otherwise when there's weather coming, when they've been on deck for eighteen hours, with no coffee and no food, trying to catch the fish before a storm rolls in, the tension mounts.

"We'll just go and go and go until we can't stand up anymore. We'll go thirty, forty hours. Straight. And the crew will start bitching if someone is in there watching TV with their feet up." To make a trip pencil so he can shoulder the cost of the crew and the fuel and the bait, he sometimes has to stack up to four walk-ons—yes, extra people—on the boat at a time. Last year he had to add a life raft just to keep it legal. The crowding can upend harmony. And fishermen, people practiced at turning inward and containing themselves in close quarters, can sometimes unravel if the quarters get too close.

Later, Harvey will say he doesn't mind. Doesn't mind that some of the walk-ons don't work at all or help him out when he needs it. They're less annoying than the crew who show up only for the money, people he has to work with through long, dogged days who complain too much and sometimes never stop talking. On one recent trip, he says, Crane put a man on a fifty-word budget and fined him fifty dollars for every word over, his chatter was that incessant. That he will never own the rights to access this fish on his own is evident. "I don't have a fair shot at it. I can't buy IFQs on what I'm making off of our lease rates," Harvey says. But he doesn't mind the extra people. They mind their business, Harvey says. And he minds his. Once, a walk-on heckled him for an entire trip, "bitching about the weather. Remarks like, 'Oh, you wouldn't have work if I wasn't here' and shit like that," and he got angry. But the rest are simply there. And while he sometimes wishes the crew had more space, thinks it would be nice if there weren't extra people playing cards or watching movies in the galley when the galley is small, it's just a part of fishing, same as hooks and bait and all the rest.

This sentiment is not at all odd. Leasing is a generation old in this market. Most crewmen are happy to have the work. They don't bother trying to plot their way to the top of this industry—it's an industry

most can't climb. Though quota was given away free to the last generation of fishermen in 1995 when the catch share started, to buy enough
of it to run a business now costs as much as a house. Most young
fishermen would rather have the house or something else they can put
their hands on. It can be a risky investment unless you've got cash to
burn, which is why the "graying of the fleet" is now a thing worried
over by industry stalwarts and overseers like the government and trade
groups. What access rights sell now tend to consolidate among people
who already own them, people who buy more just to avoid the taxes
on the revenue from the rest. The number of halibut owners in this system has fallen by 44 percent over nineteen years, sablefish by 21 percent
in seventeen. And so long as those owners keep walking on, captains and
crews fishing these seas take what they can get.

———

By the time the crew falls into their bunks to rest it's 4:00 a.m., the
Viking Spirit is on anchor, and the engine is still roaring. They have
fished for twenty-three hours. Crane doesn't sleep in his stateroom,
catnapping instead in a day bunk in the wheelhouse—the same place
his four-year-old entertains himself with a stuffed moose during salmon
trips. It's the only place Crane can see the radar. He likes to be sure the
boat isn't drifting.

The ocean is trying to get you, he says. He said this at the helm on
the drive out, a calm, clear day that wouldn't have triggered that kind
of thought in most people. He pointed at the sea from behind his screens
and gadgets—laptops pimped out for navigation, satellite GPS and
radar, depth sounders, sat phone and radios—in a gesture that was part
accusation, part statement of fact. From the moment you set out on it,
the ocean is trying to get you, he said, making clear the job of beating
it is a captain's curse. The ocean nearly claimed him more than a decade ago—a boat run aground in the night, overturned in dark water,
his father asleep at the wheel and the sea filling with rope. And since

then there are habits he doesn't break. Sleeping in the wheelhouse, the radar close, that's one. Anything that's going to go wrong, he says, "you can bet that shit is going to go down at night."

This night it doesn't.

They sleep until 9:00 a.m., the sunrise and the time secondary to the cycle of set, soak, haul. Crane calls to Harvey in his bunk, asks for his help with the anchor, and Harvey and Sutherland set out for the bait shed, grabbing bags of chips from a box under the galley table. This is food they can pour quickly into their mouths without fuss. They will devour fifty-four bags of chips in three days. And while their appetites are probably enormous, food, like sleep, is mostly a thing that waits.

Midmorning there's a forecast to outrun, warning of twenty-one-foot seas, ten feet or more inside Chatham Strait where the *Viking Spirit* is tucked behind Baranof Island. The wind is projected to blow sixty knots, almost seventy miles an hour. It's a wind that, with enough fetch, will put a boat in real trouble. At the least it will break the windows and the sound of it will tear through the eardrums and the mind.

Nobody says much about it. But the next two sets fly out of the stern. Presumably, catch shares freed fishermen from the time constraints of a derby, and eliminated the race to fish that put so many boats to sea in bad weather and so many fishermen in watery graves. Still, fishing is a dangerous business. And those gains can be erased by leasing when walk-ons jump onboard with fickle schedules and an expectation that their fish get caught on time. Baldwin is not that guy. But with ten hours of driving between Chatham Strait and the boat's slip in Sitka, the crew has got twelve hours to catch the rest of his fish before the weather catches up, or Crane risks losing the thousands he's put into bait and fuel for this trip, a loss that the crew absorbs too, their pay beholden to a game of percentages.

Baldwin reads on a tablet while the hooks soak—a mercifully short time, given the weather, but necessary, too, while carnivorous sand fleas, aquatic critters that will devour the flesh of the catch, infest this bottom as they do. Baldwin knows there's a chance the boat will turn around or tie up in some bay until the weather is clear. He is disinclined to gripe about it, nostalgic instead for Warm Springs, a bay with fifteen or more cabins and a dock where a boat can go and hide, so named for the handful of hot springs there. It's a place fishermen don't mind waiting.

He is unlike some of Crane's walk-ons in this way. He doesn't treat the *Viking Spirit* like a cruise ship and expect that Crane can pilot it on a schedule and catch his fish too. Others want to know how long it will take. When they should book their plane tickets and hotels. Sometimes they call six months in advance, before the fishing season is even announced, trying to block out dates for next year. Weather is presumed to be fair, like vacation.

"Here's a guy, literally on the golf course, calling me up and saying, 'Okay I'm coming to Alaska, how long do you think it will take? 'Cause I've got a tee time on Wednesday and I can't miss the country club,' or whatever," Crane says later, sitting in the wheelhouse. "Of course, I say yes. But I'm thinking, 'Oh God, I hope I can do this.' . . . I've been completely bitched out because guys have got to change their plane ticket." This is true for the times he's brought fish in early as well as late. Though he shoulders the cost of bait and fuel, boat maintenance, the crew, and food, some make him pay their airline change fees, too.

Baldwin is not that guy, either.

But older fishermen like him, fishermen who still love to fish, may be a dying breed. Absent buy-in from the next generation, access rights to these fish are landing with their children and people with money to burn. This system does have rules to ensure that quota goes to qualifying fishermen. But they're quaint laws, about as enforced as prohibitions on jaywalking. So that the up-and-coming generation of walk-ons includes people who couldn't catch their fish if they had to.

"You can just spot them. They got the gold watch. Their hair is perfect. They don't smell like diesel. They definitely weren't at the bar watching football," says Crane. He is sitting in the wheelhouse surrounded by pictures of his children, two tow-headed boys, often curled in his arms in snapshots. Cap-covered in these photos and squinting at the sun, Crane looks not unlike Mark Wahlberg on the set of *The Perfect Storm*, a guy inclined toward jeans and sweats, T-shirts and cutoff rubber boots. He doesn't relate to some of the quota owners he leases from. And sometimes these trips illuminate the widening cultural divide in the seafood industry.

"Their little briefcase, you know, they stroll down the dock with a little briefcase. Lot of them wear Dockers and shit. I'm like, 'Wow. Anywhere on my boat is not clean enough for you.' But it's the money. I'm just slutty enough that they will go with me . . . And, thank God, 'cause it made my boat payments."

Crane wheels the boat around, rolling two fingers on a knob near the throttle, and back to haul the first set of the morning. He climbs from the wheelhouse to the bait shed. Baldwin dons his rain gear—a navy jacket, orange gloves, and an Icicle Seafoods cap—and takes up a spot behind the neon-green Crane, now at the rail. The rain and fog persist, but the first haul is immense. "Welcome aboard!" Baldwin says to the fish. He does this with the big ones—they sell for a serenade-worthy eight dollars a pound, making each one basically a hundred-dollar bill. And they are all big. He holds each one down, reaches a finger into the gills, and pulls. Blood sputters over the chute. He tucks the fish into the dump box, sometimes pushing them into the back. One by one the fish stack up, filling the box until Baldwin can't fit them in. Before long a thousand pounds are dropped into the slaughterhouse below. He wipes the pools of blood and water away with a gloved hand, then happily tosses curiosities across the deck: sea urchins and sand fleas, little strips of red coral and petrified treelike growths from below.

Somewhere along the way, Harvey asks for music. Crane hands

him an iPod Shuffle waterproofed in a Ziploc bag. Gloved hands having no say, the crew works on to a friend's playlist. The Beatles and Bruce Springsteen. Band of Horses. An unlikely blend arranged by a keen ear. When CCR's "Long as I Can See the Light" comes through the speakers mounted inside the canopy, Baldwin sings it.

Another thousand pounds of fish come aboard, bringing the tally to eighty-five hundred pounds by 7:30 p.m. The forecast has shifted so that the worst of the weather won't arrive until the following afternoon. The sense of urgency eases, but it doesn't abate. The forecast is still severe—ten-foot seas, even in the Inside Passage, and winds at forty-five knots, more than fifty miles an hour, strong enough to toss the boat, maybe break a few windows. He doesn't fear for his safety, Crane says. But bad seas are like traffic jams—you'd rather avoid them.

He has already moved the boat north, away from the mouth of the Chatham Strait where it meets the open sea, where the weather will be worse. The fish keep coming aboard. But then with them comes a monster catch of rope—old Norwegian gear, maybe Japanese. "Small snarl," Harvey calls up the line. Crane is behind him again, Sutherland mending gear. "Small snarl," Harvey says again. Then again. And again. First these snarls are just tiny knots. The size of a hankie, maybe a scarf. Then they get bigger. Like grocery bags. Then ice coolers. When the final warped knot comes aboard, and Crane lifts it off the deck, it is larger than he is, a massive tangle peppered with hooks. He can tell by looking at it that his ship has just caught a rope older than he is. Gear left behind in the days before catch shares, when people in a rush cut their muddled lines off in the sea, ghost fishes these waters. It is now hopelessly ensnared by his own. Not wanting to be slowed, he pulls a knife from his belt—they all have one—and makes quick work of ripping through the gangions, more inclined to replace them later and get back to work. Baldwin dives in to help, and by the time they are done they have sentenced Sutherland to a purgatory of mending. But the sun is falling. And time is short.

Gulls and albatross set up around the starboard side, diving in for the odd fish scrap. Gold light dances over the sea. Baldwin and Harvey stand briefly in the bait-shed door, the water walking under the sun-lit boat like glitter. Gunning for the final fifteen hundred pounds, the crew doesn't bother with breaks. They set again, intent on heading back to port in Sitka in the night.

But within an hour or two the luck of the last tow runs out. And that's fishing. This last hopeful set brings up hook after hook of nothing. A thick tension falls over the deck. It's dark again and the crew has gone quiet. The hope of heading home tonight seems unlikely. The playlist plays on, the sound bouncing off the aluminum canopy. And almost on cue, as Radiohead roars through the deck—*Don't get any big ideas*—the line goes so cold that Baldwin hangs up his rain gear, something he does when waiting for the fish starts to feel like hovering. "A watched pot never boils," he says, and takes up reading in the galley again.

Midnight comes and goes, late enough that things start to ache. Backs. Knees. Wrists. To stand on the sea hour after hour, the water rolling the deck, is a workout in balance training. Tomorrow, Harvey will be lathering his knees in some kind of tiger balm—his wrists too, already swollen and curling. But for now it takes a few more hours before the whole set is hauled cold and two more are put out. Before the sun rises, Harvey crawls into a bunk for a nap, doubling up on socks. Sutherland takes a seat at the galley table and nods off sitting upright, his feet still in his boots. Crane doesn't sleep at all. At 5:30 a.m. they try again. Harvey crawling out of bed, Sutherland snapping awake at the table. Baldwin steps onto the deck and up to the chute too. The sun rises with the line and they burn through two pots of coffee. And finally, the fish arrive. One big one after another. Harvey swings them over the rail fast, each one the size of two gallons of water. Baldwin bleeds them all, so that the dump box fills up quick.

The *Viking Spirit* heads for port at 9:00 a.m., an albatross on board signaling a storm farther out. Sure enough, the radio reports rising seas in south Chatham. Crane aims north for Frederick Sound, where the weather is supposed to turn by afternoon, and organizes the wheel watch. Harvey will tend the wheel for long, deep straightaways through which Crane will sleep. Crane takes first shift, and plans his own driving time through the areas that require more navigation and the stretches during which the *Viking Spirit* will face a southeast wind that could be fierce. It's Friday morning. He's slept three hours in his bunk since Wednesday, save for the twenty minutes in his chair with the watch and the depth alarms on and a nap to a ten-minute alarm he hit twice. "People don't give the captain enough credit for how hard it is to stay awake. They think you're not doing any work so you shouldn't be tired. But once you get in here and it's all warm, oh, fuck, it's hard." You can string it along with caffeine and your head out the window, he says.

There's no need. In a couple of hours he gets to bed, and sleeps for two more with Harvey at the wheel. It's enough. The rest of the day passes with Crane in the captain's chair, the sea unfolding under the *Viking Spirit* as it travels a slow six or seven knots, or about eight miles an hour. The waves on the open ocean hit twenty-one feet. Planes are diverted from Ketchikan in the wind, unable to land. But the water stays calm behind Baranof Island until the Sitka port is in view, and then the harbor. The eight-foot seas Crane expected in the Inside Passage never come.

Crane's relief is plain. He starts cracking jokes. Belts out some Snoop Dogg. He sets his sights on the Pioneer Bar, a fishermen's watering hole on Katlian Street, a road that runs along Sitka Harbor speckled with marine supply stores and boat services. He says he likes to sit there surrounded by the photos—the walls are covered in them, fishing photos from every era and every kind of endeavor, even shipwrecks—and see the water through the window and know that he made it to land.

This anxiety about living and dying, and the people who could live and die with him, it wears. He admits now that he was worried after midnight, sure he'd made a mistake in not weathering in, sure he'd get caught and have to scrap his way out. And he says there is a line in the book *Time Bandit*, written by the captains of the vessel that once carried Tom Miller, that resonates deeply with him. It's about how fishermen hit the bars about as fast as they hit land. How if they don't erase the memory of the sea, they will never go back.

Gulf Wild

Traceable Catch and the Restaurant Menu

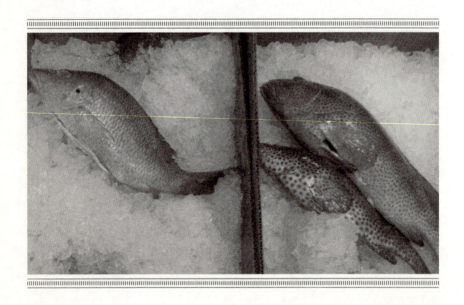

Back in Florida, Jason De La Cruz started to make a go of it in catch shares. He was still a boat mechanic by day and a part-time commercial spearfisherman by all the other days. And he had hired a captain to run a longline boat, which he planned to use to catch the fish that were his.

While he did all that, he had a vision he could not let go of. And in it, his grouper were more than just pounds of protein, hauled out of the water and towed to the nearest fish house. They were a brand that meant quality, freshness, and ecological sustainability. He believed there was a market for that—one in which consumers paid a premium. They were already paying more for grass-fed beef and free-range chickens, and the chance to know about the farms and farmers that brought them their food. He thought they'd do the same for seafood. Based on the talks he'd had with Buddy Guindon, the scar-faced fisherman from Texas, and a handful of other quota-owning fishermen, he was not alone. Now that catch shares had replaced their competition with cooperation, they had moved past talks about steadying the supply to keep prices up and sharing crews and started germinating bigger ideas.

The Gulf Reef Fish Shareholder Alliance, as their group came to be known, congealed around a core of five to ten guys, all leaders in the industry from around the Gulf. De La Cruz was not an industry leader yet, but he noticed this bunch of fishermen with plans akin to his own, then joined up as a dues-paying member. Launching their own brand was an idea they toyed with from the very beginning, in the days when De La Cruz was learning how to run a longline boat and catch a couple hundred thousand pounds of fish.

At first the idea was one of many, conceived to help them do battle with imports coming from the other side of the Gulf. Labor was cheap there, environmental stewardship questionable. They knew their fish offered consumers something better. So when the alliance, led by president David Krebs, conceived the brand as a means to hold the value of domestic fare, De La Cruz wanted to help build it. He wanted consumers and chefs to see his seafood as more than just finned fare of unknown origin. But the alliance pulled the trigger on the idea sooner than its members expected. The impetus arrived, more or less, on April 20, 2010, four months after the grouper system became rule. It was the day the multinational oil and gas company BP started spilling oil into the Gulf of Mexico.

De La Cruz doesn't remember where he was when it happened. Just that night, when he was watching stories about the oil rig's explosion on the news and details of the mess were populating Facebook. It was at the end of what was becoming a dizzying daily routine of fishing, hauling, hawking fish, and boat repair. The video he remembers best was shot on a cell phone from a recreational tuna boat. In it, the explosion of the oil rig was unfurling into the sky. His mouth fell open when he saw it. He remembers thinking: *Oh my God, what are you doing to me?* It took him less than a minute to see that his and Joswig's half-million-dollar investment was taking a hit.

Supply boats were surrounding what remained of Deepwater Horizon's drilling platform and spraying water where oil was blasting out of the drilling riser in an inferno. The boats were chugging lakes' worth of water from the sea and blasting it at the flames. Still, the fire and smoke so dwarfed their efforts that, from the air, the scene looked like an angry, burning starfish. Eleven people were missing and presumed dead. The survivors, some badly injured, were in need of rescue.

In the days that followed, efforts to seal the gusher failed. Underwater cameras captured oil spilling out of the ruptured riser in a pressurized, billowing cloud. Within a week, thousands of feet of rubber booms were thrown out over the Gulf. Birds started flying and floating ashore covered in oil. Aerial photographers captured images of the sea looking as if it had been fractured by veins, the red-tinted crude spilling below the surface like a wall of capillaries. Within twenty days, planes were spraying oil dispersants over the sea like crop dusters.

The early estimates of exactly how much oil was spilling into the Gulf started with a thousand barrels a day and pitched steeply upward until government scientists pinned it at somewhere between twelve thousand and sixty-two thousand. The translation was that every four days the *Exxon Valdez* spill was repeating itself in the Gulf of Mexico. Fishing was shut down, including De La Cruz's boats. And newscast after newscast featured guys out of work, some trying to inch around the water by boat to assess the damage, only to be threatened with fines.

It wasn't so much that the grouper was getting pummeled. On the animated maps shown on the news—maps in which the spill kept getting bigger and bigger, traced by zigzagging lines—De La Cruz could see that his fishing grounds were far away from it all. The Gulf of Mexico is more than 600,000 square miles, after all. Not much smaller than Alaska. The actual spill site was closest to the southern tip of Louisiana. The oil came ashore, when it did, nowhere near to where De La Cruz fished off the coast of Madeira Beach, southwest of Tampa.

But to the rest of America, Gulf fish were Gulf fish, and so Gulf fish were losing market share fast. Nobody wanted petroleum for dinner. And while the national news broadcast images of oil-smeared pelicans and people hunting tar balls on the beach with litter-box scoopers, consumers were doing what consumers do and just buying beef and chicken.

"We were like, holy crap, what are we going to do now? The news was nonstop about that damn oil spill," De La Cruz said. He fished one or two trips between the day of the spill and the end of that year. Maybe three. His boats tied up by mandate and his life's investment crashing, De La Cruz and Krebs took the lead among the shareholders in crafting a brand that could save it.

What they envisioned was to build a brand—and soon—with emphasis on the exact location of their catch. If they could pinpoint where in the Gulf their fish came from and develop a tool that brought home the ecological merits, quality, and freshness of their fish, they imagined they could get out from under the disaster when fishing resumed. The only question was how they would prove to consumers that their fish were domestic and sustainably caught. Solving that riddle was something catch shares made easier—the shareholders had more time than they used to, the newfound ability to work together, and allies at environmental groups eager to bankroll such questions.

———————

Turned out, one answer wasn't far. At the time, Michael Clayton, a consultant for the Environmental Defense Fund, was hanging around New England trying to figure out how to keep some of that region's most diligently cared-for seafood from disappearing into the opacity of the supply chain. In a meeting with chefs and fishermen, he'd hit on the idea of Trace and Trust, a storytelling platform that could connect diners to restaurants where seafood was going straight from the hands of its harvesters to the plate. The aim was to get past the buzzwords—"local, sustainable, small-scale, fresh"—to the tale of the region's cleanest fishermen. Through talks with the fishermen and a handful of chefs, he created a multimedia dining experience. Restaurant-goers could scan QR codes on printed menus to learn the story of their seafood. The story was straightforward: when and how their fish was caught, and about the fishermen and boats that delivered it. When Clayton launched Trace and Trust in 2011, it proved consumer appetite for traceable seafood like nothing ever had.

One of the places it hit big was 606 Congress, a restaurant within the Renaissance Hotel in the Boston Seaport where a chef named Richard Garcia had been working with Clayton to usher Trace and Trust along. A guy who loved sustainable seafood before anybody even married those two words, Garcia's interest was not so much about heeding consumer curiosity as it was about engendering it. A heart-and-soul locavore before locavore was even a thing, Garcia wanted to drive the burgeoning love affair between diners and seafood farther than it had gone yet. He'd been looking to link day-boat fishermen to his restaurant and to other chefs in Boston for a while. And like a lot of chefs and fishermen too, he believed that traceable seafood could be the next culinary revolution, and should be.

Born in Guatemala and raised in Miami, Garcia was a natural fit to pioneer a startup that paired foodies and seafarers, someone who brought exactly the kind of self-made grit to cooking that fishermen are known for on the seas. Self-taught, Garcia started working in kitchens at the age of thirteen, dropped out of high school in the ninth grade, and got a GED at eighteen. His only formal cooking training was in the Marine Corps. He was a guy with ideas and discipline who that year was spending twelve hours a day in his restaurant, at least half of them in the kitchen, unusual in an era in which most executive chefs were hovering over ledgers behind desks. That he was more apt to hire a newcomer—a blank slate of a kitchen kid who had never cooked—than the culinary school graduates he complained were outnumbering chefs fifty to one was indicative of the kind of upstart ingenuity that drew him to Chris Brown and Steve Arnold, the fishermen Clayton had been working to link to consumers.

What they envisioned together was this: Brown and Arnold would deliver fresh day-boat catch to 606 Congress and other restaurants, while Trace and Trust curated their story online. That way, Garcia could stoke a hunger for fresh local catch without much effort from his waitstaff. Instead, Clayton partnered with a software geek in Georgia (the country, not the state), so that all Garcia had to do was print the menus with the QR codes to bring the tale into his restaurant. This way, diners not only got the story, but once they scanned the code, entered their fish ID, and dove into the digital narrative of their dinner, they were just a few clicks away from the social media bonanza that could blow Trace and Trust across New England.

It worked. During what was supposed to be a one-year pilot of the program, diners tweeted their dinner plates in such volume and with such enthusiasm that the media could not ignore it. *The New York Times, USA Today*, and CNN, not to mention the local papers and news channels, were like moths flocking around the spotlight that shone on Trace and Trust meals. Before long, 120 restaurants across New England had piled on. And while Garcia would surmise it was all "pretty basic information," it was information the majority of consumers have never had when it came to seafood. And they went wild for it.

For Garcia, it was an ideological tailwind he craved. Boston chefs had long been critical of city leaders for letting chain restaurants dominate the seaport. Anchored in what used to be an enclave of local seafood, 606 was surrounded by behemoths in a supper war that had devolved into one neon-lit bowl of clam chowder after another. With cod stocks taking a nosedive, local chefs were working hard to buoy the underloved fish that still thrived off Boston's shores. Garcia was doing his part—doing a swift business in sea bass at the time, in concoctions like white cocoa bean and chorizo stew with yogurt. Hake, pollock, and fluke were also still around, all environmentally safe and all caught locally and brought in fresh.

But Garcia was getting diddly for curbside promotion. Instead, the Boston Seaport had become ground zero for a kind of Disney food scene. Chain restaurants churned out meals by the thousand, all of them featuring the white, flaky fish in distress in the Atlantic. The great lie the chains peddled, subliminally at least, was that the shores of Boston were still teaming with the stuff and that local boats still fished it. In fact, only about fifteen fishing boats were left working out of the seaport, compared to the hundreds that moored there in the days when it dominated the East Coast seafood trade. So what diners were eating there instead was mostly imports, caught in who-knew-what conditions and shipped from who-knew-where for who-knew-how-long before it hit the plate.

Ironically, seafood mogul Jared Auerbach was in a warehouse across the street from 606 glued to computer screens, hawking a glut of local catch out of the region—tens of thousands of pounds a day—all because few in Boston besides Garcia even wanted it. Auerbach's newish company, Red's Best, would be credited with keeping a lot of the remaining small boats in business during the cod crash in New England by finding markets for their catch. If the push to build local appetites for that seafood worked, it could not only keep those fish in the region, it could also buoy prices for the small boats that were struggling through cod's decline. But whether New England consumers were just drunk for cod or simply hadn't tried anything else was a chicken-or-egg kind of problem. Most of New England seafood does, after all, taste the same: white and sweet and flaky. For all chefs knew, diners wouldn't eat anything else.

Garcia thought he knew better. He thought diners would go for local catch if they could get it, and if they knew the stories of the fishermen who caught it. But if he and his colleagues were ever going to get support for their mission to buoy the local catch, it was going to require things like Twitter. And *The Boston Globe*.

Fortunately, with Trace and Trust, that is exactly what happened.

Now diners were sitting in front of their dinner plates reading about the fishermen who brought their fish to them. A couple of quick clicks and they could check in at 606 Congress on Facebook, then share the story of what they were eating. They followed with photos. Then their friends chimed in, turning up at the restaurant later to do the same thing.

It was, quite literally, a feeding frenzy. And after big media piled on, Trace and Trust proved effective at battling the bizarre unreality that Boston's seafood chains were broadcasting. Suddenly more newspapers in New England were taking an interest in the fact that those white, flaky fish had crashed hard. And they were telling eco-conscious diners they could do their part by trying something new.

It worked for more than a year. Fabulously. Then on January 7, 2012, a boat named the *Elizabeth Helen* rolled over and sank about three miles northeast of Block Island off the coast of Rhode Island. Soon afterward, Trace and Trust floundered too. It turned out that despite all the fanfare, Trace and Trust had been propped up by only three boats. It had grown far and fast, but it was already struggling with delivery logistics. Minus one boat, there were not enough fishermen involved to serve all the restaurants that signed on. Garcia, who had become director of Trace and Trust's advisory board, helped Clayton expand it to include other farmed fare. The reputation he built through Trace and Trust only bolstered his credibility as a locavore. So that when Trace and Trust receded out of Boston to concentrate on Rhode Island seafood, Garcia hung on to his street cred and kept bringing the same products to the same interested consumers.

To those watching, Garcia and the other chefs had made their case for local seafood. The consumer appetite was clearly there. And traceable, sustainable local catch could and did sell big.

For Garcia, it was also an experience that helped sell him on catch shares. Party as he is to a white-coated brotherhood that buys its pork and beef from people who can predict how much there will be for years and what it will cost, he saw that same predictability finally coming to seafood. "Five years ago, without catch shares, for example, Atlantic fluke was something that we could only get certain periods of the year, and outside of those periods it's very tough to find." Garcia says this sitting on a pinstriped chair in the lounge of 606, chefs busy off his shoulder behind a wall of glass. Now he gets fluke year round, he says. And he can buy it from more than just a few creative-minded fishermen. He can buy from anyone who has access rights to fluke.

In this equation, where fishermen have an actual inventory, chefs find consistent supply at consistent prices. It helps them plan menus. It helps them know what their costs will be. And in this world where a boat can become a more complete business, chefs can have other things, too. They can link their restaurants to their fishermen and draw consumers through the door with that narrative, all while giving local catch the fanfare it deserves. There simply is no comparable security with wild seafood managed otherwise, Garcia says. Which is why he is inclined to stump for catch shares. And why he's among dozens of chefs have who signed on to support catch-share initiatives led by EDF.

———

DE LA CRUZ was about to learn much the same thing: that because his fish came from a stable, sustainable supply, there was an eager market on the other side of the supply chain, including chefs, that would want them. Once he and the rest of the Gulf of Mexico Reef Fish Shareholders' Alliance set their sights on building a brand, their environmental partners knew exactly who to pair them with. Eager to see their work in the Gulf take root, EDF set them up with Clayton.

On a day in 2011, Clayton toured Katie's Seafood Market, Guindon's fish house in Galveston, Texas. And afterward sat in a room overlooking the bay with Guindon, De La Cruz, and T. J. Tate, the brand's newly minted sustainability director, a deeply resourceful woman who had quit a more promising gig to help them, a gesture that proved her to be exactly the person for the job.

By then they didn't just want to get out from under the BP oil spill. Or simply be known as purveyors of high-quality fish. They wanted to make a difference in seafood fraud and in conservation efforts, too. Their seafood supply stable, they could concentrate on becoming environmental innovators and advocates. But they knew they could only succeed if they could move their fish all the way through the supply chain without losing that story. They wanted help with how to do that. They had already started tagging their red snapper and grouper with a traceable tag.

And they had a name: Gulf Wild.

Port Orford, Oregon;
Pacific Ocean

Farmstand Seafood and the Left Behind

Fishermen everywhere were riding the sustainable seafood wave, not just those in catch shares. On the West Coast, while catch shares came to a badly battered groundfish industry, fishermen in Port Orford, Oregon, banded together under the banner of sustainable seafood just to combat having been left behind. It was a remedy for staying in business while trawl boats rose to power.

To ask Aaron Longton, these little boats were otherwise doomed from the beginning—politics and policy being wired as they were so that the biggest boats with the most money kept coming out ahead. As the catch-share era took hold, it was no different. The design for Pacific groundfish favored larger, more efficient vessels and sidelined the small, artisan fishers who caught this particular array of seafood with the least amount of collateral damage.

At nearly four in the morning at the port of Port Orford, a stretch of asphalt between the Siskiyou National Forest and the Pacific, it's easy to see why these boats were so overlooked. About a football field's length from Highway 101 on the south end of Oregon, the pavement is lit by a few streetlights, the light of a hoist shack, and a spotlight on the hoist. The night sky is an umbrella of stars dancing on mountains. Longton is standing out front, in T-shirt and glasses, jawing with a couple of Carhartt and cap-wearing guys, fishermen assembled for the morning ride. Two dozen boats are nearby—dry-dock style—mostly wooden and lined up on trailers, waiting like airplanes on a tarmac.

There used to be a breakwater on the ocean here, a long arm of barnacle-covered rocks to protect these boats from the open sea. There's no natural sandbar. No estuary or bay to otherwise nestle the port into its rocky post between mountain and water. Built forty-five years ago, the breakwater cushioned the port through an era of prodigious timber shipping. But like the timber industry, the breakwater trickled away too, rock by rock, so that now all that's left is a jumble of stones with waves rolling through the middle. Now storms rise out of the water and crash all the way across the dock a rough twenty-six feet above sea level, the ocean swatting at the cliffs like a cranky adolescent. Left in the sea, these boats could be in pieces in a night. Which is how it's come to be that only boats about forty feet or shorter can fish out of Port Orford—boats light enough to be lifted in and out of the water by the hoist at one of two dolly docks in the country, the other being in Los Angeles.

The line at the hoist shack is only three deep at this hour. This is the late shift, actually. Longton typically heads out earlier so he can turn his gear loose before the birds wake up and start bothering his bait. He's running late today, but still early enough that he owes twenty dollars to the man industrious enough to drop his boat into the water—a premium paid by each fisherman for boats launching before 4:00 a.m. Odd as it is to see boats lifted into the sea, suspended by the miracle that is rope, the scene plays out like anything else that's been done thousands of times—seamlessly—one boat after another lifted over a guardrail, crew inside, then lowered to the sea below.

On this September morning, the talk is about a dredge boat that's there too, moored freakishly close to the dock. Used to scrape silt and maintain the navigation channel, the thing is massive enough to withstand the steady assault of the waves, and its presence makes it so today's departing boats have to be lowered between it and the dock.

Later, Longton will compare the morning ride from the dock into sea to the child's game Operation, not ineffectively. But right now the talk is mainly about how the dredge just spent a few days scraping enough muck off the seafloor to keep the port going for a few more months or a year. And about how every time this happens, people worry it will never happen again.

Nobody in a position to pull levers on things like dredges, and, in a broader sense, the state of the fishing industry in Port Orford, seems to care much about this place. Though fishing is a primary industry in this town of 1,153, it's a place of small businesses that make big impacts on tiny margins. It takes a critical mass of boats to keep fishing alive here. Enough to keep the fish buyers coming. To keep the icehouse running. To keep the crews working. It helps just enough to keep the town a town, bringing in about $5 million in seafood a year.

But sixteen years ago, the primary fare of these vessels—groundfish— was being hit hard, chiefly by trawl boats more common on these waters than the hook-and-line boats of Port Orford. In 2000 the fishery was declared a federal disaster area. And within a decade, seven of the species in this region were deemed overfished and started being managed under rebuilding plans. Catch shares followed. And while fishing West Coast groundfish—skates and rockfish, flounder, lingcod, and sablefish, more than ninety species of the stuff in all—is the cleanest it has been in years, or perhaps ever, what's also true is that catch shares handed the spoils of the sea to trawl boats. It was a move that left little opportunity for small fishers, tiny artisan boats that have been here since the 1850s, making catch shares just one more thing in a long line of things to put this port and its fishermen on their heels. That it flies in the face of sustainability to shove small-boat line fishers off the water in favor of trawl is an inconvenient fact that few people care to talk about.

Longton is one of the few.

A crew hustles onto a vessel and vanishes like window washers lowered on a scaffold. Longton, up next, backs his truck up to his boat the *Golden Eye* and tows it across the pavement. Built from a Navy hull made in the fifties, the *Golden Eye* used to sport a house almost all the way across the deck. After a friend found the boat in a San Francisco shipyard, its house was rebuilt into a tiny cabin, painted green with twin scuttles and round deadlights like a submarine. With orange trim and blue hull, it looks like a tie-dyed, stoner twin of a tugboat. Because it's the only steel boat in the harbor, Longton is fond of telling people that his is the one with the rust on it.

He lines the *Golden Eye* up under the hoist, which quickly lifts it over the edge of the dock's wall. Crewman Mark McClelland, a rough-looking guy in a gray hoodie with a straight, stern drip of beard, slips a wooden slide between the boat and the truck. In a few practiced minutes, he and the goateed, towering Longton slide ten plastic tubs of baited lines from the truck to the boat's deck. Then Longton parks the truck and climbs aboard, his twenty-two-pound dog Rocket, a smooth-coat fox terrier, tucked under his arm.

It's a comical pairing, these two. But duo they are. As the boat is lowered to the sea, the night sky still covering the water, Rocket jumps into the wheelhouse, then to the bunk next to the captain's seat—a white leather chair on a wooden box—while Longton takes the wheel. Rocket shivers as Longton steers the boat through the rocky waters of Port Orford Heads. Longton's theory is that Rocket's gameness for the ocean is more a function of separation anxiety than daredeviltry. Faced with a day on the water or a day without his master, he will choose the aquatic life. Rocket settles soon, curled into a sleeping bag with the dozing McClelland, who smokes a little pot to smooth out the ride (it's legal in Oregon and in its state waters, and the fishing is hours away). Longton turns the boat toward the finger, a twelve-hundred-foot crimp in the seafloor about sixteen miles northwest.

As he drives, he talks about how this piece of the sea used to belong to small boats. While the bow noses over dark waves, he describes why that is changing now. "The thing of it is that the hook-and-line fleet, as well as trawl fleet, had this history of participation," he says. "But when they started divvying it up, it's like the hook-and-line guys never existed."

Hook-and-line boats have been part of this water for nearly two centuries. Many of them are bread and butter to small towns, however sniffed at in larger ports. But despite their history, and the fact that they made up more than two-thirds of the boats fishing groundfish when catch shares arrived, hook-and-line boats weren't cut into the spoils. Instead, when the West Coast Groundfish Trawl Catch Share Program took hold, hook-and-line boats were tasked with fishing out of two separate, set-aside pools that amounted to about 10 percent of the catch.

Those pools match what the hook-and-line boats were catching at the time the fishing was divided: 10 percent. But that was because 90 percent of the groundfish caught on the West Coast was coming out of the water in the nets of trawl boats—which wasn't such a good thing at the time.

Trawling was primarily what put groundfish in such a dire ecological state. Sixteen percent of the groundfish the boats hauled, save for whiting, was made up of fish caught by accident, either species too fragile to be caught or fish too young to be brought to market. Environmental groups bent on containing such damage pushed for the catch share and new rules to whittle that 16 percent down. But in a series of meetings and open houses aimed at building consensus around the catch share, protecting small-boat fleets in Port Orford and other towns like it wasn't a priority. Instead, when the catch share took hold and trawl boats got new rules, those boats were awarded enough fish to match what they had been taking. Now 90 percent of the fish that can be caught on the West Coast belong to trawl boats.

Longton puts it this way: "They took the dirtiest fishermen and they gave them all the fish. . . . Greedy and efficient was rewarded with ownership of the resource based on how greedy and efficient they were. Or how hard they worked, of course. But it's all the same."

He turns the steel steering wheel, driving over the waves, an eye on the gadgets in the helm: the usual radar, chart-plotter, depth-sounder and a handful of instruments reporting on the engine. Critics say that anybody managing fisheries should have been concerned with strengthening these little boats. Though small, they are the cleanest boats operating in groundfish. They don't drag nets on the ocean bottom. And what accidental catch they have, they find markets for. On the *Golden Eye*, for example, not a single fish is thrown back dead or wasted. But this stuff is politics, after all. And while the biggest players with the most money tend to call the shots, environmental groups intent on controlling the carnage were satisfied to get as far as they did: reining in trawl boats.

Their success in doing so is no baloney. The catch share subjected trawl boats to a set of rules that would force them to control their accidental catch. Each boat gets only so much of each fish, and the penalties for taking more are steep. Now, managing the catch aboard these vessels is like counting calories. Following these rules, less than 5 percent of the bottom trawlers' total catch were fish caught and killed by accident within three years, down from 16. Thus the catch share became the first sustainably certified fishery in the world to offer rockfish and skate, and is one of the most diversified fisheries ever certified by the Marine Stewardship Council. It offers lingcod, sablefish, sole, and flounder under the Marine Stewardship Council's blue label.

Amid all the backslapping and congratulations that followed, however, the fact that these successes marginalized the cleanest fishermen on these waters was lost. And because hook-and-line fishermen can't buy into the catch share unless they buy a trawl boat permit or rent one—both of which would add costs they say are unmanageable (a trawl permit fetches more than half a million dollars)—their 10 percent of the catch is a bit of a glass ceiling. Essentially, they can never grow. And trawl boats that drag the bottom and the midwaters of the Pacific will always control 90 percent of the groundfish. It's like trading one kind of collateral damage for another.

Longton, much like former crabber Tom Miller at another U-shaped table on another ocean, tried to fight back. He turned up at meetings of the Pacific Fishery Management Council and aired his grievances in five-minute increments before a panel of people who didn't seem to be listening. Friends joined him. They took their own five minutes. Their loss seemed preordained, he says. It was a scenario that repeated itself in court when a judge ruled that, while federal regulators could have gone about things differently and avoided at least some of the issues that drove small-boat fishermen to sue them, it all looked pretty legal.

"When I'm talking about losers, I'm talking about entire fleets of small boats in places like Port Orford. Little by little, you watch," says Longton. He eyes his course in the chart-plotter and navigates the boat through an especially choppy patch of dark waves. "We're going to do everything we can to try to hang on. That's why we're trying to redesign the way we sell our fish and wean ourselves off of dependency on that program—the bigger fish houses and stuff. But it's an uphill battle. We are rolling the boulder up the mountain all the time."

Longton is a champion boulder roller. His efforts come in the form of a nonprofit he founded called the Port Orford Ocean Resources Group, which is now dedicated to keeping what fishing resources they can access, like permits and boats, in Port Orford. He is also a fishmonger, running a community-supported fishery called Port Orford Sustainable Seafood, a direct-to-consumer operation that's funneling fresh seafood to Oregon's I-5 corridor, where money and urban do-gooding translate into a premium from households and restaurants in cities like Portland. What consumers get in exchange is traceable, clean-caught fish, fresh off day boats, and a chance to know their fishermen. And right now, the extra money it commands is one of the only things keeping small boats in Port Orford alive.

The *Golden Eye* reaches the edge of the continental shelf and the ride smooths out as the boat slips off the edge of North America into the deep sea. There's a blue glow in the sky as the sun presses up. And the Siskiyou forest and mountains back on land become visible over the water. Longton grew up on the Umpqua River on the other side of the mountains. His father was a Navy man and a boat builder, so that Longton spent much of his life on water. He fell in love with Port Orford as soon as he could drive, jumping in the car and speeding to the rocky headland at Cape Blanco to salmon fish in the late seventies. Eventually one of the fishermen he met there sold him the *Golden Eye*. In between, twenty years went by. Twenty years of fighting forest fires and working at a nickel smelter tending furnaces. The heat got to him. He came to the coast to cool off, knowing he was destined to fish, some days wishing he'd done it sooner.

Now he calls to McClelland, napping in the bow. "Twenty minutes," he says. And McClelland rouses, steps out onto the deck and into a pair of two-tone oilskins, the suspenders over his sweatshirt. He starts lining up the tubs of line, connecting the lengths, and after twenty minutes of this he walks to the stern and drops an anchor and a buoy—one end of the fishing line, a rope, really—tied to both. Longton rolls the boat forward as the first orange wisps appear in the sky. The rope uncoils from the first plastic tub, its squid-baited hooks whipping over the stern, about three thousand hooks in all. McClelland switches the tubs—ten of them, a thousand feet of rope in each—as the lines uncoil.

A crowd of gulls and shearwaters—ducklike save for an absolutely hulking wingspan—start collecting around the boat, clamoring for the odd squid that's pitched skyward while the rope uncoils. It only takes about fifteen minutes before the full line is set. There's no glamorizing what happens next: they wait. For three hours. Mc-Clelland crawls back to the hull and Longton into the bunk. Rocket, who has been huddled on the bunk throughout, dives on Longton for a morning cuddle, then skips out onto the deck to vacuum the last few bits of squid that haven't been claimed by birds.

Things are not necessarily better in the catch-share era of trawl-boat towns. Though the fishery is cleaner than ever, places like Newport, once a fishing stronghold in Oregon, look more like Kodiak, Alaska, than the home of catch-share beneficiaries. Only a handful of hake and whitefish boats really won big, their profits soaring with the new sustainability certification from the Marine Stewardship Council. Midwater trawlers all of them, they are rapidly turning their catch into a hyperefficient, near–industrial-scale fishery, a tiny cousin to the Bering Sea pollock industry, funneling a rough 109,000 tons of fish into West Coast ports in 2014.

Trawl operators who fish the seafloor for groundfish, however, say their market has been so retooled by catch shares that it's impossible for some to make a business work. It requires access to a mix of species to fish legally—something not all the boats have. Now, twenty boats have stopped fishing groundfish. Pacific Seafoods—the largest seafood buyer in the town—has collected others, along with attendant rights to the fish, and become a regional landlord. Between circumstances like these and an embraced trend toward leasing, more than 20 percent of trawl boats were being skippered by renters in the program's first year, the only year for which data is available.

Walk the docks in these towns and fishermen who bottom-trawl will tell you they are starting to shrug off groundfish for good, opting for state-run fisheries like shrimp instead.

While what comes aboard the *Golden Eye* is some of this same fish, the product is nowhere near the same. When the three hours are up, this is plain. The boat's been drifting while Longton and McClelland nap, outriggers lowered so that the *Golden Eye* looks like a bobbing green tern in the sea, its wings outstretched to steady its roll. Longton shakes out of his bunk and unsettles the dozing Rocket, who has returned to napping after the scavenger hunt on the deck. Rocket's white eyebrows arch up. Longton crosses the plywood floor of the wheelhouse and settles in the captain's seat again. He shifts his eyes from the sea to the instruments on the helm, searching for the anchor buoys. McClelland climbs past him from the cushions in the bow to the deck. Behind the steel cabin of the *Golden Eye*, he raises the outriggers so that the boat begins to list from side to side.

Longton spots the pink buoys bobbing on the water and turns the boat around, so that the Pacific comes at the *Golden Eye* in an unfurling blue roll, the water breaking over the bow. The boat sidles up to the first pink buoy and McClelland leans over the rail and grabs it with a pickup stick, a pole with a little plastic hook on the end. When he lays hands on the line, he hoists the buoy in first. It takes the two of them then, Longton on the deck and both leaning hard against the rope, to feed the end of the line to a hauler—a metal wheel that cranks the thing in, anchor and all, much like the comby aboard Vern Crane's *Viking Spirit*.

The rest is seemingly easy. One by one, the fresh catch roll aboard. Longton stands on the starboard side, unhooking each, with McClelland sorting them into plastic buckets on the green metal plates over the boats holds. There's one for sablefish—that's the earner. The rest are a mix of groundfish—rockfish and skates, tiny sharks, and lingcod.

The scene is peaceful enough: the ocean rolling in soft, steady currents under the boat, the *Golden Eye*'s green steel cabin bobbing on the water, its round scuttle windows bouncing and the fish stacking neatly in the tubs. But, again, fishing is death. Each fish that arrives meets the grim truth of the gaffe—the piercing metal spike that seizes each by the head—picking them off the line in swift, swinging strikes wielded by whichever fisherman is nearest. Few are missed. That means few hit the crucifier. There is very little bleeding. Most of the fish arrive in the tub heads intact, as sharp looking in the sunlight as they are in the sea. There is not a single bit of waste. Every fish on this boat is used.

Rocket sits it out. Back in the wheelhouse, he is perched in the sleeping bag wearing his usual worried expression. When a sablefish jumps the hook and gives a last, heroic fit on the floor of the wheelhouse, Rocket springs to life, hopping down to dance around it.

But what seems like an easy run for fish today gets harder when it turns out the hydraulic system is cranky. For reasons unknown it will only run in one direction, so that the hoses have to be switched and then it will move only in the direction that is least convenient. Every few minutes as the fish come aboard—turning and twisting for the last moments of life—the hauler chokes on some knot or hook in the line. And because there is no way to haul it out again, the engine has to be cut instead. The job of disassembling the hauler and relieving it of hooks and knots falls to McClelland. He is bravely trapping all of the words he might be shouting in a furrowed brow. On the third leg of this exercise, his brow knits deeper in the direction of his beard.

Chefs like Kali Fieger at the Loft in Bandon, a tiny restaurant on the water over the bay, say that there is nothing like the quality of fish that comes off of these small hook-and-line boats. The fish arrive frozen fresh—not after three or five days in a hold, then another few days at the processor. And they have no bruises, something the best of chefs can spot and taste. These are important qualities for somebody whose sablefish dish—called butterfish on Fieger's menu—is such a hot seller that she will sometimes turn her entire thirty-seat dining room nearly twice a night on it, burning through eighty-five pounds a week. Though the bulk of Pacific sablefish is still shipped overseas for lack of markets here, as it is in Alaska, it is doubtless one of the most incredible-tasting fish on the Pacific Coast. And if the day comes when trawl boats control it completely, that may make it harder to get this fish to customers aching for this kind of quality. Guys like Longton serve the small markets that keep chefs like Fieger in premium seafood.

Now eager to capture the higher prices line catch commands, trawl boats are fishing closer to shore under new rules that allow them to switch to using pots to catch these fish. What that means is that trawl boats now compete directly with smaller hook-and-line boats for the same tiny marketplace that used to be theirs in shallow water. So Longton and other small-boat captains now have to steer around pot gear in what used to be their part of the sea. The market for sablefish, their biggest earner, is collapsing as more trawl boats enter in, dumping a lot of small fish into the market and lowering the price for everybody. And with less mechanized operations—no auto-baiting machines aboard these small hook-and-line boats—they spend more to catch less.

"My story is every small-boat fishermen's story. A lot of them don't get into the politics of it; they don't really understand what's going on. They just know it's getting harder and harder," Longton says.

While 10 percent of the available fish was set aside for mitigation of what might go wrong in the catch share, politics at the U-shaped table have routed it to trawl to fish for years, so that now trawl-boat owners are fighting to keep it for good. Those owners are also organizing to dismantle a conservation area for rockfish, arguing it is no longer necessary since catch shares will foster the recovery of those fish. While their operations consolidate—and they do—there are fewer jobs in trawl. And there is always the threat that icehouses, fishmongers, and other peripheral services will disappear with consolidation, potentially killing off smaller fishermen, too, when they can't afford another ten miles to the icehouse or find another buyer for their fish when the one in their port drops off. Worse, there's the threat that the sidelining of small fishing boats, one by one by one, will sideline fishing towns.

That's why Longton works to sell his seafood through word of mouth and a roving drive up Interstate 5. He buys from about twenty of the boats in Port Orford, then drives the catch into Oregon's Willamette Valley, direct-marketing line-caught fish to foodie-conscious Portlanders and their equivalents to the south. Slowly, he's putting Port Orford Sustainable Seafood on the ground in places like Eugene and Salem and a handful of restaurants, food co-ops, and farm stores. The extra dollars he raises with this sea-to-table approach are returned to Port Orford fishermen and create up to nine part-time jobs readying the fish for sale.

Without this mongering, it's unclear how long the tiny fishing industry of Port Orford can survive. Meanwhile, Longton's ability to capture premiums on the same foodie momentum that has galvanized brands like Gulf Wild is instructive. It shows that higher prices are available for sustainable seafood with or without a catch share. And that capturing them is as easy as this farmstand seafood model, the antithesis, really, of commoditizing the sea to scale brands for mass appeal in grocery stores and restaurants. And it brings something more than just quality, sustainable seafood, traceable to the boat. It engenders support of inland Oregonians for their coastal neighbors and for those fishermen they now regard as their emissaries on the sea.

His hope for its success is something Longton wears like clothing. On the drive back to Port Orford, the Siskiyous hovering in the distance, Rocket leaning over the rail at the first whiff of land, Longton looks at the Port Orford dolly dock as it comes into view: "We just want to maintain what we have. We just want to stop the erosion. . . . Here we are, we're adjacent to all this beautiful water. But can you imagine maybe thirty years from now, maybe fifteen with the way things are going? Maybe there will be an RV park on that dock," he says.

It's a future in which Port Orford would be just a town on the coast, and not a coastal town. The fish in the ocean would still be there. But not the fishermen. And there'd be no relationship between the community and the water. Just a strip of pavement between land and sea and a bountiful market off Port Orford's shores that belongs to somebody else. If it happens, it will be a very hard thing to reverse.

Gulf Wild

Walmart, the Environmental Defense Fund,
and the Multimillion-Dollar Idea

B UDDY GUINDON WON BIG. HE knows it. He also believes deeply in catch shares. And as he worked to build the Gulf Wild brand, he had backing from people who count. That was clear the day in 2009 when Sam Robson Walton, an heir and chairman of Walmart at the time, arrived in Galveston for a fried chicken dinner. The Walton Family Foundation board, the philanthropic arm that spun out of the Walton family's success, was in tow, most of its members family. They tumbled out of a bus in the Texas sun near Guindon's fish house, ready to see what he was doing with their money.

"I was shocked," Guindon says. He points toward where he met them, just a few blocks down the sidewalk, and describes the whole thing as a no-frills affair, typical of the low-key charm that's endeared many a consumer and a banker to a Walton.

"You would think these multibillionaires would be driving up in a limousine and all that. They showed up in an airport kind of bus thing. Wearing clothes like I wear." Guindon looks down. He's in his signature jeans and T-shirt, a baseball hat with something nautical above the rim. He says some of the Waltons seemed a little eccentric. But there was no gaudy jewelry, nothing that screamed money.

"If you saw them walking down the street, you wouldn't think anything of it," he says, a wistful look and a shrug.

It impressed him, this understated style, given that the Waltons are, doubtlessly, the wealthiest family in America—one of the wealthiest in the world, in fact, worth an estimated $149 billion by *Forbes* in 2015. Two years prior, Politifact had ranked their fortune as equal to the wealth of the bottom 42 percent of Americans.

Walton money was fueling much of what was happening on the Gulf when the Waltons came to Galveston. At the time, the family's foundation was putting tens of millions of dollars into the Environmental Defense Fund's oceans program. And as the Gulf Wild brand started to develop, EDF paid half the salary of the brand's sustainability director and gave the fishermen behind it $400,000 to conduct scientific testing. It had also seeded the Gulf of Mexico Reef Shareholders' Alliance. By then, those fishermen had decided to pass on the Trace and Trust platform, wanting more than just a storytelling vehicle.

Instead, as they tagged the fish at the dock, they gave each catch a unique number and started tracing its journey through the supply chain using their own tracking software. A portion of their sales—which would be buoyed, they hoped, by traceability—was being funneled toward conservation efforts. T. J. Tate, the new sustainability director, was implementing those efforts from Galveston.

Before long, fishermen who fished for Gulf Wild would be asked to sign conservation covenants requiring them to fish clean, mind science-based limits on catch, and follow rules that protect turtles. They agreed to be monitored and to submit to random enforcement checks. Tate would also debrief them at the docks, gathering information about where they fished, what kind of gear they used, and how many crew members were aboard. She ultimately used the information to build a database for regulators. And she also put cameras on their boats to ensure compliance and helped to develop small markets for the catch those fishermen might otherwise throw back.

Lacking faith, or interest perhaps, in PowerPoints, the Waltons turned up in Galveston to see for themselves. They wanted tours of the boats and the fishing tackle, and they wanted to see every step in the process of unloading and tagging the fish.

Guindon happily obliged. He believed the Waltons just wanted to help the oceans. And to do it while preserving those businesses that make a living off the sea. They are businesspeople, after all. "When they look at a problem, they look at a problem through making you a better steward of your own business. So by allowing fishermen to have . . . a percentage of the catch, our incentive is to make the amount we can catch bigger. And that's a huge incentive," Guindon says.

Whether there are other incentives, like impacts to the freezer aisle at the Walmart, is unclear. Walk the no-fuss concrete floor in any Walmart and you can find at least some catch-share fish amid the frosty seafood selection. Flounder fillets in bland, brandless packaging hail from those hulking trawlers on the Bering Sea. The Alaskan halibut comes from that same icy water—it's the cheap cut of the halibut catch, where distance from retail markets makes pricier fresh fillets impossible. Catch shares helped commoditize this wild fare. And commodities are, after all, bread and butter for big retail chains like Walmart.

Beyond what Walmart publicly releases about its seafood policy, however—which is that the company is committed to sourcing seafood sustainably—the Waltons say little about why they are such ardent supporters of catch shares. The staff at the Walton Family Foundation say the family's love of the sea and of sport is a factor, as is the Waltons' inclination to retool economics in favor of conservation rather than to simply throw money at saving the environment. That's because they believe nature is forever at risk without financial rewards linked to preserving it.

Teresa Ish, a marine program officer at the Walton Family Foundation, puts it this way: "Coming from the business perspective, they know if it doesn't work for business and if it doesn't work for the economics of what you're trying to do, it will not last. . . . If you can identify a solution where there is actually an incentive to have the right environmental protections in place, a financial incentive to do that, the likelihood of undermining that conservation becomes much lower, because people start to lose out."

Whatever the motivation, the Waltons' commitment to catch shares is clear. Since 2009, they have emerged as one of two top funding sources of the catch-share effort in America, along with the Gordon and Betty Moore Foundation, giving roughly $10 million annually in support of catch shares over seven years. That's a small portion of what the Waltons give to charity every year, but like most of their donations, it is directed at seeding economic solutions to social woes.

There's no fancy office out of which this money spills, at least none with a street front and a public address on the brick sidewalks of Bentonville, Arkansas, where Walmart is headquartered. Instead, the foundation operates—in typical low-key Walton fashion—from a post office box somewhere within the town. All that's otherwise visible of the Waltons' empire is located inside a low, sprawling building on Southwest Eighth Street, looking less like home to one of the most profitable corporations in America than like a dull maze of industrial bulk. Half a mile away are the Walton Suites, the corporate apartment and office space on South Walton Boulevard. And right near it is another building, emblematic of the philanthropic tornado that has engulfed the catch-share effort: the Bentonville office of EDF. It's one of eight outposts of the organization's New York headquarters. A conservation powerhouse, EDF had more than $225 million in total assets in 2014, drawing from a mix of member and private donations and philanthropic grants. The Bentonville office was established to help Walmart green its supply chain. Outside of those efforts, the two organizations also have a long relationship on ocean policy.

How the Waltons and other conservative backers came to be involved in the plan for America's oceans is a story that dates back to

2000. And to the day when EDF chose to adopt a purely economic strategy to fix the ocean's ills. The aim was not, initially, to foster brands like Gulf Wild. It was to save the seas—and the fish inside them.

At the time this same mission unified a lot of conservation groups and fishermen. Overfishing plagued the American seas. And EDF was a member of the Marine Fish Conservation Network, which had been brought together in the nineties to try to change that. The network's initial aim was to safeguard the Magnuson-Stevens Act, the seafood equivalent of the Farm Bill, offering a single voice for conservationists, scientists, and fishermen on Capitol Hill. Since then, its members had started using the network as a place to cultivate a long-term vision of what the seas ought to look like. By then the first catch shares had hit America. And the question before the fish network was whether its members ought to have a vision for how catch shares fit in.

The assumption was that they would agree. Or at least be able to come to a consensus. But instead of consensus they hit gridlock. An ideological fissure reared up, one with catch shares at its center. While everyone agreed the nation needed to do a better job regulating fishing, the agreement stopped there. EDF wanted fewer boats. And to award fishermen with the rights to fish in order to give them a financial stake in conservation. But its leaders had a tough time selling its pure economic strategy, one in which catch shares would function as a panacea for the seas. The network's fishing groups wanted protection from related fallout. Like high rents. And consolidation. They also wanted provisions for the young to be able to enter the industry, and mandates for conservation initiatives, too. The sticking point was that those fishermen also wanted access rights to be a privilege that would expire in time and revert to the government. They were opposed to private property rights on the sea. Leaders of EDF's new oceans team didn't agree. Drawing from economic theory dating back decades, they reasoned that private property rights would be key to engendering a culture of conservation. And they would also bring about the safety and economic gains catch shares had become known for.

Not everybody believed that economic and environmental gain would end up as bedfellows. Giving people a bunch of fish and betting they would take care of them was like giving people houses and betting they would all cut their grass. There was no way to know. And silver bullets made some people in the fish network queasy. They had long ago learned that conservation work is like a long and frustrating game of Jenga. There are wrong moves and whole plans topple, and it can be hard to move a single thing without messing up a lot of others. What EDF proffered sounded too easy. Like the kind of thing that gets funded by philanthropists who move on before there's a mess to clean up. Downstream economic consequences were already rearing up in catch shares. In New Zealand and Alaska, primarily, they had crushed jobs and instituted a renting class. And while big industry was providing economic development funds to the native Alaskans who had been left out of catch shares off their shores in western Alaska, initially from pollock, it looked to some more like buying agreement than actually getting it.

Then there was Angel Braestrup and her case of déjà vu.

Braestrup joined the Curtis & Edith Munson Foundation in 1989. Today she is the executive director of the philanthropic foundation, which funds about $1.4 million in ocean conservation annually. When it came to policymaking and politic, she was a sure-footed sort. Through the eighties, Braestrup, a Yale history grad, had worked for the US House of Representatives. Her stint on Capitol Hill included a tour as legislative assistant to Tom Petri, a Republican congressman from Wisconsin. And during that tour she had been tasked with busting up a rights-based program of another kind: tobacco. As the catch-share conversation kicked up, its pitfalls bore similarities she found hard to ignore.

"When the quota system was established for tobacco, you could not plant a tobacco seed without owning enough quota to plant that seed," says the straight-talking Braestrup. She's on the phone from her DC office in Dupont Circle. The program did some good in places like Kentucky, she said. It guaranteed income so that people who farmed a couple of acres got a set price for tobacco without foreign competition. But in North Carolina, where farmers had to rent the land and rent access to the tobacco, too, once a rental market took hold, the system had thinned profits. Dramatically. Tobacco farmers were shouldering the cost of every aspect of tobacco production, and paying two different sets of landlords besides. Meanwhile, "the guy who was probably now a doctor in Philadelphia was still collecting from the tobacco allotment he had inherited," Braestrup says.

Catch shares didn't look much different. Rather than the market-based solution that was their billing, she worried they would end up as tobacco had: with people divided into winners and losers until Congress had to rewrite the Farm Bill. Pushing tobacco back into the free market took ten years and cost the tobacco industry $9.6 billion, paid for by manufacturers and importers.

"My concern was this: One, that over time, you would have a displacement of owner operators, for lack of a better way to put it, and that people would be paying for the right to fish as they paid for the right to plant tobacco," Braestrup said. And she also worried that ocean properties would become so valuable that they could only ever be consolidated in the hands of the rich. Such a scenario would create enormously powerful lobbying groups. And their interests would likely come to dominate policy until nobody even remembered why they were regulating fishing in the first place.

There were other examples of what could go wrong. And when some of the people in the fish network pictured these dynamics coming to the oceans, they didn't like the picture. As dozens of conservation and fishing groups found common ground in repelling private property rights through catch shares, EDF's oceans team took a hard line: it wanted the property rights. The infighting reached Capitol Hill. When the fish network lobbied to extend a moratorium on catch shares until consensus could be reached, EDF lobbied against it. It broke a golden rule: network members could disagree, but not in public. The fish network's board began taking steps to oust EDF. But before it could be cast out, EDF withdrew. The day it severed ties with the fish network was the day its oceans policy took a decided turn toward privatizing the seas.

EDF then paired with conservative funders for early support. The Charles Koch Foundation (of Koch brothers fame) signed on, as did the foundation of free-enterprise thinker Alex Walker, the libertarian-leaning Reason Public Policy Institute, and the Montana-based Property and Environment Research Center. The more progressive David and Lucile Packard Foundation provided early backing, too. Ultimately, EDF drew two of the biggest conservation funders in America to catch shares: the Walton Family Foundation and the Gordon and Betty Moore Foundation. And it kept them.

Its oceans program was only a $2.5 million annual program in those early days. In 2003 the organization hired former Capitol Hill staffer David Festa, a Harvard-educated consultant who had been a policy director in the Clinton administration's Department of Commerce, to lead the charge. Publicly, Festa, who looks like a clean-shaven Abe Lincoln, would become one of the country's most strident supporters of catch shares. And his experience leading policy and financial initiatives proved a good fit. Under his direction, the oceans program grew to $24 million.

Over the next decade, EDF gathered and produced a body of catch-share science to promote its agenda. The science supported a lot of what was already known. Catch shares continued to produce economic benefits, with fleet-wide revenues in the United States and British Columbia climbing 27 percent over ten years. Fishermen who had succeeded within catch shares had more freedom over when to fish and how to plan their businesses. There was less accidental catch in some catch-share programs, like the West Coast trawl program and the pollock cooperative. And preassigning the catch had also steadied the supply of seafood and made fishing abundantly safer, with rescue missions in halibut falling from thirty-three in the last year of the derbies to only two in 2010.

But the benefits of preassigning the catch, and limiting how many fish could be caught based on science, were being conflated with the notion of privatizing the seas. There were lots of ways to preassign catch. Not all of them came with a private property right. And science that showed that catch shares ended overfishing failed to acknowledge that the features of the programs—hard caps on catch, defined by quality science—were the chief achievers of those goals, rather than the privatization itself. In 2009 University of Washington professor Timothy Essington drew the line quite clearly. After reviewing metrics across all the nation's catch shares, he found that catch shares had no significant ecological benefits. Their chief advantage was their ability to make fisheries more predictable and fish more valuable.

Meanwhile, the social science around catch shares was becoming more alarming. While Alaska's halibut, sablefish, pollock, and crab gained a combined $234 million in value between 1992 and 2009 ($94 million when adjusted for inflation), those catch shares were bleeding jobs and boats, and the rental economy they spurred was only getting more entrenched and costly for workers. Elsewhere in the world, fishing access had started to consolidate deeply among the wealthy. Over the course of a decade, 86 percent of the fishing access in New Zealand came to be controlled by its twelve largest fishing companies. In Iceland, the twenty largest companies controlled 66 percent of fishing after four years.

Scientists like Bonnie McCay, an anthropologist at Rutgers, indicated that this would be the future of catch shares: corporatization of the seas by big companies that controlled everything from dock to dinner plate, with downstream impacts to workers and communities.

The kicker was this: in 2006 another reauthorization of the Magnuson-Stevens Act would accomplish what conservationists in the fish network had dreamed of all along. It forced federal regulators to put hard caps on the amount of domestic fish that could be caught, then firmly tethered those caps to science, capturing the two best tools in the catch-share arsenal. It was a move that underscored how "overfishing" had really been "under-regulating." And it was a solution that made the very thing catch shares do best a federal law, minus the private property rights so many conservationists opposed.

It didn't matter. By then, the catch-share movement was being propelled by an immense amount of cash—hundreds of millions of dollars over a decade—to push policy and new programs. It was enough money to drown out opposition while EDF's oceans program spun out public relations missives in staggering volume. Though conservation groups like The Nature Conservancy and Ocean Conservancy would jump in and out of the catch-share movement, EDF became a catch-share powerhouse. It built a catch-share design center in San Francisco to help regulators build new catch shares and developed a database and maps of catch-share programs around the world. It continued funding pro–catch-share science. And it secured seats at the U-shaped tables around America.

In 2008, after Barack Obama was elected president, Festa was tapped as part of a sprawling transitions team tasked with dispatching papers for the Department of Commerce's next iteration of fisheries regulators. The Obama administration then picked Jane Lubchenco as its new head of the National Oceanic and Atmospheric Administration. An Oregon State University scientist and a catch-share proponent, she was a longtime friend of Festa and a board trustee of EDF. Two years later, she would make it national policy to consider catch shares in fisheries in America.

But when EDF hit the European Union with its ideas in 2009, it finally faced opposition. As it was trying to get a catch-share concept into European nations' fishery management plan, the organization was confronted with something new: a countercampaign. Client Earth, the environmental law organization based in the United Kingdom, fought catch shares hard. And it fought them in public, dispatching white papers raising questions about the legality of privatizing public resources. The group told its constituents that assigning property rights in fisheries was economic and social policy, not fisheries management.

"That didn't happen in the United States, and a big part of it was there weren't very many funders left," said Mark Spalding, president of the Ocean Foundation, the DC-based nonprofit that operates on a lean $7 million a year. "If you get Walton and Gordon and Betty Moore . . . that's a huge percentage of the money for marine and coastal conservation in the United States. No one was excited about speaking out for fear that it would affect their funding from those sources for other activities."

Thus, American conservation groups stood down on the privatization of the seas. No countercampaign took hold. A few outliers would be openly critical, like Food & Water Watch and Ecotrust, but that was all. Where there used to be cohesion around ocean policy, there was now unyielding tension. In a conservation community that had always worked in concert, meetings were being convened where either catch-share proponents or detractors were invited, but not both. And the rapid adoption of catch-share policy in America, as it coincided with a lack of journalistic scrutiny, raised the stakes daily.

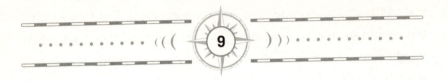

Kake, Alaska

The New Colonialism

E CONOMIC SOLUTIONS TO ENVIRONMENTAL PROBLEMS call for one key ingredient: an economy. And places that didn't have one, or much of one anyway, lacked the resources to play along. So while small towns like Port Orford, Oregon, were getting sidelined by how the lines had been drawn, rural native communities in southeast and south-central Alaska had another problem: even when they were cut in, they didn't have the economic resources catch shares required for success. Instead, one by one, whole communities were commercially cut off from the sea. And in those places, people started losing their fishing heritage. Some were places where that heritage stretched back centuries. Far from Port Orford, Aaron Longton's worst nightmares had already come true.

This was the aftermath of catch shares in Kake, Alaska, a Tlingit (pronounced clink-it) village on Kupreanof Island, at least with regard to halibut. Kake's fate is shared by dozens of other communities tied to halibut in this region. They are places where the only way out is by sea or by air, and even then only by prop planes. And because of their rural character, they lack the commerce and financial backing to build the kind of robust fish markets that catch shares nourish.

On the other side of Kupreanof Island, the contrast is plain. Petersburg, Alaska, a town settled by Norwegians and an American fishing stronghold, is home to three major fish buyers, a pile of marine-service suppliers, more than one shipwright for boats, and—the mother of all imaginings—banks that give loans to fishermen. That there is jet service and enough trade in permits and fishing access to support two brokers says just about everything you need to know about Petersburg fishing. That the town has ice and bait and fuel at the ready—things that cost people in Kake big and still come with logistical problems—means that Petersburg's advantage is built in from the start. Two downtown seaports showcase as much to anybody who comes looking: rust-free boats, gleaming and gadgeted, their captains in spendy North Face and driving new whatevers, even though the town has only a few miles of paved road.

In Kake there is no such bustle. No hype. It's the kind of place where civilization backs off rather than crowds in. Cell service is an open question. The Internet is spotty. The nocturnal soundscape is but sea and eagles. People from outside this place can find the quiet so unsettling that the matron of the tribal lodge says some guests lie awake at night, stunned by the absence of noise, and look forward to leaving. Sometimes you can see it on their faces, she says: *What am I doing here?*

In the daytime there is airplane traffic—sometimes—and a handful of drivers who get to where they're going quickly for lack of roads, but at speeds so slow that seat belts go unused and babies ride in the laps of bigger babies. The airport is a slightly large version of a bus stop. There is one taxi. And the culture of the town unfolds in such intimate circles that the chief experience of the outsider—and perhaps many insiders too—is that of the landscape, a thing that outsizes humans as the sustaining force of the place. The wind alone will remind you—all day every day, the salt pecking at your skin—that you are at sea. The land underfoot is somewhat beside the point.

Kake is a white man's take on *Keex' Kwaan*, a Tlingit phrase indicating tribe. "Tlingit" itself means "People of the Tides." And these people are, indeed, of these tides.

One look from a hilltop makes plain why their ancestors settled here thousands of years ago. Waterways surround the island's northern tip so that the original Kake village, arranged at the bottom of the hillside, is ensconced in mossy shore and barnacles from which the water unfurls like a kind of welcome mat. The Tlingit nation once commanded the ocean beyond it in canoes, its trade routes running south to California.

What lies at this intersection of sea and land is nothing short of a kitchen made by gods. Salmon run six streams to meet the sea here. Clams and mussels, gumboots, and crab burrow in the tide pools and in the soft, shallow seafloor ringing much of the town. Seaweed abounds. And the gulls that nest in it lay eggs as good as any chicken's. All have been a food source for as long as anybody has been marking time here. So, too, has the bounty of Kake's inland.

In the forested hills of Kupreanof's interior, berries grow quite literally by the ton. Blueberries and salmonberries. Gray currents and huckleberries. Elderberries and thimbleberries, too. Skunk cabbage and wild rhubarb and fiddlehead ferns make for greens. Starchy vegetables come by way of spruce roots and potatoes. Moose and deer, ducks and porcupines, all have been part of a subsistence diet that reaches back through time to underscore why the island's founders chose this place. Oral history describes a search for a perfect ecosystem; Kake's founders discovered it.

Before white people came along and rearranged things, the culture of this place was a rhythm of sustenance and harvest. Food was society. The potlatches were the stuff of legend. Reverence for both was once strong enough to end wars between clans. Kake's first people harvested salmon through summer and stored the bounty of the fish for winter. They spent the dark months sustained by smoked salmon and salmon eggs dried and stored underground. When food ran low, it was halibut that replenished supplies in spring. The meat was light then, and easiest to dry.

In times past, halibut was not such easy prey. Today, the juvenile fish are often dubbed "chickens" for their eerie resemblance to poultry. But centuries ago and even decades ago, halibut was the size of an average fifth grader and twice as strong. Tlingit people hooked this fish on a special hook designed to "drown" them underwater so they would not have to fight them in canoes. They carried spears, too, so they could stab the fish if they lacked the strength to hold them down from the rocks and kill them.

These fish woke the village from winter with meals forged of proteins and fats. Halibut heads boiled in seal oil. Halibut chowder and halibut soup. Halibut cheeks rolled in flour and fried. And there were other uses too: halibut skins were used as bags. A fresh halibut could be sliced thin and applied to burns like a salve.

That life isn't lost from this place. But Kake's last 157 years are a litany of religious occupation, persecution, and shaming that drove its culture underground. Even still, halibut, along with salmon, was a life force. Commercial fishing allowed the people of Kake to rise up again. For a while, they captured their piece of the ocean economy. Thirty-five boats in a portage in a cove put four to five crewmen to work aboard each one every season. It was a big number in a town of barely more than six hundred people. But it was brief respite. Save for salmon fishing, Kake is commercially cut off from the sea now.

Most of the time you don't feel the things that happened, that are still happening, to put this culture on the defense. But today is not that day. It's a cloudy evening, somber weather to accompany a somber ceremony. The first of the elders steps into the road of Kake's old town in regalia, his red cape waving against a backdrop of dusty roads and ocean. He drifts between the buildings, the weather-beaten boards washed smooth by wind and rain, an embroidered eagle wafting homage to people long gone and to the eagles that can congregate here by the dozen, along with ravens. Kake is like this—its structures and roads so immersed in the landscape, it has the look and feel of a washed-out watercolor. The white hair beneath this man's headpiece and the blue embroidery of his cape pop vividly, as if he has arrived through some portal from somewhere else, somewhere Technicolor.

Soon there are more people: a woman with a tambourine drum, a man in a veterans' cap from the Korean War—five eagle feathers in the back—and a row of well-dressed children. They circle a narrow trench in the road, where yesterday a backhoe unearthed the edges of a human femur and a skull, and file along a skinny strip of land between the trench and the side of a tan building. The bones are covered now, an archeologist having already pronounced them hundreds of years old, his involvement a great irritation to these people who would have preferred their ancestors stayed buried in the first place. There used to be markers for these graves—totem poles called funeral poles. But after whites descended, courtesy of naval operations and a steady stream of church- and government-sponsored meddling, the poles were removed. The ancestors were lost in the soil. So as the ceremony begins, the man in the cape describes how the bones will be mapped with GPS this time.

Back before this person was laid in this earth, the people of Kake nailed a silver spike into a nearby boardwalk on a day in 1913 and agreed to cloister their culture to survive the unrelenting attentions of militaries, missionaries, and other brands of the self-righteous. It was a day that followed years of war, if you can call it that, with the US Navy. What really happened was that naval ships started getting into people's business after the United States purchased Alaska from Russia in the 1860s. When a Kake native was shot by a non-native sentry in Sitka in 1869 and two prospectors were killed in retribution, the Navy sent the USS *Saginaw* to Kake to settle things. Sailors shelled the town, torching homes and burning food stores while Kake's residents took to the hills. People spent the next winter starving and freezing to death. It took about twenty years for the survivors to regroup. By then, missionaries had arrived to tell them how to save themselves.

What they said was get civilized and govern yourselves. Become a legal town. Quit with your witchcraft. Burn your totem poles. Dig up your dead, burn their coffins, and move them somewhere where they will not cause disease. Banish the unsavory sorts. Swear off alcohol and fights and the people who indulge in them. Send your children to school.

So on that day in 1913, the tribal elders buried a box somewhere near the spike. In it, they said, they placed their old ways. This symbolic end to their culture was far from a casual move. It was a civic crisis. But the decision by then was not to live with the rule and religion of whites or Tlingits. It was to live at all or die Tlingit. And because smallpox and other diseases brought by whites were killing them too, religiously speaking, Kake's people had started wondering whether they ought to be having some of what the whites were having. Maybe their culture was silly, they thought. Maybe they did need a new god. Fear made getting one easier.

The echo of all that is still here. The drumbeat is steady and doleful. The mourners stand, backs to the wall, wedged on the island of land between it and the trench. They sing. The songs are Tlingit. The bare skeleton in the soil, somehow still intact after the assault of the backhoe, lays covered. The archeologist found a layer of shells above it and declared it food waste, evidence of a few centuries between the time these bones were laid down and this day in late spring. The state requires such exams to be sure there's been no killing, as there was once in Kake, quite famously, a short time ago. But these remnants are of another era, a better one. And they clearly summon the heartbreak of the in-between. Most days this place has a lot of happiness. People so friendly that passing drivers standardly wave. But there is that reverberation of the time the silver spike drove hard into the boardwalk. Of the time Kake's culture was locked in a box.

A lot of culture has been lost since then. To the canneries that came next. To the timber industry that followed. To the contractors that still come and go. And to the television that came alongside all that, to tell people what it is they ought to want instead of what they had. When you look at the history, it seems that so much came at this place so fast, it's hard to parse what was forced on Kake from the path that people found on their own. But in the middle they built the harbor. And they took to the seas in ways they had not. They fed themselves, and they fed a cannery with salmon by the tens of thousands, while hundreds of immigrant workers lived in dormitories there until the compound shuttered in 1977. When cannery begat cold storage—a fresh fish house—they fed that too. No more.

When halibut was divided into catch shares and handed out to those who had fished it, Kake's boat owners got a piece, but not much. Timber had come by then so that recent fishing history didn't look like history at all but like an interlude punctuated by a lot of wood. The pieces of the halibut harvest that were awarded, called individual fishing quotas (IFQs), were small. Then the pieces trickled away. The town's single fish buyer—the cold-storage facility run by a succession of different operators—had been blinking on and off for years before it fluttered out in 2014. It was the only supplier of bait and fuel and ice. But owing to the fact that the electricity on Kake is powered by diesel, it proved impossible to keep the cold storage running at a nauseating sixty-three cents a kilowatt. Energy prices had tripled in the twelve years before it shuttered, so that the bill at the cold storage ran as high as $80,000, sometimes $90,000 a month. Various entities tried to keep it up. They all failed. And they especially failed to compete with towns like Petersburg that paid a lean eight cents a kilowatt for power and zipped products to the lower Forty-Eight with daily jet service while the same shipments from Kake took two weeks.

Catch shares added a liquidity to the slowdown. When a businessman came to Kake to run the cold storage, but then never paid the boats, those who lost tens of thousands that season sold their quota—their access to the halibut—to get through winter. When an elder who drove the catch to Petersburg for a fee passed away, that cost spread itself out again too, to the detriment of a few boats. Their owners sold as well. Quota was quick cash when the bills got high. Or when people didn't see one coming. Some didn't realize that they wouldn't be able buy it back again, or that when they tried, the quota would cost twice as much as they sold it for. Who could blame them? For thousands of years their people had lived off this land and these wilds. It did not immediately register that the government had given it all away.

Only five people in Kake own quota now. Twenty years ago, that number was forty-two.

"If you do the research and went to every village, you'll see that the IFQs are almost nonexistent," said Robert Mills, president of the Kake Tribal Corporation, who holds out hope for a biofuel-powered smokehouse in Kake so that the salmon industry can recover. It's among the first visions for the town to rely on something the people here are good at, instead of the larger public works projects Kake has survived on in the recent past. Things like roads. Infrastructure repairs. Pots of money doled out by governments that produce just enough jobs to keep the community limping along.

There's still a town smokehouse, with or without industry. And subsistence fishing carries on, and is legal in halibut if the aim is to eat rather than sell it. And people still hunt, still gather berries, still collect eggs and the riches of the tide pools. Food is still the culture of this place. In fact, what little cash circulates in Kake tends to make its way around via food sales, the direct-sale economy that stands in for brick-and-mortar retail. Custom meals are made in home kitchens, so it is not at all odd to come across a crab cake meal advertised on a bulletin board, at the basketball court, or on Facebook, which has infiltrated the lives of people even here. Homemade Big Macs. Sushi and sundaes. Pizza and baked goods. Bread and spaghetti. All are part of the quiet, calm weekends marked by rummage sales and basketball games, bingo, and, yes, church, while every dollar in town gets worn out good.

Halibut is there too. For those who still catch it to survive, it's legal to sell a portion of the subsistence catch. Fried with fresh-cut potatoes and driven to your door, it's a fish that has belonged to this land, and to these people, for longer than anyone really knows.

The amount of halibut quota in Kake has dropped more than 88 percent since catch shares began. And much of that quota has migrated to white towns, sticking to the fish houses, rust-free boats, and the same retirees who then lease it to captains like Vern Crane. Although in fewer hands, it ends up in southeast Alaskan towns, mostly, places like Petersburg, Sitka, Juneau, and Wrangell. Meanwhile rural native communities in southeast and south-central Alaska struggle to hang on. There are no halibut owners left in Angoon, forty air miles away from Kake, where in 1995 the fish brought more than $773,000 to the local economy. Same in Metlakatla, where all of eleven quota owners have divested. In Pelican, all thirty-nine owners divested over the last two decades. Many continue to rent quota and fish in Pelican, but on average they bring about half as much revenue as they used to. All told, forty-four Alaskan villages have lost 66 percent of their boats and 82 percent of their catch, and 57 percent of the people who used to have the rights to fish halibut no longer have them. In 2004 there was enough concern about the related economic and social fallout that forty-two nonprofits were authorized to buy and hold halibut quota on behalf of the communities. Only three ever came up with the money.

And while there are other ways to get along in Kake now, for a while there weren't. So between 2008 and 2013 the town's population dropped by half. School enrollment dipped from 210 to 97. Whole families—aunts, uncles, cousins—left for places where they could find jobs and cheaper energy. Over 2014, intent on cleaning up, in part from the exodus and neglect, the town demolished twenty abandoned houses and carted off 116 abandoned cars. Now people are coming back—slowly. And now that they're returning, the town's leadership is listening hard.

There's not as much talk about big plans for big projects anymore, or big dreams that will lack buy-in from the state and federal agencies that pay. Not as much talk about reviving industries. Now the talk is about using biofuels to make their own electricity, maybe firing up the cold storage again and using its waste heat to power greenhouses. It's a conversation that's less about keeping up with other places and more about remembering who you are, who your people are.

"We have lived here for thousands and thousands of years relying on ourselves and our trade," says Adam Davis, the soft-spoken director of community economic development for the Organized Village of Kake, the tribal government that serves the town. Kake's first people were once such robust traders that oral history has them traveling past California into Mexico for slaves, gone for years at a time, he says. This in large canoes on an ocean locals say you have to practically write your will before you paddle on. Davis grows his food and lives on subsistence harvest. He heats his home with wood. He leads by example. He believes his town can recover this culture.

"When you spend so much time watching TV and you're told you have to buy these things to be a good consumer, it's hard to get that across," he says, sitting in an office in an old cannery building under towering pines. He knows there is still depression and anxiety in Kake and that it still hits hard among people who have lost the ability to consume, or have been so ashamed of their culture for so long that they don't know how to reclaim it. "There is more scarring than the people know," he says. But he welcomes the day when the town can set aside the temptation of money, if not the need for a little of it. It won't recover the losses Kake has taken on halibut and on timber. But it could return people to what they really need: the permission and the desire to live fully on their land again, and in their culture.

As the ceremony in the old town winds down, the Ravens remind everyone that they all got here by working together. The rain is falling, but no one is particularly hurried. There are offerings. Feathers.

Tobacco. Anywhere on the ground will do, someone says, as people begin to step forward. There could be other people buried—likely there are—and no one wants to disturb anything else on the unstable slope. There's a profound sadness. Everyone stands in it. For a long time, things are just quiet.

The last songs that follow are rhythmic and heartfelt. The woman with the tambourine drum beats it steady, holding it by the crossed rawhide strings behind its skin, a mournful expression on her face. The drumming is strong, stern, the stick improvised from what looks like a horned spoon.

When the ceremony is over, several people climb the hill to a community building where there is bingo. Though games are supposed to be held at somewhat regular intervals, in reality the intervals are irregular, owing to the unsteadiness of cash. Though it's about the only entertainment in Kake that costs money and isn't the diner or the liquor store, bingo is a big expense. It costs forty dollars to play all night. But the games, when they happen, are just as you would expect a good night of bingo to be.

There are coffee and snacks. A woman calls the numbers from a sprawling Bingo King console, a wall-sized flashboard behind her, lighting up one number at a time, and a game-indicator screen too. There are Dabbin' Fever bingo markers and rows and rows of recyclable cards. They play straight diagonal and double bingo. Coverall and block of six. There's anticipation. There's suspense. Gasps and sighs and a lot of laughter. There are near misses and close calls.

And in the end, people walk away happy, a few of them winners. That is the glorious thing about bingo in Kake. It's a fair fight. When people come here and they bet against each other, someone in this town can win.

Gulf Wild

White-Collar Foodies

THOSE STILL STANDING IN THE catch-share economy faced their own struggles. Back in Florida, in 2013, Jason De La Cruz was about to square off with his most formidable foe: seafood buyers. And he would soon have to decide between doubling down on his bets or forfeiting at least some of his dockside dreams.

By then Gulf Wild was a bona fide brand—religiously tagged aboard fishermen's boats, so that consumers could find out when and where and how their fish was caught. But while De La Cruz and his colleagues had customers who wanted Gulf Wild fish, the local seafood buyers weren't willing to bridge the gap. Doing so required them to keep Gulf Wild fish separate from other fish, and to track and sell it accordingly. And unless you had a sea-to-table business of your own, like Port Orford seafood or the boats that used Trace and Trust, seafood distribution was a business that ran on high volumes and tiny profits. Nobody in it had the time to coddle the catch.

De La Cruz stumped hard to convince them that they should. He even rented city hall for an event exercise in persuasion, passing out free lanyards with a couple of folks from the Gulf Reef Fish Shareholders Alliance and talking in his breathless verse. They could all capture extra money on Gulf Wild fish, he told them. They just had to be willing to peddle a tagged-at-sea brand.

But no matter how many chefs and high-end consumers waited on the other side of the supply chain, or how many fish the Gulf Wild fishermen caught, De La Cruz had hit a wall. "It pissed me off," he said. He owned boats that were out fishing. But his brand was at the mercy of the buyers who would take the fish, unless he wanted to be a distributor too.

Almost by default, De La Cruz's business began to change. And as he began to wrest control of Gulf Wild distribution from local seafood buyers, he was building exactly the kind of vertically integrated seafood company that makes investment firms drool. Not so much those buyers that American catch shares had seen so far—individuals who'd come hunting for fishing rights and for boats. But big investors. Marquee Wall Street firms and multinational corporations that wanted to own companies that straddled the seafood supply chain, controlling everything from the dock to the dinner plate. De La Cruz could do all that and more. He could also control the fish in the sea. And Wall Street types were beginning to understand just how delicious that was.

To understand his investment appeal is to understand his problem. De La Cruz was up against the middle of the seafood supply chain. This section of the fish market has a lot of names. In the Gulf of Mexico, seafood buyers are known as fish houses, which tend to buy and sell their products fresh. On the West Coast, seafood buyers are called processors, for the slightly different tack they take in canning, packaging, and whipping fish into products. Regardless of what you call them, they're the center of the supply chain. Below them are the fishermen on their boats. And above them are the grocery stores and the restaurants, then the consumer. They're an opaque center. Several such distributors might lay hands on a given fish. And these were the actors that De La Cruz began to fight for control of his fish, so that he could preserve the integrity of Gulf Wild's path through the marketplace.

The reason why the fish houses would not play ball was really pretty simple: the middle of the fish market had been dealing fish like widgets for years. All the conversations about traceability, about great brands, about how to fish right and keep consumers coming back—that was just chatter among chefs, policy wonks, and conservationists, and inside De La Cruz's head. The stark reality is that consistency and volume are not up to those players. They are up to seafood buyers. And their job is to make wild, erratic seafood supplies look as accessible and predictable as hotdogs and candy corn.

It's not really that way. The oceans are fickle beasts. We know astonishingly little them, about aquatic life, and why populations of fish ebb and flow as they do. And we control none of it. Not the temperature of the water, not the movement of the fish we consume or of the predators that compete with us for them. The supply of wild seafood fluctuates naturally, and even more so with regulation organizing things into seasons. This is the stuff the supply chain has long been glossing over. Snapper season shut down? Time to scare up some imports. Not enough white fish? Call a haddock a cod. Once filleted with the heads off, one fish can look quite like another, which might account for the number of fish that get mislabeled and renamed once the heads come off. Though it's never been quite clear whether fishermen, retailers, or the players in the middle are the biggest offenders in the seafood shell game, a 2013 study by the nonprofit oceans champion Oceana found that a third of all fish were frauds by the time they got to consumers in the United States. Gulf Wild's chief fare—grouper and red snapper—were among the most widely impersonated, a problem the Gulf Wild tags could cure.

But there was little De La Cruz could do to get his fish through the middle of the market without support from fish buyers, at least at first. Then one day he turned up at the docks to settle a question. His boat and his captain were coming in with a haul of grouper. And he decided to wait around. It was a lot like any other day except for one thing: he'd told his captain not to tag the fish. No more Gulf Wild. Just plain old grouper. He didn't give the fish house a heads-up, either. Instead, he just showed up at the place, the kind of building in Tarpon Springs that looks like the back of a hollowed-out thrift mart, and he watched.

Buildings like this were scattered all around the region, industrial dots on a landscape facing a wiggling series of bays and salt lakes. The rest were whitewashed or pink, many of them home to restaurants keen on local catch like his. And this might have accounted, in part, for why Gulf Wild fish were being treated the same as all the rest of the fish coming off the Gulf. Locally, they still were.

What De La Cruz wanted to know, however, was whether that was true nationally. Whether there was, in fact, a difference between his fish and all the rest once the middlemen sold them to far-flung buyers who would have only the Gulf Wild tag to work with. He'd been looking for a payout on that tag, reasoning that traceable seafood could fetch more money. And he wanted the fish houses to pay him that money, a fact that had them treating him like a man who had lost reason. De La Cruz pressed on. But really, he wasn't sure that money was there. He sure wasn't seeing it. But he figured maybe somebody else was.

While his captain unloaded the first hundred pounds of fish, nothing happened. The owner of the fish house was standing there, watching the fish come in. And De La Cruz was watching the man. A couple hundred more fish went by. Still, no reaction. But there were at least eight thousand pounds of grouper on the boat. All untagged. So he waited some more. And after about a thousand pounds, he got his answer.

"They, all of a sudden, magically noticed there weren't tags," De La Cruz says. "And. They. Freaked. Out. 'Uh, where are the tags? Your fish are always tagged.' And I go, 'Well, you won't pay me any more for them so I just told them not to tag.'" The fish house owner shot a look across the room then that De La Cruz could read plain. It told him he had just cost the man a pretty good pile of money. "I said, 'Yup, that's exactly what I wanted to know.'"

De La Cruz tagged the fish after that. But he started selling some on his own, calling around to customers that he knew wanted trace-able seafood. He got regular updates from his captain via satellite phone. And he started using the information to cut the fish house out of the haul. It was just a bit at first. A few hundred pounds here. A hundred there. He let the owner of the fish house know it, too. "About the sixth or seventh time, you could tell that he was not happy with me." But by June, De La Cruz took a whole boat out of the mix. The fish house still didn't offer to pay him more, though, or to get his fish where it was going. So he kept on going rogue. Theirs was getting to be an expensive game of chicken with a guy who barely blinked. And De La Cruz, meanwhile, was building market demand.

Soon he would not be able to meet it, so that he would have to start building his very own middle—a fish house of his own. The bank would come to like him. And to any other investors he probably looked like a dream—a guy with guts and vision who had a whole lot of equity floating in the deep sea. That equity was a thing that a handful of smart people had been thinking hard about how to leverage. They knew that seafood—not just seafood brands but ocean properties, too—must be bankable. And in the hands of people like De La Cruz, people who were willing to capture a market premium with a conser-vation ethos, the returns for investors could add up big.

———

IT WASN'T THAT thinkers in the conservation world wanted to turn the sea into a kind of floating stock market. Their chief aim was just to promote conservation in the first place. Within the Environmental Defense Fund, an effort to draw on private capital to transition more fisheries into catch shares, called the oceans enterprise effort, was at least two years old at the time. The theory was this: if conservation groups could get deep-pocketed investors to place bets on catch shares, they could amass a pile of money that would privatize seafood and thus conserve more of the world's oceans faster.

David Festa, head of EDF's oceans program, was deeply involved. His résumé was fitting. In addition to his stint with seafood regulators in the Department of Commerce, he'd worked with national governments, the United Nations, and multilateral development banks, including the World Bank, on issues that married money and policymaking. In 2009 he was tapped, along with a handful of others, to serve on a panel at the Milken Institute's global conference. There, he rolled out a strategy for capital growth much as De La Cruz had at city hall.

The audience was a little different: several thousand CEOs, international investors, policymakers, tech tycoons, boutique fund reps, and academic and government sorts. They were all milling around the Beverly Hilton in Los Angeles, where the intellectual fare ranged from well-lit theater presentations to panel talks in rooms with oppressive drapes. Despite its ties to junk bond king Michael Milken, the conference was and still is attended by a lot of heavyweights, blurbed by the likes of Google CEO Eric Schmidt, former California governor Arnold Schwarzenegger, and media mogul Rupert Murdoch.

Festa was fresh off a stint drafting white papers for the next iteration of the Department of Commerce as part of the Obama transition team when he spoke. After a crash course in fisheries, he pegged the present-day value of US fisheries at $5 billion and estimated that value could quadruple if those fisheries were converted to catch shares. Then he laid out a plan by which private capital could hasten the transition. Behind him was a line graph that showed the fifteen catch shares in America ballooning to seventy by 2030 with the aid of private investment. At an axis point before the line arched up, a navy blue box proclaimed the catalyst for this transition would be the new administration in the White House. A separate flow chart clarified the maze of regulators on the seas under US jurisdiction, with arrows showing investors in league with seafood buyers, fishermen, and trade groups as they lobbied for more catch shares. As he talked, Festa compared the oceans to factories making a decent product. But the workers are undertrained and the equipment is out of date and the marketing plans basically suck.

"I know that if I fix all that, I can be profitable in the future. So I pull together investors and I buy the factory and I sink a whole bunch of money into it and, you know, retrain workers and then get paid back on the profits on the other end. Well, why can't we do that with fisheries?"

When a transcript of the talk hit the Internet, it rattled the American fishing community to its core. EDF doesn't like to speak about it to the press. And Festa doesn't do interviews about his financial ideas, at least not lately. Today, catch-share proponents say these strategies are meant for overseas fisheries, where communities are less able to fund the transition to catch shares than in the United States, where some combination of government loans to industry and taxpayer money tends to do the job.

But fishermen who heard the references to the United States made at Milken bristled loudly and publicly at the idea of well-dressed people talking about giving them "an honorable exit" from the fisheries. Nobody really argued that good points were made, for instance, when the panelists talked about the capital needs to do things like daylight the middle of the supply chain, or develop better ways to monitor the catch, or come up with more sophisticated trading for ocean access than Craigslist. But the notion that fishermen would happily "give away the upside in the fishery if the fishery happens to recover and the take doubles," as one panelist put it, made people irate. A good many fishermen were not planning to give away anything. And they recognized themselves as the "marginal performers" and "incumbent industry" that Festa and Larry Band, the panel's moderator and a consultant for EDF who had spent nearly twenty years on Wall Street with Lehman Brothers, hoped to get rid of.

What was whispered among philanthropic funders later was that this talk was part of what caused some of the larger conservation funders, those still on the fence about catch shares, to confirm their lack of interest, unable as they were to reconcile their environmental aims with the privatization subtext laid bare at Milken. Instead, they started congregating around more philanthropy-focused endeavors, including Fish 2.0, a *Shark Tank*–styled business competition convened a few years later by brainiac seafood investment consultant Monica Jain at Stanford. There the fare ranged from aquaponic and aquaculture farms to direct-to-consumer ideas. Funders started using it as a hunting ground for less controversial things to throw money at.

Yet the vision described for investors at Milken, one in which the well heeled could make big money supplying the capital to convert fisheries to catch shares, is still alive. A good place to understand why is at the IntraFish Seafood Investment Forum, the preeminent incubator of private-capital seafood deals, convened twice a year, in London and New York.

The union between seafood companies and Wall Street is perennially on display there, where investors like J.P. Morgan, Paine & Partners, and Merrill Lynch turned up to shop around roughly six years after the Milken talk. Though the main fare is typically salmon—farmed salmon—there's an incredible amount of high-dollar dealing that goes on here. Convened by *IntraFish*, a publication owned by the Norwegian equivalent of the *Wall Street Journal*, the attendees—about 140 of them—are largely institutional investors, mostly white men in black suits on the loose from Wall Street offices, making deals and listening to panel talks on the future of aquaculture, with segue pitches from businesses on the hunt for capital. The investors glued to panel talks are essentially in Seafood 101, brushing up on a topic that's of increasing interest on Wall Street. The rest is like speed dating for money. In this place of gold foil and dim chandeliers, where speakers are backlit by their own PowerPoints, the real action is elsewhere. Organizers estimate about fifty private meetings go down in the Roosevelt

Hotel throughout the day, so that suited industry reps are floating in and out of the conference room between face time with money people. Those people include the bespectacled and elusive Band, who spoke with Festa at Milken in 2009, a great ducker of the press, in a tweed jacket, pecking away at a cell phone. Since leaving Lehman Brothers, Band has quietly built a reputation as an oracle of private-capital seafood deals. The meetings also include representatives from a couple dozen multinational seafood companies.

There's a good reason why Wall Street investors like seafood. The United Nations predicts the world is running out of food and that, by 2050, its protein needs will have outstripped the ability of land-based farming to produce it. These kinds of dour statistics are like soft sales pitches floating throughout the day. By lunchtime, the buffet table is cleaned of salmon and the chicken goes mostly neglected. Educated people speak frankly about the disgusting amount of water and land consumed by beef and the hideous feed conversion ratio of land-farmed livestock. It's talk that might not play well at any other business lunch. But with the almighty farmed salmon now converting feed to protein at ratios better than even crickets—yes, the insect—it's popular chatter among institutional investors placing bets on aquaculture and toe-dips into wild seafood.

Things get briefly Orwellian, though, when Glenn Cooke, the CEO of the family-run Cooke Aquaculture, a $1 billion-a-year salmon and sea bass producer, points to wild fish, among other things, when asked where investors ought to be putting their money. "There are a lot of good MSC-certified fisheries that have really sustainable quotas. The proteins are limited. . . . But if they are managed in a sustainable way, they are very positive investment vehicles."

Bingo. The moment is brief. But it underscores the possibilities that institutional investors and the financial conservationists now visualize in wild seafood—that they could own not just the facilities, but the rights to the fish. And that such things are extremely good investments. Right after Cooke says this, he tells the investors, in polite terms, not to dive in like idiots. He talks about storms and weather and disease and reminds them that they have no idea how to manage any of that stuff. And that if they think they can stand alone in any seafood business—wild or farmed—without an industry partner to manage all but the money, they are going to be very sorry.

Investors know this. Which is why most stick to buying companies. And why such companies turn up in places like this looking for money, armed with the bar graphs that people who speak money understand. Revenue. Production. Operational costs, alongside planned cost-saving maneuvers. So far, buyouts of wild seafood companies are not wildly popular—not yet—and are instead the fare of a particular set of investors who are busy making seafood a portfolio specialty. But as such firms slowly consolidate fishing rights, talk about privatizing seafood for conservation's sake hasn't acknowledged the consolidation, even while its pace quickens.

In the year leading up to Cooke's remark, for example, the European private equity firm Bregal Partners and the Boston-based Falcon Investment Advisors paid an undisclosed sum to buy a piece of struggling American Seafoods Group, a pollock and groundfish company that controls a chunk of the seafood supply in the Bering Sea. Paine & Partners raised half of an $850 million fund for food and agribusiness deals, which it previously used to buy the Seattle-based processor Icicle Seafoods, through which it controls a good bit of crab. And the Bangkok-headquartered Thai Union, a publicly traded fish products company with production in nine countries on four continents, tried to buy Bumble Bee Seafoods, also a fish access holder, for $1.5 billion. That deal was nixed after the US Department of Justice started sniffing at whether it would harm competition in the seafood industry.

There's nothing insidious about these deals. Profit seeking though they are, the fact that the deep-pocketed see protein as a way to ever deepen the pocket has positive consequences for people who still plan to be eating in another three decades. But this is not the transition capital that EDF and its leadership envision. It's not saving the world. It's just an outgrowth of privatization. An outgrowth aided by that trifecta of issues—consolidation, ballooning rental markets, and a class of elite owners—that has helped make big businesses the next logical inheritors of fishing rights. The vision to save the world hit the ground overseas instead, after the ideas expressed at Milken in 2009 were floated internationally.

These were not just ideas exclusive to EDF. The nonprofit ultimately became part of a larger worldwide coalition of groups promoting catch shares, called the Global Partnership for Oceans, under the tutelage of the World Bank. It was one of thirty-five organizations in the partnership to set a worldwide goal of bringing 50 percent of the world's fisheries into sustainable management, chiefly by catch shares, in ten years. Quirkily called the 50in10 initiative, it acknowledged that achieving ocean sustainability had been hastened by philanthropic donations. And that someday those donors were going to disappear. By transitioning the oceans to financial models, believers in 50in10 aimed to keep ocean conservation moving forward with or without donations. The fact that investors could then stick their fingers in was just a by-product more welcomed by some than by others.

In 2014, as part of the initiative, Band partnered with The Prince's Trust (the prince being the Prince of Wales) on behalf of EDF to develop a playbook for seafood investors, one that followed on the 50in10 thinking. Today it helps seafood companies make themselves more attractive to investors, and fosters the development of improvements in the supply chain's middle to help harvest and distribute seafood sustainably and transparently. But it also makes clear that "secured tenure" or "rights-based management"—catch shares, in other words—reduce the risks in seafood that investors see as impediments to jumping in. Just like they want to know that Nabisco will always have sugar for the Oreos, investors want to know that seafood companies will always have fish.

Secure tenure, sustainable harvests, and robust monitoring and enforcement are all considered key ingredients in the recipe for saving the oceans now. As the playbook itself notes, "These conditions, particularly establishing secure tenure, provide the platform for unlocking greater social, economic and environmental value in fisheries and are vital to investment activities."

These ideas jumped the playbook to became a reality in the lobster and conch industry in Belize, where two cooperatives that control access to fishing through a catch share are now being positioned as investment vehicles. Belize is one of twelve countries EDF targets for catch shares. Those efforts partly follow new Walton Family Foundation investments in catch-share programs in Indonesia, Peru, Chile, and Mexico. They also dovetail with strategies being pushed by the Rockefeller Foundation and Bloomberg Philanthropies in Chile, Brazil, and the Philippines.

This work opens the door to Wall Street and to international investors to advance their missions. And while investment firms come to this market looking for the kinds of vertically integrated companies they're comfortable with, sea-to-table companies like Gulf Wild are an obvious choice.

———

ALTHOUGH HE LIKELY did not think about it at the time, this is exactly what Jason De La Cruz was building. By then he had a marketing guy. And he was still peeling fish off his own boats—one or two thousand pounds at a time for the customers who wanted Gulf Wild. The marketing guy kept putting out press releases, which gave De La Cruz more demand than he could handle. There was more desire for Gulf Wild fish than he could pull away from his boats and still deliver to the fish houses. If he cut them out completely, he was on his own. Yet the marketing guy was dangling carrots. Big carrots. He had a place that really wanted the fish. It was a distributor that supplied two or three really high-end restaurants. The chefs were big deals. They were winning Beard Awards. And they wanted Gulf Wild.

De La Cruz was sitting in a parking lot with his phone lighting up when he made the decision. He was at yet another fish house. And the images before his eyes were about to sear into his memory for good. The boatyard. A twenty-foot ice tower. Traffic on Gulf Boulevard zipping by on his right. He was on his Bluetooth. And on the edge of a cliff again, he realized. It was another one of those moments where he was either going to leap or back away.

The marketing guy was in his ear. Carrots, carrots, carrots. And De La Cruz was unlike a lot of people in this way: enticed by the gap between his best ideas and the reality of implementing them. He was a leaper. He considered what he was hearing only briefly. And then, "I said, 'You know what? Screw it. Let's do it." He would start his own fish house in Madeira Beach. He would buy from his own boats and supply his own product so that Gulf Wild could reach the top of the food chain unencumbered. From the marketing guy, he got the phone number of a man who wanted Gulf Wild fish and who could link it to the chefs. He called him up. Then he took his first order, right there in the car.

Gulf Wild was hitting the white tablecloth.

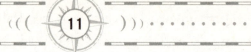

Southern Ocean, New Zealand

What's the Worst Thing That Could Happen?

A factory trawler hauls its net on the Bering Sea.
PHOTO BY DAVE WAGENHEIM

On the other side of the world, an opposite kind of product was making headlines. And the catastrophic sinking of a vessel was about to upend fishing politics in New Zealand and send a shudder through the global seafood economy. The sinking of the *Oyang 70*, while it fished for the soon-to-be sustainably certified southern blue whiting, exposed the tragic gap between sustainable seafood's branding and its labor practices. Turns out whiting was being had cheap, including by Americans, on the backs of people who worked long and dangerous days, often in horrible conditions, for unfathomably low pay.

Later, when police tried to find out how the *Oyang 70* sank, they conducted forty-four interviews with survivors and created detailed maps of each man's movement through the ship in its last hour. The narrative that follows is an account that derives from those records. And in it the names of surviving crewmen, but not officers, have been changed to protect the safety of those who remain at sea. These pseudonyms employ only one name, a practice common in Indonesia. And no quotes are used, since the documents are summaries of translations. The story unearthed from those pages is shocking nonetheless, excavated as it is from the bland white sheets of police papers.

Some who survived the accident that day said the net hanging off the *Oyang 70*'s stern contained the biggest haul of fish any of them had ever seen. It was August 18, 2010, and the whiting were spawning. The thirty-eight-year-old factory trawler was four hundred miles off the coast of New Zealand in the Southern Ocean, hunting whiting for export for fish balls and surimi, the fancy name for fake crab.

The ship was a hulk of a thing: its black hull towering out of the water, lettered in Korean, its masts and lights immense, more aircraft carrier than Love Boat. On board were eight Korean officers, a Chinese cook, and forty-two Indonesian and Filipino crewmen. The latter two groups would later describe themselves as the vessel's second class. And they were. They worked an average of eighteen hours a day on six hours of sleep in three decks, one a factory just to process the massive amount of fish they were catching.

Parmin, an Indonesian crewman, realized the day was something other than ordinary while hauling the trawler's net. He was on the port side of the deck, holding a camera while a crew wrested the net aboard, steadying it with ropes while a winch tugged it onto the stern. Parmin was the captain's eyes on the fish, dangling the camera deep inside the net from an iron step. This, so that Captain Hyonki Shin, by all accounts an angry man and a yeller, could bellow his instructions from the wheelhouse to his navigation crew and to the deck below. Except that it was 3:00 a.m. So Shin was sleeping. Two and a half hours earlier he had left first officer Min Su Park in charge of the wheelhouse and slipped away for a nap.

Their objective was a big catch. And this catch was enormous. The whiting's tendency to cluster during summer spawning was so reliable it was possible to catch 100 or 150 tons of them in just a few minutes. By some estimates, plumes as large as a thousand or two thousand tons of fish were normal. And though the fishing had been mediocre on this trip—a haul of squid, a dud of a catch, and a ripped net—Shin was gunning for a winner. He'd called for a bigger net earlier in the day, then dragged it for eight hours. He opted not to worry about the dead batteries in a sensor designed to tell him how full it was getting.

Reshoot the net, he told his crew, flying blind. Then he went to bed.

So it came to be that ten men were on deck of the *Oyang 70* wrestling a monster of a catch. It was the usual number of guys against what seemed to be an unusual number of fish. Four of them were on the port side of the stern. Another four were starboard. And all were leaning against the wires that, on a normal day, helped to keep the net on course. Today they looked like Lilliputians dogging Gulliver on his travels—helplessly small, battling a giant. Under floodlights in a dark sky, they strained while half the boat slept below.

Parmin held the camera low. The idea was to keep the captain, or in this case Park, aware of exactly how much fish they would be dumping onto the factory deck below. As it was, the factory had been churning for hours. Part of the reason Shin had dragged the net so long was to give the workers a chance to catch up. Fish were already everywhere.

But the more the deck crew reeled the net in, the more awestruck they all were. The net was absolutely stuffed with whiting, towering over the deck in a gigantic wad of mesh. Few had ever seen anything like it. Mere men aside the behemoth, they were powerless to move it far. And before long it was hopelessly stuck. Not half of it on the deck, the rest dangling in the water. Even the boat was cowed. It started squatting in the sea.

The bosun—the deck boss, a Korean officer—finally paused. It's too many fish, he said. He asked for permission to open the net and drop ten or twenty tons back into the water. Park hesitated. He was already a bit confused. Later he said that he hadn't known that the captain had switched to a larger net. And that he'd been a bit surprised to see, as he commanded it aboard, that the net was bigger than he knew, and so full. He called Shin in his cabin, roused him from sleep. Chain of command, he later explained. It was a loose way of confirming what the crew would tell the police: that Shin was a man concerned with fish and not much else. And that nobody aboard the *Oyang 70* would cross him, not even his first officer.

So, they waited.

What happened next wasn't the fault of catch shares. It was the fault of bad leadership, of inexperience, of recklessness, and of the sheer neglect of the maintenance of a ship and the training required to keep it from sinking. None of those things can be blamed on fishing policy. But they can be blamed on the dynamics of a privatized market, a market that had prompted, much like Alaska's halibut and sablefish, a race to the bottom of the rates paid to the boats that competed for the work.

The *Oyang 70* had come to New Zealand to fish some of the forty-nine thousand tons of southern blue whiting up for grabs off its shores. The fish was one of thirty-seven species divvied up among private owners. Most of those owners were leasing their shares to one of nineteen corporations that rented the opportunity to fish, the 2010 reality of a system that was privatized in 1986. That season, those corporations had fifty-six boats trawling in New Zealand's waters. Twenty-seven of them were foreign ships leased for the work. In other words, the foreign ships were renting the opportunity to catch fish from the entities that controlled them. Their laborers were contracted, adding yet another layer of hired hands, most of them cheaply acquired from poverty-stricken places. Those workers' wages had already been gouged by the unscrupulous middlemen who recruited them—an industry reality in the global seafood economy, a marketplace rife with problems, most occurring on underregulated seas between nations.

It was a scenario bred of top-down economic pressure, in which those eager to grow profits on ocean properties didn't want to know how those profits were being captured. Or that they were being captured through the exploitation of workers whose treatment was breaking national laws that couldn't reach aboard the foreign-flagged ships. Though New Zealand officials had known for years that conditions on these boats were dicey or worse, they failed to act. And the longer they did nothing, the more the prices paid to these foreign ships and workers fell.

Operated by Sajo Oyang Corporation in New Zealand, a Korean

company with tentacles in several international jurisdictions, the *Oyang 70* was squeezing its workers hard. The average wage was US$180 a month. The crew ate the same fish day after day, often left over from the day before. Sometimes they were fined if they didn't eat it fast enough. They slept in unheated cabins so leaky that every week they bailed water out of them in pails. The engine was infested with cockroaches. There was a leak in the portside bow. A broken refrigerator was pooling water in a fish hold, so that to work there, crews waded midcalf in muck. None of the commanding officers spoke a language the crew understood, or, if they did, they didn't use it to communicate with them. So while the boat sank, the people aboard would divide— as they had on all other days—along racial lines.

Even on regular days, their catch was huge. The net was more than ninety-eight feet long, nearly twice as long as a basketball court is wide. When the crew could haul it normally, they hoisted it all the way out of the water and led it along a slipway on the deck so that, stuffed with fish, it looked like a whale on a waterslide. The idea was that the tail end of the net—the cod end if you're a seaman—would then dangle off the end of the stern into a chute that led to the factory floor. When opened, it sent fish flowing into a hold, from which they were pushed down a series of conveyor belts. A trouble-free haul took an hour, and processing the fish took twenty-one people in the factory below.

The net was inching aboard when Shin got to the wheelhouse. He told the bosun to dump a few tons, then pull the rest. The man did. But while the crew kept hauling like they were supposed to—at a slight angle, not too straight—it was just too big a catch inside, the chute too small. The more the net climbed from the water, the more immense it appeared. When somehow the crew got the end into the chute and opened it, at first the fish poured out like normal. But then they stopped flowing, their passage clogged by a mass of their own making. Fish piled up behind fish. The extra weight made it so the net shifted fast. It rolled to port hard. The boat listed.

Later, when investigators tried to calculate exactly how full the net had been, they surmised that the cod end alone was the size of six tennis courts, holding 120 tons of fish, or about the size of an adult whale. At a coroner's inquest in Wellington, an expert would testify that only five or six tons would have been on the slipway on the deck where it belonged, and next to where Parmin stood. The rest of it, he said, was "trailing in the sea like a big silver sausage."

As the net dangled to the port, the crew scrambled to right it but could not. The ship bowed, tipping dangerously low. Below deck, water suddenly seemed to come from everywhere. Inside the factory, a portside door called an offal, the place where fish waste fell from a conveyor belt back into the sea, stood open. The ocean rushed in along the conveyor belt like a waterfall, filling the factory floor with seawater. The portholes leaked. The portside drains started flowing backward. And in a space between the factory and the fish pressing room, where two Indonesian crewmen named Wahyu and Samsuri were working, water starting bubbling furiously through a floor drain.

On any other day, water on the deck was nothing new. The operation itself was propelled by hoses. Every hour they sucked some forty tons of seawater from the ocean and pumped it into the holding tanks where the fish were stored, pressing the catch out into the factory for production. But while water filled the factory this time, washing in from the portholes and offal, those hoses kept running, too. They kept pouring water into the holds, where, combined with the seawater that was filling the boat, the two pumps designed to cope with it were overwhelmed.

The water climbed and ran to port toward the engine room. Three of the engine workers started racing to stop it. One was Harais, an Indonesian crewman. He rushed to close a door, trying to divert the water around the temperamental machinery powering the ship. His colleagues Tarmidi and Sarwo started covering machines, using boxes to protect some, and plastic to cover the wires. Sarwo dashed to the factory deck and turned off all the pipes, but water was still flowing through the offal. It was an avalanche of sea.

Tarmidi raced up the stairs. Above the deck, Parmin saw him stick his head up and call to the bosun. Water is coming in the engine room, he told him. The bosun turned and followed him down the ladder. Below deck, he found the water in the factory up to his knees. The bosun dashed back to the deck and radioed the captain on a ship-wide intercom. Parmin heard the message: water is in the engine room. The captain told the winch operator to keep hauling anyway.

The winch operator, Idris, had worked for twenty-seven hours before the three-hour nap that preceded this haul. He followed the orders and kept trying to pull the catch aboard. But while he did, experts said that the weight of the net must have shifted to the winch's lifting block some twenty yards above the boat, pressing the *Oyang 70* even lower in the water. Parmin watched from the iron step where he still held the camera. He could hear the winch straining, but the net barely budged.

Someone woke the chief engineer. He dashed below deck, where he found the three engine workers, now with their supervisor, trying fruitlessly to pump water away from the engine. By then the water was rushing down a portside staircase. The chief engineer ran back to the deck and told the crew to let the fish loose. He climbed to the winch room, where Sarwo and Samsuri had broken all protocol to run, and started yelling at Idris. Cut the net, he said. But Idris wanted the captain's order. None came. Samsuri started begging him. The boat is sinking, he said. But when Idris started to let the net go, Shin ordered him to stop.

Shouting broke out. The crew would later describe how the chief engineer had screamed at the captain, in tears. And how, while none of them understood what was said, they could see that the engineer kept yelling until the captain gave the order to cut the net and let some fish loose. By then the deck crew could see the boat listing into the water, and they scrambled to open the net's doors. But the catch as heavy as it was, the haul was immovable, the doors unreachable. Parmin watched as the bosun strapped a harness around his waist and climbed out onto the dangling mesh like an acrobat. With a knife, he started slashing, trying to cut the fish loose. The chief engineer climbed after him, and some of the crew followed, all slicing, panicked. It was little help. The small portion of fish that dribbled out to sea caused the net to slide farther to port. The ship sank even lower.

Shin ordered the crew to grab hoses. They did. They pointed them at the net and cranked on the water, trying to blast the fish free. It didn't work. They started kicking. By then the boat was listing so badly it was hard to walk.

Communication gaps would cloud a uniform narrative of what came next. Some Indonesians understood Korean, but most just watched, then did what the officers did. This was normal aboard the vessel. But as the Korean officers failed to take charge of the boat's sinking, or responsibility for the crew, emergency descended into chaos. There was no alarm, no evacuation, little leadership, and few commands.

The bosun and the engineer climbed off the net and ran to the winch room, taking hold of the controls and trying to shift the weight of the net. By then Idris had left, still without orders and frantic in search of a life jacket. The captain told him to wait on deck with the chief cook for instructions. Again, none came.

The engines started to cut out. Inside the wheelhouse, Shin urged his navigator to turn the ship hard to port, like a driver turning into a skid, but the engine did not respond. Shin grimly told the man to get a life jacket.

Beneath the deck, inside the cabins, people were waking up. Some woke on their own, the boat's listing snapping them from sleep. Others were knocked awake when the boat's list rolled them from their bunks into the walls. Some were gathered up by friends as the crew began tearing through the decks with words of warning. A Filipino electrician climbed to the upper deck and saw the net falling to port and six or seven Indonesian crewmen talking fast. He couldn't understand, but he could tell the boat was in trouble. He dashed through the listing halls for a life jacket, then to a room where the other five Filipino crewmen slept. He woke them and they made their way toward the lifeboats together.

People would continue waking up as the ship sank, some just a few minutes before its final keel. One said that when he opened his cabin door he saw water rolling down the walls. A small group of Indonesians made their escape through the captain's dining room, where they stopped to pray and panic both. They included twenty-five-year-old Heru Yuniarto and thirty-four-year-old Taefur, who was so frightened that he couldn't get his life jacket on without help.

Below deck, the water started flowing through open hatches toward the bow and into the holds where the fish were stored. When he saw it coming, Amir, who had been inside counting boxes, turned and ran. By his last count there were seventy-two hundred boxes in the hold, each one weighing fifty-seven pounds. Experts would later say this meant the vessel was already in trouble. Facts like these pointed to a captain who didn't know how to balance his ship. He had 410,000 pounds of fish in one hold, rather than spread over two. And one of the gas tanks was half full, so that the ship was listing to begin with.

These same experts, weighing in during a coroner's inquest, found other problems. Basic safety precautions like closing watertight doors were either routinely ignored or not enforced. The crew had no training in how to close overboard valves and keep the doors and hatches shut. There were no emergency procedures in place. No one even knew how to abandon the ship.

Many said Captain Shin never gave the order anyway. What they reported instead was Shin standing on the bridge still trying to direct the massive catch aboard while half the crew ran for the life rafts. Parmin was still feverishly trying to cut the net's wires when he heard a voice over the intercom. Go to the bosun's store on the upper deck, it said. Some thought it was the captain. Parmin did not, hearing instead what sounded like the first officer, Park. Others were just confused. They thought the captain was shouting at them to save the fish, and kept trying. One Indonesian crewman thought he heard Shin give the order to abandon ship, but he wasn't sure. He didn't speak Korean, just heard Shin say something that sounded urgent. Whatever the words were, they were few and late. The boat was clearly sinking. And everybody seemed to be figuring that out for themselves.

People started running from the deck around Parmin until he realized he was alone. He took his shoes off and he ran.

The exact moment that factory workers abandoned their posts is unclear. But by the time they did so they were standing in three feet of water. The reason would be made obvious later by a trio of researchers from the University of Auckland and the former deep-sea fisherman who assisted them. Together they amassed a frightful pile of paper— employment contracts, observers' diaries, pay slips, bank statements, and reports from immigration, fisheries, and labor departments. The paperwork, combined with 144 interviews with crewmen, painted a jarring portrait of what life at sea had been like on the *Oyang 70*, and aboard other foreign boats that were fishing in New Zealand's rental economy. All the workers faced heavy fines for ducking out on contracts, no matter what the circumstance. Most had already forfeit a portion of pay or paid security or finder's fees to the middlemen who recruited them. Most had also left family behind, family who depended on what bits of their paychecks dribbled in from those recruiters, and who would be devastated if those checks stopped coming. Deserters could look forward to having their photos broadcast in their hometown newspapers, alongside promises of rewards for their capture.

Across the industry, the researchers also discovered astounding conditions aboard foreign ships, particularly the Korean ships. Beatings were administered like a kind of sport. Random violence and torture were ready tools for control. Crews were made to bathe in salt water and drink rusty water. One ship's crew was fed rotten fish bait. Several crewmen reported being hit hard, without warning, in the back of the head for no reason. One such victim, hit with a steel pan, required more than twenty-six stitches that no one in authority would administer, owing to his being Indonesian. On one ship, the bosun threw a rice sack over a man's head while he ate, then punched him in the back of the head until he struggled to breathe. A helmsman who turned the boat the wrong way was kicked so hard in the groin that he bled and required a doctor. Others were made to stand on deck in unbearable weather for hours without reason. People worked days without rest and were often so tired that they injured themselves, cut on wires or in the factory in accidents that were never reported. Those with severe injuries were kept out of sight in port, and those who spoke up were taken to a cabin and beaten.

These circumstances in New Zealand were born out of its catch-share model. "What was happening was the foreign-chartered vessels were coming in fishing in New Zealand waters on behalf of New Zealand companies and quota holders," said Christina Stringer, one of the three researchers. She said the practice began in the 1970s, before catch shares, and increased over the next two decades once privatized fishing took hold. The ships were initially welcomed to help New Zealand companies build out their capacity to fish. "That never eventuated. Because, of course, the foreign vessels, the South Korean vessels, employing migrant crew was a very cost-effective model."

They were fishing for species linked "to commodity-oriented value chains and dominated by large retailers and business models that are typically cost driven," the report read. New Zealand firms earned prices commensurate with low-value commodities, a factor that pressed them to recover costs through cheap labor.

New Zealand officials had been aware of the dynamics for years, and of the working conditions aboard the boats, even debating them in parliament in the nineties. But the country never adopted the handful of rules that would have allowed it to enforce better conditions. Not until after the *Oyang 70* sank. Instead, over seventeen years, 550 crewmen deserted foreign vessels in ports in New Zealand. Most ended up deported.

Aboard the *Oyang 70,* while the last of the factory crew finally ran for deck, the water hit the stores hard. The power went out. The main deck went dark. The last to reach the upper deck groped to find the lifeboats in the black of night. Because they could not see each other, they talked to stay together. They picked their way along the ship chattering and holding the rails.

Now on the upper deck, Parmin and a handful of others surrounded the safety gear and started scrambling to untether it. The water was still at bay, the sides of the vessel clear. The sea was calm, but cold. The fog thick. They tried to get the floating rings loose first but couldn't budge them.

Their training consisted of a few fire drills. And the only printed instructions on how to deploy the life rafts were in Korean. Or English. Either way, no one understood. Someone lit a torch so they could see better and they fought to free the boats as best they could. One man later spoke of working so hard and so ineffectively that he broke his fingers on the straps. Parmin went for a life raft on the starboard side and managed to release it. But by then the *Oyang 70* was listing so badly that the raft fell limply back onto the deck. Gravity. One man later said he could see the captain through a window in the wheelhouse, watching.

Sarwo tried to count everyone and, realizing that Harais and Tarmidi were missing, ran back below deck to find them but could not. Two others would also try. They carried a torch for light and descended into the factory, but found the sorting room hip-high full of water. They called, but found no one, and turned back.

Somewhere along the way Captain Shin had issued a distress call, but only on a short-range radio, having failed to press the single button that would have sent the call zigzagging through a satellite back to shore. Fortunately, there were other boats nearby, including the New Zealand–flagged *Amaltal Atlantis*. Its officers heard the call and headed for the *Oyang 70*'s last position. By then, Shin had refused a life jacket and sat down to cry, hugging a pole. He told his navigator to leave.

The crewmen pushed the first of the life rafts into the water as it rose over the port rail. Some carried the rafts from the starboard side to port, unable to toss them to sea as the starboard rail turned skyward. The water climbed fast then. And as the crew fell portside, people started jumping. The Filipino crewmen jumped together, and from the frigid water they climbed into a raft with another man, then paddled hard away from the ship.

Parmin was still on the upper deck. The lights were out, the engine silent. He looked around and saw that he was the only one without a life jacket and felt terror. He reached for a friend and held tight to the back of him until a wave hit them and they were separated. Afterward, when he found that the *Oyang 70* was still somehow beneath his feet, he tried to run from the water, but the water was everywhere. Parmin was alone for those last few moments until the water took him too.

The boat went down soon after. Its mast landed on one of the life rafts, so that a handful of the crewmen had to dive underwater and pull it free again in order to climb in. The first engineer was hit hard by an antenna that pierced his right hand and pushed him a long way underwater before he came out again. When he did he saw the ship's oil glisten over the sea.

No one really knows how they lost Samsuri.

Taefur had been standing at the back of the bridge in a thin zippered sweater, O Chung trousers, and rubber boots, right before he jumped into the sea. His last stance, his clothes, this final leap, seared into the memories of those last to see him alive.

Yuniarto had been on the bridge too, in a black freezer jacket and rubber boots before he jumped. By then the *Oyang 70* was mostly under the surface, and the water around him was a mess of rope. Hours earlier, this same rope had been innocuously piled by the bridge, a supply for fixing nets. As the ship sank, however, it unfurled on the ocean in a deadly, waterlogged snarl. It drowned him.

Parmin swam hard. The sea was gentle, at least. The waves were small, even if too cold. The temperature at the time was about forty-five degrees, cold enough to kill a man in two hours. Though there were sixty-eight survival suits aboard the *Oyang 70*, and they would have lent another four hours of life, no one ever distributed them. Experts could not account for why—the boat's sinking had taken a rough hour, long enough to pass them around. Other unsettling facts would emerge: the Korean officers knew how to deploy the life rafts, but didn't do it. And the total sinking time of the *Oyang 70* had been long enough for an orderly evacuation, the kind that doesn't send people into the water.

When he reached a life raft, more than a dozen people were inside, and some pulled Parmin aboard. Nearly an hour passed before the *Amaltal Atlantis* drifted through the fog. When it did, its crew found only the wreckage of the *Oyang 70* and rafts carrying forty-five live men and three bodies—Samsuri, Taefur, and Yuniarto. A single raft carried three other men lying in a mix of fuel, oil, and water, two in an advanced stage of hypothermia. They survived. Three people would never be found. They included Shin, the captain, and Tarmidi and Harais, the latter two having fought hard to save the ship's engine and keep the vessel from sinking.

After they pulled the survivors to safety, some aboard the *Amaltal Atlantis* would note that the *Oyang 70*'s officers stood apart from their crew without mixing or speaking following their ordeal.

All this wasn't just something that happened in some aberrant bubble in New Zealand. The United States had been importing

7 percent of New Zealand's seafood exports about this time, and in the early part of the millennium had been buying about a third of its southern blue whiting, in combination with Japan. The whiting was landing in grocery stores and restaurants as an upscale kind of surimi, populating California rolls and snacks. By 2010 this fish started disappearing into the opacity of the global seafood supply, exported primarily to China for processing, then reexported around the world. When the *Oyang 70* sank, more than 80 percent of whiting was being caught by the foreign boats that were found to have been violating New Zealand's labor laws.

Whatever portion arrived in the United States was likely a sliver of the US$14.8 billion in seafood imported from other countries that year. But those dollars mattered. The roughly NZ$11.2 million earned by ships on exports had been forfeited by New Zealand trawlers that couldn't capture it at a profit if they paid workers the minimum wage required by New Zealand law. The downward pressure on laborers came from markets that consumed those products cheap. What let the ships that exploited them in to meet the demand was the catch-share rental economy. The same type of rental economy is now coming to US waters through catch shares. And US policy continues to encourage catch-share implementation nationwide.

Between the time the *Oyang 70* sank, killing Shin and five crew members, and when a criminal case against the Sajo Oyang Corporation washed up in the New Zealand courts, the southern blue whiting was certified as sustainable by the Marine Stewardship Council, a fact that underscored how little these certifications have to do with labor or human rights.

In the days that followed the *Oyang 70*'s sinking, the crewmen who survived were shuttled between a hotel and a police station for interviews, paired with interpreters. Their Korean officers, meanwhile, arrived flanked by lawyers. Most had been sleeping before the ship sank. Some could even proffer their regular sleeping hours, unlike their charges, who, police noted, seemed confused about when they had even last slept.

When crewmen complained about lost pay and possessions, and about the captain most easily identified as at fault, the officers accused them of lying. They claimed the crew members were better paid than the officers themselves and got bonuses to spend in port. They said other things, too: The ship was in perfect working order. An alarm had sounded. There had been a proper evacuation and everyone had known what to do. They said Korean officers woke the crewmen in their beds and distributed life jackets. No crewman ever corroborated any of it.

One Indonesian worker said this instead: that he had watched the Korean officers as they deployed, dropping into the sea in rafts and leaving the crewmen behind without a word. "Shows," he said, "what they think of us."

Still, attorneys in the case struggled to hold the Sajo Oyang Corporation responsible for what happened. The business, it turned out, was a web of entities on paper, and straddled several international jurisdictions that made prosecution for the lost lives difficult and costly. There were complicated contracts between those entities. And the difficulty of tracking information through Korea and other countries obscured the business relationships and the roles of individuals even further. It also kept corporate profits far away from the businesses with any relationship to the hiring of the crews.

This is not unusual, according to attorney Craig Tuck, who is the founder of Slave Free Seas, an organization that leads the world in identifying and advocating for crews. "Well-resourced and sophisticated businesses that have a no-cost, low-cost exploitation model know that the chance of a poor and itinerant crew obtaining competent legal representation is unlikely," he said in an email. The crew continues to try to collect wages for the ill-fated voyage. Meanwhile, a settlement was paid to the families of the lost by the nation of New Zealand.

The following year, when thirty-two crew members walked off the *Oyang 75*, the replacement ship for the *Oyang 70*, citing abuse, the Sajo Oyang Corporation was successfully fined NZ$420,000 for fish dumping in relation to the case. The boat itself, worth NZ$9.6 million, was seized by the nation of New Zealand. The person-to-person crimes were never prosecuted but were settled privately with crew members, who received money to withdraw from the legal case. The following year, a second ship, the *Oyang 77*, was also seized for alleged illegal dumping of fish and fishing in forbidden areas.

A ministerial inquiry in New Zealand meanwhile led to an avalanche of recommendations to strengthen the country's control of fishing vessels from foreign nations. The recommendations called for everything from rewriting policies and legislation to practical changes within the agencies tasked with overseeing the boats. Among those adopted were new laws requiring chartered boats to flag as New Zealand ships, making them fully subject to domestic law. Now wages are up and abuse is down. Advocates for crew say they are vast improvements, but that their level of effectiveness is still undetermined.

Gulf Wild

An Industry Retools

DESPITE WHAT HAPPENED IN THE New Zealand rental market, two years later and halfway around the world, Jason De La Cruz began to prove the business case for American catch shares.

He rented a rough wooden shop under the boardwalk in John's Pass in Madeira Beach, where the foot traffic rattled overhead. A small building with a metal roof, it was tucked into the shade, the door side by side with a hefty ice machine. He called his new fish house Wild Seafood. And out its front door, past the ice machine, was a parking lot where delivery trucks came to load up Gulf Wild fish.

As Wild Seafood grew over the next two years and De La Cruz became the seafood industry's next generation of middleman, Madeira Beach was changing. On the heels of catch shares, grouper was being remade in much the same way as any other catch share. Consolidation hit hard. And a rental market took hold so that the rates to go fishing started climbing alongside the dock price for grouper, now worth more while the catch came in steadily rather than in erratic clumps. Guys who used to hit the water and go fishing were suddenly staying home, newly minted landlords trying to figure out how much money they could make from the couch. The captains and crews were getting younger, with older guys unwilling to pay rents to go fish.

Wall Street had not exactly moved in—equity acquisitions in fisheries don't start with a bulk sale of assets to big firms. But small investors began to turn up, aiming to add ocean properties to portfolios that they could cash out in a few years. Some were well-established fishermen. Others were new to the game. Either way, they were people who could pay the highest prices as the privatized grouper market took hold, and they quickly outstripped the means of the upcoming generation of workers who might otherwise have become owner-operators like De La Cruz.

People didn't easily separate De La Cruz's new fish house from the outside money that started trickling in. Or from the Environmental Defense Fund, which was funding the development of Gulf Wild, of T. J. Tate's job as its overseer, and of the Gulf Reef Shareholders Alliance that devised it. Thus began a period of his life that De La Cruz now refers to as "not boring." The naysayers and detractors went at him whole hog.

Salty though it is, Madeira Beach is an unlikely place for the seafood dustup that followed. Though it's part of the Grouper Republic—one of three major seaports along with Cortez to the south and Tarpon Springs to the north—it's not like New England or Alaska. It's not a place where quaint Victorian houses and bungalows popped up around the seafood economy and stood for hundreds of years while whole towns grew up on fish dollars. Instead, the ports along this stretch of Florida line a series of skinny islands to the west of St. Petersburg, islands that make it a hotspot for sailing, sport fishing, and bikini lounging on white sand. People come here to cultivate cases of skin cancer, not join seafood empires. But empires were building nonetheless, and there was a hell of a lot of complaining over it.

The scratchy, sun-bleached fishermen who harvest grouper in Madeira Beach are not an especially visible part of the town. They're not an economic driver. More like economic pedestrians in an area where more than 20 percent of the workforce is employed in service jobs, partly to fawn over tourists. Hotels. Restaurants. Bars. Even while grouper dominated the menus at each, fishermen were camouflaged behind sea-weathered fish houses, cleaning boats and offloading totes facing the suboptimal water views on the city's east side, the side without the white sand.

Knowing as much makes it easier to understand how, right after the grouper catch share took hold, a fisherman named Jim Bonnell ended up at a coffee shop trying to give a stranger $10,000 for grouper access. At the time, though swift trading of grouper rights was under way, there was no infrastructure to service the exchanges, save for one broker in Cortez that had its own boats and grabbed the good stuff. Without brokers to handle the deals, there was nobody to the hold bets, which is what trading was. When trading sprang up without any attending services anyway, people did what they do when they have a thing to sell and no place to sell it: they posted it on Craigslist.

Coffee shop rendezvous aside, access to fish was never something a person could put in your hand. Most of these systems arrived in America after guys like Steve Jobs and Bill Gates did their thing in the garage, and the Internet was around by then, too. Fisherman or not, society had long expected a person to have a computer, and once the grouper catch share was established, these transfers were done online through portals maintained by the National Marine Fisheries Service. There was no equivalent government portal to take payments, however. And without brokers, the absence of a venue through which one could buy and sell fostered a logistical problem that drove Bonnell, and probably a lot of other people, to meet total strangers at random retail establishments and consider giving them amazing amounts of cash.

People were reluctant to take checks—there was nothing to do if they bounced. There was no way of knowing, beyond drivers' licenses, if the buyers were even who they said they were. Cash deals were shaky too. Bonnell could turn up carrying five figures in tidy Benjamins and have it grabbed out of his hands while he watched a new acquaintance make a transfer on a laptop. There was no real way to verify that the person actually had fishing rights, not unless you watched them give it to you online. Bonnell was frantic he'd be mugged while staring at a screen. These meetings played out all over the region. And they were like staring contests over coffee and computers, where the guy with the money and the guy with the access sat there wondering who would make the first move. This particular meeting concluded at a bank. Bonnell did not bring the ten thousand after all, so the duo ended up, laptop in tow, making the awkward transaction there.

This is the long way of saying that by 2013, while the price of access was rising and money was flooding Madeira Beach and elsewhere, the vibe among the fishing community was distinctly paranoid. Which is partly why, as De La Cruz built his new business in the tiny building under the boardwalk, people were not readily separating his endeavors from your garden-variety hostile takeover.

"It's like just a personal invasion," said Johnny Stalides, who had fished for twenty-five years before catch shares, but wasn't awarded enough fish to stay in business (the qualifying years were not his best). Bob Spaeth, executive director of the Southern Offshore Fishing Association, upon seeing fishermen like Stalides start renting, began championing their cause. His organization funded a congressional lobbyist while Spaeth pressed the Walton Family Foundation, trying to cut off funding for more catch shares and for their promotion. Disgusted with rapidly rising rents, he lamented the fisherman's downfall from storied artisan to retail chauffeur. "All we are is a taxicab for the non-fishing public," he said.

It was not long before the fish-house owners in the middle—the people who used to buy the fish before De La Cruz showed up—were getting worried, too. Really worried. In his first year, De La Cruz bought about one hundred thousand pounds of fish. It was no small amount, all of it siphoned away from competitors. A year later, he was well on his way to tripling it. People were peeved. The way he did it was unlike anything they had ever seen. He'd set a tiny margin for himself to operate on. Then he gave the rest to his fishermen. De La Cruz's idea was to push the value of his product high. And to do it, he needed to build the supply volume so that Gulf Wild could be a player upstream. To build a brand, he didn't need grouper in a restaurant or a single grocery store. He needed grouper in thirty restaurants and a dozen grocery stores. That meant his fishermen had to want to keep coming back. If he could pay them enough, and a premium for tagging the fish, he figured they would.

Before catch shares, it wasn't like this. A fisherman on the water was a slave to the fish house. If the guy who owned the fish house didn't like you or had too much fish that day, he could let your fish rot on the dock, no problem. Didn't have to give you a dime. Now the supply was spread out. So it got to be that a fisherman was in demand. He could sell to whomever. No more ridiculous games, like the one where the fish house would triple the price of the ice, just for you, over some perceived slight. All of a sudden fishermen had power. And once they could sell their fish wherever they wanted, a good many of them started selling to De La Cruz. It was simple math—he had the best prices. In translation, it meant De La Cruz was peeling fish off of other fish houses like mad.

"People were really, really pissed," he said. But he had tried to enlist their help in selling the Gulf Wild brand. It hadn't worked. And while he wasn't a huge fan of conflict, didn't much like being the center of the kind of drama that his life was turning into, he didn't like being told what to do either. So he kept doing what he wanted. Which was to build market share. And he was building it fast. So was Buddy Guindon, with red snapper in Galveston.

Guys like Randy Lauser could see as much. Sitting in the garage of his home, a man cave a club's throw from the edge of a golf course, Lauser notes: "It's a business world. Hey, good for them. They've seen it coming and they jumped on it and they got it. It helps keep the price up because there's another fish house on the market now, and they pay good money for their fish." That money helps fishermen pay their rent, he says. The more the better.

But Lauser has other worries. The double bay doors are thrown open in the spring sun on a warm spring day when he describes them. "The way it's going now, before long you'll be working for investors," he says. Tucked in a corner of the garage, he is sitting on one of a pair of black barstools at the helm of a workbench. Behind it is a pegboard lined with wrenches, two tall Craftsman boxes, too. Seeing them makes it easy to imagine why Lauser is a guy in demand on a boat. So much in demand, in fact, that he now captains the boat he sold. In a deal that illustrates the ways in which industry assets began consolidating among small investors, Lauser sold his boat and seventy-five thousand pounds in grouper access after the catch share took hold. To his surprise, the new owner, having no interest in fishing, asked him to stay aboard *The Brandy*, a thirty-seven-foot canopied longliner, and run it.

It was as good a deal as Randy Lauser could ever get. No more maintenance. No more insurance. No more risk. Plus a paycheck to keep on fishing. Quite a lot of boats ran this way—sans rent—in the pre–catch-share days, taking a 40 percent cut for profits and maintenance instead, with captain and crew dividing the rest, after expenses. It was an expiring model as the rental market crept in, one that better rewarded captains and crews. So for Lauser it was hard to say no. The financial incentives aside, Randy and *The Brandy* went together like grouper and breading, like ketchup and fries. It was hard to know if anyone at the dock even knew that his last name was Lauser. He was Randy on *The Brandy*—that was it. And if you doubted it you only had to grab him by the arms and find the two loves of his life tattooed on opposite biceps. On one, his wife Erika. On the other, the boat, wrapped in grouper with a fan of sun rays over ocean. Man and boat presented with a second life—he took it.

But to a guy who no longer owns access, the future does not look very good. "There are a lot of captains out there, they've been fishing all their lives," Lauser says. A lot of them worked for boat owners and weren't awarded access when the catch share took hold. Now those same guys pay a rent of a dollar a pound to go to work. And it isn't so much that the former owners are capitalizing as aging out, and their replacements are new investors who are busy pushing the line on leases, seeing exactly how much fishermen will pay to work. Lauser says only about five boats aren't charging their captains the new lease fees now, *The Brandy* included. Just recently, it sold to another investor. And he suspects his days of rent-free fishing are over.

He's right.

————

A FEW MILES away at the Madeira Beach Seafood Company, Shawn Watson, the new owner of *The Brandy*, soon climbs aboard. He likes to watch over the boat, even if he doesn't often fish it. The sporty little vessel is snug up against the seawall alongside the company's driveway. On the other side is another wind-worn fish house, a sun-bleached series of rectangles and cubes, the main office standing over it on stilts. Pallets are stacked along one side and the frontage is littered with plastic totes, a forklift driving in and out.

Watson is not exactly out of his element here, having rented quota to fish in the Caribbean a few years ago. But he's not exactly in it, either. Relaxed in a jaunty blue pullover, sharp in eyeglasses, Watson has all the hallmarks of a serial entrepreneur. A former track athlete, he cut his teeth on professional sponsorships in his days on the US national team (Adidas, for long jump, triple jump, high jump, and the 400 meter). It was an experience that ruined him on working for anyone else. He's since leapt from one business opportunity to the next. Invested in gyms. Worked as a personal trainer. And used his time with business clients like apprenticeships. He picked up skills. He spread some money around. Restaurants. Stock investments. After tournament fishing for big game in the Bahamas and Costa Rica—marlin, swordfish, tuna—he tried his hand at commercial fishing and took, after catch shares took hold, not a bath, but a bit of a shower. He was a renter, with no access of his own. "I was having to lease everything," he said.

When he met a fisherman at a marina, Jack Golden, who explained to him how it worked, Watson threw in when Golden offered to sell him a boat and fishing access. Now Watson has five boats. The magic number is seven. Even on this spring day aboard *The Brandy*, Watson is being offered other boats. Golden walks by. Shouts he's got a boat in Tarpon Springs. And while fishermen in these parts will grumble about investors like Watson, there's no question that he and his ilk have become a go-to for people looking to cash out.

By this time in 2013, grouper access was fetching fourteen dollars a pound while the fish itself sold for about $3.40 a pound at the docks. And while Watson sees how, over the long term, he will make the bulk of his money on grouper as the dock price of seafood rises, he is also a guy who wants a return on his investment in the access rights, too. He forecasts about a year, maybe longer, before he will have to start charging Lauser a dollar a pound to fish, the lease rate he thinks the industry ought to hold. He says it's a number that means both fair wages for fishermen and returns for guys like him.

"Pretty much in every business you're going to have investors," he says, whether it's crabbing or computers. "I consider myself a working investor, meaning that I'm not just buying things and sitting back on them and looking for a return. I actually work the business. I come down here. I'm with the guys. I'm involved, I'm not just sitting on the couch saying 'pay me.'" Last year he was 270 miles offshore fishing with his employees. He likes it. And he says he takes the job of keeping these boats maintained and safe seriously. He's already thinking about how to direct-market his catch so that he can pay the captains and crew better prices like the folks at Gulf Wild, following the lead of dozens of other seafood businesses around the nation as they cut out the middlemen to build traceable brands that fetch better sums.

But like any investor, Watson expects to make money. Returns on investments in grouper are averaging about 6 percent, compared with 1 percent if he had stuck his money in a bank. He says that's not a bad deal. Guys on the other side of the fish house, Florida tan with long hair, say it's not such a bad deal for them either. There's more fish to catch as the industry consolidates. And the dock price is good enough that investors can skim a bit off the top and it still turns out okay for everyone.

"The only thing anybody might complain about is people getting greedy with the leases," says Ed Maccini, standing aside a freshly unloaded vessel while a crewman with a cigarette tidies up the deck.

Whether that remains a good deal, or is someday superseded by greedy lease rates, is an important question. A study by the nonprofit watchdog Food & Water Watch found that the dynamics fostered by privatizing fishing closely mirror those of factory farming in America. As farms were "pressured to get big or get out," it resulted "in the near death of the family farm and the loss of food quality, food safety and consumer choice." While profits rise for landlords, the report found, rents "can become the single largest operating cost for the fishermen out on the water. Essentially, catch shares turn a fishery into a stock market," where access rights have higher values than boats, equipment, even fish.

As more investors, restaurants, and hotels buy up access to guarantee their share of grouper, costs may rise for fishermen. And fish houses that once survived on a loyal base of local boats are limping while the industry redistributes geographically, as the new generation of fishermen choose new ports and new points of sale, a realignment that may also cost those fishermen more when they have to travel to make sales. Right now, "They say, 'It's not worth it to go fishing, Karen' . . . rather than go actually work they just lease them for $1.25," says Karen Bell, whose family has owned the A.P. Bell Fish Company in Cortez since 1940. Some who can't get access have ported boats in Nicaragua, hired crews cheap, and gone back to catching the same fish without the headaches of the catch-share program. They're combatting Gulf Wild from overseas with imports. Same fish.

Observers of the industry say this wasn't supposed to happen. What was supposed to happen was that those who stayed in would help to foster a more sustainable fishery, a goal that seems lost while crew pay starts to fall and longtime fishermen who can identify the forty-three species of reef fish in the Gulf are leaving boats. Without firm limits on rents and a bank to help new entrants get in, people on the hunt for the financial upside of the transition will have a financial advantage that could lead them to take control of the access. It's a recipe for industry shrinkage, one that threatens to destine its labor force to renting and funnel the catch toward bigger, more corporate businesses.

———

WHILE DE LA Cruz builds one of the most dominant companies in the region, he is becoming the kind of owner-operator the Environmental Defense Fund hoped for when it pressed for this program. His fishermen make firm commitments to conservation and sign agreements to do so along with the rest of the Gulf Wild suppliers. And after a while, he and Guindon started putting a nickel in the kitty for every pound of fish they sold so they could break free of EDF, paying their own way instead and still funding conservation efforts. His innovations in the supply chain allowed him to get sustainably caught fish to consumers who will pay for that, and trace its path along the way. And his decision to buck trends by paying fishermen well eventually forced other fish houses to do the same, or lose out on fish.

But here's what's really important: banks started to look at De La Cruz's business and see it as something they could put money behind. That's not so common in fishing, not for anything other than boats and gear. And all of the things he was doing—tracing the fish, pushing the pay for fishermen, starting a new fish house, and taking up conservation initiatives—those things cost money.

"You really had to see the world in what I thought, and what I still think, is the new way that that world exists. Which is if you don't try really hard to differentiate yourself, and then also to support your boats at an incredibly high level, somebody is going to get it from you," said De La Cruz.

He was swiping business from the other fish houses for sure. So much, in fact, that there were days when a refrigerator truck idled in his parking lot overnight, stuffed with a hundred thousand dollars' worth of fish that he had not yet found takers for. And days when the fish came in so fast and in such volume that he could not make ice fast enough. Guindon sent him an ice machine and he powered on.

De La Cruz didn't own that property under the boardwalk, though—not yet. And it was all his competitors had against him. They told fishermen that De La Cruz would be gone any day. When the city briefly made a move to buy the building that housed Wild Seafood, it looked like they could even be right. Some fishermen didn't sell to him for fear he could be fly-by-night. And that, if he was, they would suffer for their lack of loyalty to other buyers when he disappeared.

So with quota in hand, he wrote a business plan. And in it he detailed the amount of fish he was guaranteed to catch every year, translating for the bank how his assets in the deep sea would provide steady income, year after year. The bank took a look and gave him a loan to buy that wooden shop under the boardwalk. And afterward, he started marching along that plan like a soldier. More quota. Work on the shop. Improvements to the docks. His growth was steady and assured.

"One of the reasons that the bank was willing to go let me do this and give me the loan for this facility was that I could show that, no matter what, I could still land, every year, 300,000 or 400,000 pounds of fish because of the quota that I own. And with that, that number works for me to be able to pay the bills," he said.

To say that Gulf Wild was a buzz in the town as Wild Seafood grew was an understatement. People were huddled up in diner booths grousing about Jason De La Cruz like it was a full-time job, cornering one another on the docks and in fish houses just to bitch about whatever he had last done. As he retooled the Madeira Beach seafood scene for good, De La Cruz became a locally mythic bad guy, a symbol of all that had changed and all that would change. The fighting didn't stop at the docks. It followed him around town, too. On the days when the other fish houses wouldn't sell him bait, for example. Or would gouge him badly on the prices for it. The theatrics even followed his wife, who joined Wild Seafood as a 50 percent partner and its bookkeeper.

His life, De La Cruz said, was "a full drama like you would see on a TV show."

It didn't matter. He was absolutely killing them all in business.

New Bedford, Massachusetts

Foreign Equity, Domestic Seafood

J OHN MILLER LEANS OVER A conveyor belt, grabs a quahog, and smashes it on a pole. A couple of sturdy strikes and the shell—five inches of gray-black armor—shatters. He plucks the shards from the meat inside and works his fingers around the edge.

"That's the muscle, right there," he says.

He has to dig to bust the meat loose. When he does, the quahog fills the palm of his hand. He's a big guy—taller than six feet in a baseball cap and hairnet—so it's no small hand. He offers it up. The meat is tough, with barely more give than a rubber ball. Miller takes it into both hands, then tears it in two.

"This is what they call the cone," he says, pointing to the rubber ball. "They separate the cone." Behind him, machines are doing this same work. Faster. Much faster.

In the shucking room in the New Bedford plant of Sea Watch International, Ltd., one of four facilities Miller oversees, washers and shelling contraptions are grinding their way through 160 cages of quahogs. Each cage is like a chicken-wire milk box on steroids, the metal as thick as a finger and the frame as tall as a person, so that thirty-two bushels of quahogs fit inside each. In five and a half hours, the machines will work through all of them. Eighty-one people on shift today—mostly workers from Central America—will do the rest, the majority hovering over conveyor belts and sorting for things the machines can't see.

Fresh off the boat, the quahogs that haven't yet been fed to this mechanical array are sitting in their briny cages like an army at attention, stacked two high and in rows in a storage area off the shucking room. On each one: two tags, one for state regulators and the other a federal tag with a ten-digit number. Those ten digits make clear who owns the rights through which these quahogs were caught.

Later, workers in a room with stainless steel tables will tediously examine the numbers on these tags. They'll count all ten digits, every time, and make sure none are missing from what's supposed to be an exact numerical sequence of 160. Those digits will have to square with the captain's log on the ship that harvested the quahogs. And they will have to make the federal regulators at the National Marine Fisheries Service happy too. The service oversees the Surf Clam and Ocean Quahog ITQ (individual transferable quota) program, making sure nobody catches more than they should, or catches it in the wrong place.

At the end of all the accounting, federal regulators can chronicle who harvested the quahogs, where they came from, and which facility processed them into foodstuff. It's likely to be enough information to qualify them for some green or blue ecolabel if the controllers of this resource were willing to pay for it. But the story of who those controllers are—in other words, who owns the rights to harvest the surf clams and quahogs in America—is one federal regulators can't quite decipher from the ten-digit numbers on those tags.

It's not a reassuring tale. Instead, it illustrates how—amid all the buying, selling, and trading—federal regulators have already lost track of who owns the rights to catch America's fish, paving the way for foreign and investor control of US seafood. As catch shares consolidate those rights into lucrative seafood ventures, and as private equity firms and international corporations increasingly eye those ventures for investments and acquisitions, access rights are more and more subject to the whims of the global food market. These tough little mollusks off the coast of New England are the seafood that tell the story best.

This was never a glitz-and-glamour trade. And that hasn't changed. A slab of pavement lies between the shucking room and the seawall separating it from Buzzards Bay and the Atlantic. On the blacktop, empty quahog cages are stacked beside a crane that has already done the job of hauling them off a boat. Semi trucks come and go. A bay door is thrown open in the rain, heat and salty vapor wafting into the air as a forklift scuttles in and out, honking its comings and goings.

Such blandness and industrial bulk is not at all out of place along this stretch of coast. From the road it looks like a super-villain district, a combination of towering brick depots with boarded and shattered windows mixed with a smattering of more modern, corrugated-metal rectangles. Along the seawall, a single dredge vessel is docked between tidy rows of scallop boats, their white masts reaching skyward with a kind of stiff New Bedford pride. When most people think of this Massachusetts fishing town, they think of it as the scallop capital of the nation. And it is.

The quahog and its close cousin, the surf clam, however, are also players. Harvested by hydraulic dredge boats like this one, they garner much less fanfare, denizens as they are of the increasingly passé clam strip. In New England, the surf clam still enjoys a kind of shrink-wrapped glory in the frozen-food aisle of the grocery store, its shell stuffed with breading and chopped meat, doused heavily in paprika. The quahog is more a stealth product, chopped for chowders and sauces or stewed as a base for clam juice. Both come from the seafloor off the coasts of New Jersey, New York, Massachusetts, and Maryland. Together, they produce most of the frozen and canned clam products in America and are the ambassadors of all things clam: canned clams, clam chowder, clam juice and sauce, clam nuggets and concentrate. Too tough and chewy to eat without boiling, they underpin a mostly industrial marketplace.

Today only nine companies process surf clams and quahogs. There used to be more. But after the mollusks were parsed into the first US catch share in 1990, many of the independent fishermen and small seafood buyers disappeared. It happened in much the same fashion as it did in Alaskan crab: heavy consolidation among boats and buyers, with many quota owners ultimately turning to leasing, earning income on seafood without fishing it.

Besides the catch share, other factors contributed to the trend, mostly labor and environmental problems, plus market forces. Sea Watch International and Snow's, the clam chowder king, own the processing facilities that capture most of surf clam and quahog harvested from the Atlantic. Both own a substantial number of boats, too. But only Snow's owns the rights to access the mollusks.

That wasn't always true. Four of Sea Watch's shareholders, former fishermen, owned access when the catch share got started. They gave their quota to the company when it began, making Sea Watch the largest processor of surf clam and ocean quahog quota in the region at the time. But when Sea Watch was acquired by the Japanese Nichirei Corporation and held for over a decade, those shareholders reclaimed their access rights. They were adhering, they thought, to laws that prevent foreign ownership of seafood rights. So they kept them in the hands of Americans. Since then, Sea Watch has paid tens of millions of dollars to rent access to the clams and quahogs it harvests. Company officials won't say exactly how much, but some have pegged the figure in excess of $50 million over ten years. It's a number that now eats at Sea Watch's bottom line and doubtlessly affects prices for consumers.

That's not the case about 350 miles to the south. That's where Snow's runs an 86,000-square-foot facility probably not much different from this one. Anchored in Cape May, New Jersey, it's where Fred Snow created F.H. Snow's Canning Company in 1920 and rolled out Snow's now-famous creamy white chowder. Still based in an area known for its pastel Victorians and cedar-shingled beach houses, Snow's has all the look and feel of a good old American company. It still produces its famous chowder en masse, along with minced clams and clam sauce.

Since 2005, however, Snow's has been owned by Bumble Bee Seafoods, the purveyor of a dizzying amount of canned and pouched fish, everything from tuna to mackerel and ready-to-eat fare. And Bumble Bee is not so all-American. In 2010 it was purchased by Lion Capital, the London-based private equity firm, for $980 million. Which is why whenever anyone sits down to a can of Snow's clam chowder in America today, they are likely padding the profits of a British investment manager.

Snow's owns the access rights to nearly a quarter of all of the quahogs in America, "the largest allocation for fishing and harvesting ocean clams in the United States," a fact touted on its website. Though Snow's has been indirectly owned by foreign equity interests for more than six years, albeit through what is technically a legal US subsidiary, it has yet to divest of its rights to catch quahogs. And nobody in the government is trying to make it happen.

It may not be an elegant haul. Back in New Bedford, that's clear as the first briny cages of quahogs are ferried from a towering collection via the honking forklift. White-aproned and hairnetted workers scatter out of its way as the forklift feeds cage after cage of quahogs into the arms of the first stainless steel contraption. Like a robot mother greeting her young, the machine grips the cages, hoists them up in twos, then tosses the quahogs onto the first of many conveyor belts. Still shelled, they travel under a magnet at the speed of a slow-walking dog, because who knows how many bottle caps meet brine. From there they undergo a whole lot of washing and are dumped into what looks like a giant coffee percolator and then a cauldron and a shaker to separate them from their shells. The heat and steam make for a moist and toasty place that smells like wet salt on a few hundred pounds of seafood.

Despite the grit and the heavy machinery, these clams and quahogs are valued at more than $50 million, accounting in part for investor interest in Snow's. To the global companies that amass empires of shelf staples, a quarter of a nation's quahogs are an asset worth having, especially when you consider the kinds of products that come out the other side. Snow's produces four kinds of canned clam chowder today, plus canned minced and chopped clams and clam juice. All are big retail products, dialed in to the consumer diet. Other products fed by the US supply of surf clams and quahogs include all of the clam-based Progresso soups, half of Campbell's soups, the Rhode Island–based Blount Fine Foods clam products—five kinds of chowder and the frozen and refrigerated soups sold as Legal Sea Foods and Panera Bread brands—plus clam strips, stuffed clams, whole clams, and clam cakes served up at its New England restaurants and markets.

Though laws prevent foreign investors from owning rights to American seafood, and from using those rights as investment vehicles, there is a distinct lack of enthusiasm for sniffing out foreign ownership and monopolies. That in turn leads to a lack of enforcement of the rules, making them quaint laws that few trouble themselves to follow.

Part of the reason the government has not fussed over the ownership of these clams is because the National Marine Fisheries Service doesn't really know who owns them, nor do the folks at the U-shaped table in this region. Records indicate that there are 111 registered owners of the rights to surf clams and quahogs. All are tangled up in a web of corporations and registered agents, making it impossible to understand who actually controls what. The most obvious players are banks, with 28 percent of the catch, acquired as collateral for loans, a fact that underscores how difficult it would be for the US government to ever reclaim control of this resource, should it try. Lawyers hold another small chunk, insulating their true owners from visibility. And of course Bumble Bee stands out as the largest holder of the quahogs with 23 percent. Economists at the U-shaped table have indicated they're not too concerned about who owns what, reasoning the money is all green.

But whether the profits derived from these resources ever translate into American dollars is an open question, one that matters to some. Dispassion about foreign ownership of these mollusks has not always been the norm. In 2002 there was enough concern about lost profit from natural resources and a loss of control over the food supply that a Senate committee headed by John Kerry, then a Democratic senator from Massachusetts (and later secretary of state in the Obama adminis-tration), and Olympia Snowe, then a Republican senator from Maine, asked government auditors to look at whether foreign companies could take control of US seafood—or their value—by buying up access rights. Those auditors quickly sounded the alarm about surf clams and qua-hogs, which at the time had the most lenient ownership rules, now rivaled by golden tilefish.

Despite that 2002 report, there was never any fix. Instead, the folks at the regional U-shaped table—the Mid-Atlantic Fishery Management Council—have spent more than a decade plotting how to collect data about who controls the mollusks to guard against monopolies, foreign or otherwise. They only recently approved a method for collecting the data. And they haven't started to do it yet, instead giving owners a year to adjust.

Though regulators do check to see that direct purchases of the rights to fish are tied to a corporate registration in the United States, they don't sift through the myriad LLCs and corporate structures that can hop-skip all over the world through investments and acquisitions in the global food trade. They also don't research the inevitable family connections, legal entanglements, and corporate partnerships that allow owners to stockpile access rights in seafood dynasties, through which they may obscure how much they really own.

Instead, how this plays out is that anyone can hang a shingle over American soil and claim a right to own a piece of the ocean here. As long as there is a US-based subsidiary that holds the access rights and its CEO is an American, along with most of its board, it meets the loose requirement for US ownership. Such is the arrangement at Bumble Bee, where a majority of the company's board and its CEO are US citizens. It is also how the Japanese conglomerates Maruha Nichiro and Nippon Suisan Kaisha are among four companies controlling 77 percent of one type of Bering Sea crab through legal subsidiaries.

At the Bumble Bee headquarters in San Diego, president and CEO Chris Lischewski defends the arrangement. He rightly points out that the company and its subsidiary Snow's have been American brands for more than a hundred years. And despite their ownership by Lion Capital, they still process their clams in New Jersey. "We pride ourselves of being one of the last U.S. companies that actually process most of our canned seafood in the United States," he said in an emailed statement in 2013.

But Tom Alspach, attorney for Sea Watch, calls it all window dressing. "They need to appoint a majority of US citizens to their board. And that seems like 'Oh, well then they're giving U.S. citizens control.' Well, that's true. But then as soon as the board does something they don't like, the shareholders . . . have the absolute right to fire the board and put a new board in place. That's where, indirectly, there can be foreign control. If not in effect, it's kind of unspoken control."

There's a tendency to overlook this fate for the American quahog. Rubbery as they are, they don't sit in the fish case in smooth-skinned fillets. Inconspicuous in a can on a shelf, they don't inspire much consumer concern.

Miller reaches over a belt and scoops a pile of odds and ends from a woman's hand. Yet another machine has blown the bellies out of the quahogs before they were spun in a pair of martini-glass washers and a rolling drum. Women with broad cheekbones, dark hair, and almond-shaped eyes are plucking undesirables from the remains: leftover belly material, the odd crab leg, the hinge from the back of the clam, and the little black strings that run around the outside of the shell.

Miller picks through his palm and raises one of the black strings. It's thin, like a medium-sized rubber band, and most unappetizing. Black on one side and fleshy on the other, it has the consistency of something one would not want to swallow and that seems destined to be stuck between human teeth. "Having that in a can of chowder is not real attractive," he says.

Shifts in the American diet—less fat, less fried, not so breaded—and competition from imports from Canada and Vietnam have caused the market for surf clams and quahogs to slump. In the post–clam strip era, not all the available mollusks even get fished every year. Instead, in the lobby of the upstairs office in which Miller tends the Sea Watch empire, a place where the briny odor of the factory is dampened but not tamed, copies of the company newsletter highlight efforts to revolutionize this industry.

For the eighth year in a row, Sea Watch scoured its broker network for clam recipes, then picked chefs to star in a kind of reality show cook-off at the spring Seafood Expo in Boston in 2015—the Indie 500 of the seafood world. Hundreds of people cast ballots for one of two burly men in white coats who threw down over clam concoctions a novice could never fake. In the end, the rival dishes were a clam cocktail in a ginger pepper broth and a bucatini pasta in a roasted poblano and corn cream sauce, sprinkled with whole clams and applewood bacon. The bucatini, an oversized version of spaghetti, took the crown.

But while the quahog and the surf clam may be a long way from bucatini most days, they're lucrative properties nonetheless. And their present-day migration out of US control should not hinge on whether they can rebrand as something flashier, more Chef Ramsey than Chef Boyardee. After twenty-six years, the fishermen who still own access to these mollusks are aging out. In another decade, maybe two, the entire resource could be controlled by people and companies that otherwise have nothing to do with it, or even with this country. "Yet you have to come back to them and pay them something for the right to fish," said Alspach. And while Lion Capital was likely less interested in controlling mid-Atlantic quahogs than in controlling Bumble Bee itself—and industry observers say such deals are less concerning than the push for direct investment in new catch shares—such deals are nonetheless a backdoor to the same outcome: banks and corporations and investment funds controlling access to the sea.

No one who plans or engineers catch shares today considers this story a success. Instead, proponents of catch shares like to call this situation an outlier, the result of poor design before anyone knew better. The mantra that the United States can plan around this endgame is well worn. A simple fix, people say, when catch shares are designed with limits on how much an entity can own. In the face of mounting criticism of catch shares' pitfalls, the Environmental Defense Fund has invested heavily in the thesis. But to claim that proper planning can ordain what the marketplace does with intangible assets is like saying an architect can control who lives in the apartment he created twenty or thirty years after it's built.

And what makes the focus on design particularly worrisome is that such controls are regularly beat back by lobbying at the U-shaped tables. In New England, caps on quota ownership may soon be set at 20 percent despite severe public opposition, so that five entities could control the entire East Coast groundfish fishery some day. And efforts to set caps on how many surf clams and quahogs one entity can own have been argued over for years, to no effect. Such opposition to controls is normal, and it lands in courts too. A seafood company in California, for example, is currently litigating what caps exist for West Coast groundfish.

Catch shares are politics. And the people at the U-shaped tables who enact and tinker with them, while far better than the regulatory authorities and advisors in some countries, are not a safeguard against politicking. Absent federal transparency rules, lobbying requirements, and adherence to universal conflict-of-interest rules—basic safeguards that attend many other rule-setting authorities in the United States—there is no reason to believe they can resist the pressures that will attend the growing investment interest in American seafood.

Gulf Wild

*Chefs, Fishermen, and Policy Wonks
Descend on Capitol Hill*

THIS IS THE GOAL: EIGHTEEN thousand square feet of seafood nirvana. Plush white booths wrapped in wood grain. Brushed chrome walls and a sparkling bar. Recessed lighting and curtains that peel back onto more booths, more wood grain. There's a dimly lit second floor. And the menus both upstairs and down are every seafood lover's dream.

Plate after plate of succulent oysters from a raw bar. Farmed caviar and a spicy *escabeche*. King crab *nigiri* the size of a baby's arm. Scallops hand-fetched from the Atlantic, soft and tender on the tongue. Sustainably caught *maguro*, dressed in tiny balls of crunchy garlic. Kona Kampachi like firm butter. Red king crab garnished in plum wine gelatin, a subtle sugar over the salt of the sea. All of it flown in fresh. All of it sustainably harvested.

This is the vision of chef Rick Moonen, a longtime proponent of sustainable seafood, who was permanently lured to Las Vegas from New York in 2005 with the promise of this oasis in the desert. Backed by Mandalay Bay casino, a dystopian maze inside mirrored glass, RM Seafood is a sprawling seafood haven that somehow sidesteps the ringing, bleeping, clattering flash of the Las Vegas strip. Black-shirted servers. Polished glasses and linens warmed by wood tones. And some of the most gorgeous seafood presentations to hit the plate anywhere.

The stardom of the salt-and-peppered Moonen, an upbeat guy with zany haircuts and eyeglasses to match, has only ascended since taking what used to be his New York seafood schtick to Vegas. Since arriving there, he's appeared in two seasons of *Top Chef Masters* and as a judge on *Top Chef Las Vegas*. He made a guest appearance on the *Oprah Winfrey Show* (feeding Gayle King his catfish sloppy joe). He was a semifinalist for a James Beard Award in 2010. And he hosted the salmon episode of the James Beard–winning *Chefs A' Field* on PBS.

He's always loved seafood, drawn to it since early days while fishing with his father in New York, when being on the water meant family and life all in one. But it was his time as executive chef and a partner at Oceana in New York City, a gig he started in 1994, that typecast him as a seafood chef. It was the same year the Food Network started. After that, chefs became more important, he says. "You weren't just the asshole in the back, cooking food." Instead, it was chic to tell your diners what you believed in. And Moonen had a vision of ocean sustainability that was close to heart even then.

Two-thirds of the planet is ocean, he likes to say. All of us walking around being human, we're just skin wrapped around sea. He believes in the human connection to water in a way that goes deeper than food, much deeper than what he serves on the plate. And when he runs through all the reasons he likes catch shares—they track bycatch and, like all systems that preassign catch, they keep fishermen safe and end the insanity of derbies on the water—he follows up by saying that all of it is taking too long to explain. That one of the major reasons he likes catch shares is that they simplify a lot of complicated stuff. And he thinks consumers deserve that. That they deserve to be a part of ocean conservation even if they want to eat seafood.

This gets at two reasons why Moonen loves Las Vegas. The first is that he can make a difference in the culinary community while it's still developing here, unlike the one in New York, where he was one among thousands in a foodie universe with no limit to the sophisticated chatter it could support. And the other reason is that he could walk into US Senator Harry Reid's home office while Reid was the majority leader of the US Senate, as he had been since 2007, and talk to him about catch shares.

By then, Moonen had done all kinds of talking. In the Philippines. In South Korea. Since 1994, he'd missed few opportunities to advocate for sustainable seafood. He dispatched columns to local papers and to *The New York Times*, columns that now cover the walls outside the bathrooms at RM Seafood. They were interspersed with interviews and feature stories for magazines like *Parade* and in local press. Educating people about ocean sustainability had been like a second job. And right around 2013, a lot of the people Moonen wanted to be educating were in Congress.

That's because saving the oceans had become big politics. By then, another reauthorization of the Magnuson-Stevens Act—the nation's seafood act—was looming in 2015. And catch-share proponents wanted more federal support for catch shares. And more money, too. Through 2013, as they fought to set the stage for both, Capitol Hill would see a tornado of effort in the form of lobbying, advertising, food events, and public relations campaigns all aimed at wooing Congress toward catch shares.

The timing to try to expand support for catch-share implementation was good. Central Washington Republican Richard Norman "Doc" Hastings was chairing the House Natural Resources Committee and on the edge of retirement. Working with coastal constituents, he'd put another seafood act reauthorization on his to-do list before leaving Congress. At the time, Alaska Senator Mark Begich, a Democrat, was chairing the Senate subcommittee tasked with ocean and fish matters. Begich also wanted another seafood act reauthorized, one with input from Alaska fishermen. Both were invested in working together. And with Democrats controlling the Senate, they were optimistic they could get things done.

What the seafood act had in it already was good conservation policy. It did not require catch shares. Instead, it had mandated limits on ocean fishing and tied them to scientific assessments since 2006. That meant that American waters were already getting more eco- logically sustainable every year, with or without catch shares. Though not everybody agreed that catch shares could best help the govern- ment meet the new benchmarks, most considered the law itself to be a conservation lovers' dream. It was so good in fact that a chunk of it would be adopted by the European Union in new fishery policies in a couple years.

What the law had was this: Protections for hundreds of thousands of square miles of ocean habitat. Firm limits on fishing. Requirements for quality science. And while the question of where to source sustain- able seafood hit the American dining scene, it was a law that paved the way toward some of the most conservation-minded seafood in the world. Development of gentler fishing gear and electronic monitoring that could improve the oversight of boats was also making progress. Even the folks in the fish network—the people who had clashed so badly with the Environmental Defense Fund over catch shares a decade earlier—were happy with where American ocean policy was headed. Hastings and Begich wanted to reauthorize and strengthen those poli- cies already in place.

Whether catch shares were to become the primary delivery vehicle for all the law promised was still very much on the table, however. Although a framework for how to implement catch shares was part of federal law, there was nothing that said that catch shares had to be used to achieve limits on ocean fishing. Many catch-share proponents thought they should be required. Jane Lubchenco, the administrator of the National Oceanic and Atmospheric Administration, was among them. Absent a law, she set her sights on using policy to implement catch shares nationwide. By then she had led the nation through the Deepwater Horizon oil spill, all kinds of record weird weather, and the restructuring of the program that was going to build the nation's next generation of weather satellites. When she talked, people tended to listen. By 2010 she had developed a policy for NOAA that required fishery managers across the nation to consider using catch shares whenever they made management or ecological plans for fisheries. It was a policy more likely to take root with a robust budget backing it.

Under her tutelage, thirty-two new catch-share programs were envisioned for development. She had requested $108 million in 2011 and 2012 to implement the first batch but received just less than $70 million. Although this was big money for fisheries, she needed more. Expanding catch shares beyond the few already in place was going to take a lot of meetings at U-shaped tables, and a lot of scientific and policy analysis. It had already cost $25 million just to move New England groundfish into its catch share. And the West Coast groundfish catch share was eating tens of millions in its early stages. Lubchenco had managed to garner all of it, exploding the budget for catch-share programs from just $1.7 million before she took charge to nearly $36 million in 2011. But it would take billions to implement the other thirty-two catch shares that were possible.

With another seafood act reauthorization imminent, supporters of her vision saw a prime opportunity to weigh in for funding. There were a lot of them. The Walton Family Foundation and the Gordon and Betty Moore Foundation were still spending heavily on catch shares. And the Environmental Defense Fund was still leading the charge to expand catch shares in the United States, lobbying for congressional support. When talk of a new reauthorization began, the force EDF brought to the lobbying effort on Capitol Hill was fierce.

Ads landed in capital journals and the Capitol was papered with leaflets. When important votes took place, EDF flew catch-share–supporting fishermen in from around the country. Many came from the Gulf of Mexico Reef Fish Shareholders' Alliance, as well as from other associations seeded by EDF to back catch shares. When supporters looked thin, EDF managed to corral new ones into new associations. Websites popped up almost overnight and letterhead rolled off the press, with testimony dispatched from these new industry backers in support of Capitol Hill proposals. Trade groups from catch shares like pollock and groundfish were solicited to sign on, and did. Fishermen were given expense-paid trips to DC to testify. And around the nation, catch-share proposals found their way into briefing books at U-shaped tables, as fly-by-night industry coalitions sprang up to propose them.

Lobbyists came on strong, too. EDF hired the largest law lobby firms in the country—K Street heavyweights, like K&L Gates LLP and Liberty Partners Group—and some smaller ones, too, and spent more than $500,000 on catch-share lobbying in 2013. These and other pro–catch-share lobbyists quickly outnumbered those representing more traditional groups, and the scale of the effort soon drowned out dissenting voices like the Southern Offshore Fishing Association from Madeira Beach.

"It was pretty serious juice," said Rick Marks, a lobbyist for the association. "The NGOs have the lobbying connections and the money, spend a lot of time here at Capitol Hill, pay for certain fishermen to travel up here, pay for certain fishermen to travel around the country and look at catch-share programs elsewhere, and then they bring the dollars and the lobbying force."

EDF was also hiring public relations firms. Those firms made efforts to germinate support for catch shares and to use bipartisanism as a political golden ticket. One example was the pairing of retired politicians Slade Gorton, a Republican who had represented Washington state for nearly twenty years, and Democrat Bruce Babbitt, the former Arizona governor who served as interior secretary under President Bill Clinton, in a catch-share promotion campaign. To political insiders it was near comedy. The duo's ideologies were so far apart they could have fought over the color of their own shoes. Thus, when they started making the rounds on behalf of catch shares together, either Capitol Hill insiders or the Capitol press—hard to say which came first—started calling them the Odd Couple.

Moonen joined the cast too. In February 2013 a fish-spangled blue leaflet started circulating on Capitol Hill inviting all to a plush dinner: "Please join Top Chef Masters Finalist Rick Moonen and fishermen chefs and seafood suppliers," it said. It was an all-caps bulletin "seeking sustainable, effective management of our federal fisheries, at a Congressional reception featuring seafood dishes from nationally acclaimed chefs." And politicians weren't going to say no to a seafood dinner cooked by some of the best seafood chefs in the industry. Dining companions—young and hungry congressional aides—turned up in force. More than a hundred fishermen and suppliers were flown in from around the nation, too, the majority from the Gulf of Mexico. And when diners arrived, they were at the ready, shaking hands and telling their stories of catch-share success, building the contacts and connections that were nudging national policy in favor of catch shares.

Teams of fishermen and chefs had already been set up with face time with congressmen, stumping for cash to get catch shares rolling. Moonen delivered an impassioned letter signed by a consortium of pro–catch-share chefs, dozens of them, some with names big enough to have their own tags on EDF's website. To boost exposure in the effort, Moonen's name was broadcast alongside quotes in the press releases accompanying the affair. Missives to the press billed it as a moment of unity between fishermen and chefs. And for the most part, it was.

Moonen framed it this way in his letter: "Catch share programs naturally create an incentive for environmental preservation and species stewardship by the fishermen who rely on their health to succeed.

Restaurants will then get to experience a more consistent supply of properly handled fish, more stable prices, longer seasons and more species diversity."

Whether catch shares naturally created an incentive for environmental preservation was still an open question. Some Gulf fishermen later complained they felt pressured to turn up and say so. That if they didn't throw in in favor of catch shares they might be blacklisted from buying access rights to the grouper or red snapper or from selling to certain fish houses. Hard to know whether this was exaggeration or truth. The paranoia and backbiting were still on high in Florida, so to think of one's business as under siege had become entirely normal. And the fishermen who had not yet taken sides were playing both, some of them simply full of hot air.

Regardless of all that, to the conservation groups that picked up the tab this effort was worth it. More than half the value of federal fisheries was controlled in catch shares at the time. In the conservation world, that translated into the largest wild seafood supplies left off America's shores—large portions of cod, halibut, bass, crab, clams, and dozens of species of groundfish—saved. By 2013, 117 species of fish were being managed in twenty-four federal and state catch-share programs. EDF was throwing all it had at pushing those numbers higher and capturing more.

But while saving the oceans is big politics, 2013 was perhaps the apex of the catch-share effort on Capitol Hill. Lubchenco resigned in February 2014. Hastings retired and Begich lost his next election, both without getting another seafood act through. Meanwhile, Republicans made huge gains, grabbing twenty-two seats in both the House and Senate in 2014. By the time elections were over, the tone of congressional legislating shifted so decidedly that conservation groups stood down in pressing for another seafood act reauthorization. The risks of undoing all the good that had been done by the last were deemed too great in a more conservative Congress. After a dizzying number of hearings, the effort simply fizzled. Thus, the hoped-for funding for new catch-share programs continued at a trickle, settling in at about $25 million annually through 2016.

This, to Moonen's irritation. "We're not seeing the forced march on Capitol Hill that we were seeing before. But we know that these groups are looking to spread catch shares where they can."

Those efforts have instead moved on to the U-shaped tables. Pilot programming for a groundfish catch share started in the Gulf of Alaska. On the South Atlantic coast, fishermen began organizing efforts to develop their own catch share for grouper. And lawsuits started popping up, too. Buddy Guindon sued the federal government, arguing that the United States was hurting fishermen if it didn't convert the last vermillion snapper stocks to private ownership, and that without a catch share, the nation would ruin the value he and others had built in a seafood commodity they couldn't yet control.

By then, Moonen had started daydreaming about aquaculture, having thrown in with developers on the idea of farming several species at once, perhaps with veggies, in tanks in the desert. Gulf Wild remains on his menu, along with the seafood he's spent twenty-five years learning how to source to perfection. Sablefish from British Columbia. Wild salmon and halibut from Alaska. Maine lobster. Oysters and scallops from Nantucket Bay. Farmed trout and sturgeon from Sacramento. Gulf shrimp. New Bedford sea scallops.

Trawl is off the menu, he says. So is dynamite, a point he feels compelled to make because, however ridiculous, dynamiting for fish is actually a thing.

He is not an evangelical. Not everything on his menu comes from a catch share. But he's still a supporter. He's also an anomaly in that he will speak plainly about what that means. He knows that catch shares cost jobs. He knows that they kick people off the water. And he knows that in this game of building reputable, conservation-focused businesses on the sea there will be people who lose big. And that the markets that spring out of these dynamics are not always fair. He still thinks that it is worth it. "Nothing is fair," he says. "And if we do nothing, we will end up with nothing."

It's a sentiment that underscores one of the deepest drivers of the catch-share movement: real fear of where inaction on ocean policy could lead.

Chatham, Massachusetts;
Nantucket Sound

History and Its Outlaws

T HE *LESTER F. ELDREDGE* FLOATS UP on the first trap of the day, having just cut a course from Cape Cod's Stage Harbor toward Nantucket Sound. The morning air is still chilly, so that diesel smoke chugs out over the water in frosty gasps. It's a small boat, about as long as four grown-ups lying down, and made for a small and ancient task—weir fishing.

At the *Lester*'s bow, a ring of what looks like vertical driftwood rises from the water, nets hanging in between. It's like a stick tribute to the Western Abenaki, the Algonquin-speaking tribe believed to be the first to set these primitive weirs in this swath of sea. To see it from shore or land, it looks like a series of knitted twigs. Which is basically what it is.

This stretch of Cape Cod is about the last place one might expect to find such a thing. Once a bustling fishing hub, the Cape is so gentrified today that whitewashed lighthouses and million-dollar Cape homes are more the norm than a fishing trap. The few working docks left are hemmed in by the symbols of weekend tourism: cedar-planked retail strips, rented bikes, and beach umbrellas. Most of the restaurants here serve the white fish tourists clamor for—like cod, imported from places like Iceland. The crash of the local cod off the coast of New England means fishermen here are catching scup and sea bass, monkfish and skate instead.

The *Lester* hails from a trap dock on Stage Harbor, a place that's become a gathering spot for the locavore movement: potlucks and suppers attended by foodie devotees. It's the ardor of Shannon Eldredge, who insists that some of the hickory trees holding the weir together are older than her father. You would have to know that these tree trunks are ten feet into the seafloor, twenty through the water, and another ten above sea level to think of them as anything other than oversized twigs. Standing there with mesh dangling between them gives them a fragile look, like they could be knocked over in a wave. But the largest of these poles weighs 250 pounds, and in the month during the weir's assembly every spring, each pole is a man's stubborn burden to carry.

Small wonder then that the more industrious have abandoned this ancient way of fishing for lines with hooks and drag nets. However unpopular in the United States, though, weir fishing still offers about as intimate a relationship between sea and land as fishing gets: a sturdy cage of timber bound with rope, placed in the water by humans willing to tackle the job. It's why this type of fishing is passion to Eldredge, who is deeply committed to shifting the food system back to this kind of artistry and to empowering people who are as mindful of their place in the water as of the fishing itself.

In this way, she is representative of a global phenomenon. As catch shares took hold in thirty-five countries, enclosing more than 850 species in 275 private market programs by 2010, she joined a global network of small-scale fishers in pressing for human rights and fair wages on the oceans and for food security in the communities tied to them. Called Slow Fish, an outgrowth of the Slow Food movement, it's asserting its own claim on the oceans, one that asks whether it's really justified for privatization to displace those fishermen by the thousands.

These fishers are her people. Eldredge is thirty-two. When her father was her age, he had a crew of ten guys, three or four boats, and two decades of experience. He has been weir fishing since he could stand. He's fished full time in summers since age twelve, and ever after out of high school. He learned to fish from his father, the *Lester's* namesake, who started weir fishing in the late thirties, launching what is today Chatham Fish Weir Enterprises. This makes Eldredge a third-generation weir fisherman.

When she was a child she hated this job. But one summer on a break from doctoral studies in American history, exploring women from fishing families, it sank in for her, in an intellectual way, what her family had been doing all these years. When she decided she wanted to do it too, and for the rest of her life, she quit studying history and assumed her role in its progression. Now she and her partner, Russell Kingman, are apprentices to her father.

"I feel like otherwise, if nobody else is going to come out here, this incredible knowledge is going to be lost forever because we're the last people doing this," she says.

On Cape Cod, they are.

From the late 1800s through the early 1900s there were hundreds of these traps, standing in the ocean like stick-figure soldiers. Now there are two off the shores of the Cape, both operated by the Eldredge family. Weirs in this area of the Atlantic and on Cape Cod Bay used to provide 25 percent of the seafood on the Eastern Seaboard, feeding an area the size of New England. They were owned by local families and a few corporations. Eventually, though, the fish dried up, in part because of too many weirs. And when fishing started up again, bigger boats with better gear made it more profitable, and an era of predatory fishing replaced this passive precursor.

The reason to continue weir fishing is because it's about the cleanest type of fishing in the world. To describe a weir simply is to say that it's an ocean corral for fish. Fish swim into it on their own, directed by a net in the water. And once inside, they are basically penned in a kind of at-sea aquarium, from which they are harvested with a dip net. Every fish taken is alive. Too young? Returned to the sea. The species imperiled? Same. Undesirable. Ditto. There is no collateral damage here, no injury from hooks or machines.

It's a type of fishing that comes with challenges, though.

Today is full of them. Modern times, primordial problem: the seals are hanging around. Thus Eldredge is leaning over the edge of the *Lester* stitching a new mesh panel to the outside of the weir to keep them out. This panel is like a second layer of insurance—the kind no one is sure will really work. Her father points, directs. She calls for a knife. Kingman, who until now has been holding the *Lester* steady by clinging to an overhead rope, feet planted on the bow, produces a blade from his pocket and passes it back. Eldredge gives the panel one last stitch and cuts the thread. The father-daughter duo stands back, not so much admiringly as perhaps relieved. This is the third day the weir looks empty, the third day without a catch. Maybe the panel will turn their luck.

Eldredge steps to the bow. She and Kingman, side by side now, begin lowering the flap of the entrance. Untying first one string and then the next from a panel of mesh just wider than the *Lester*, they let the top of the mesh slip into the water. The weather starts to cooperate. Sun pricks its way through the gray clouds that have been pinning cold to water, then brightens until the Grundéns begin to shine. It's enough to boost morale about the losing streak, and the weather, which is forty-five degrees or so on the water, chilly for summer, even in oil skins. The *Lester* slips into the weir.

Eldredge used to feel isolated in this job. And it wasn't just because her family was the last of the weir fishers on the Cape, or because gil-netters and trawl boats were more the norm. It was more because small-scale fishers seemed to be on the losing end of everything in the fishing industry, some trawl boats and gilnetters included.

In 2012, when catch shares—dubbed sectors—arrived in New England, they were ushered in with help from the Cape Cod Commercial Fishermen's Alliance, a local nonprofit group supported in part by the Environmental Defense Fund. Afterward, fishermen were irate, anxious, sad, and raging all in one, less about catch shares than the fact that the alliance didn't seem to be advocating for the local people. Groundfish—among them the cod that helped lure the first Europeans to America—were in steep decline. And the dustup over catch shares was blurring the already blurry lines between what was going wrong and what was going right for the region's waters. The government was spending $16 million to make the catch share run well and to help the people who would inevitably be out of work. And the fishermen's protest over the new system seemed mostly unheard.

Law required a vote of the people for catch shares in New England. Thus the new program was presumably voluntary. As one local put it, however, in practice it was about as voluntary as Stalin's collective farms. Its arrival amid such protest left Eldredge gobsmacked.

She and her family weren't subject to catch shares—they didn't own a trawl boat—but a lot of the local fishermen were. Between those offloading seafood at her family's dock and what Eldredge heard in the local fishing wives group, where she volunteered, the stories were the same: people were losing businesses, houses, marriages, too.

While she still believed in all the things that her family had been doing since the thirties—capturing fish cleanly and putting them in the hands of the people that eat them—she could see that those simple things were losing social currency in the catch-share era. It pained her. She discovered she was not alone, however, when she was invited to Terre Madre, a Slow Food conference in Turin, Italy, where she and Kingman were asked to serve as delegates on behalf of small-scale New England fisheries.

It turned out to be the largest gathering of the Slow Food movement up until that time, a loose network of people just like her, volunteering to organize and share knowledge about producing quality and fresh food with human rights and equity in mind. It was only the second time fishermen had been invited to convene at Slow Food within their own space, soon dubbed Slow Fish. The convener, heeding requests, had specifically shaped discussions around privatization. Among the goals was to develop voluntary guidelines for sustainable small-scale fisheries for the Food and Agriculture Organization of the United Nations. And people wanted a voice in how privatization fit in.

So it was in Turin that Eldredge went from being one in a lone-weir fishing family in an increasingly industrialized, corporatizing world, to being one fisher in a global community of small fishers. Fishers from Peru. From Thailand. From the United Kingdom. From Senegal, Canada, France, Italy, and the Netherlands. In this melting pot, she discovered there was a shared heartache. Fishermen were losing ocean territory to privatization, to industry, and to ocean grabbing for tourism and other interests. An awful lot of that loss was being perpetuated by catch-share policies, called rights-based fishing elsewhere in the world. There was a shared goal as well, however: to make small-scale fishing work. She arrived ready to figure out how. And what happened at Terra Madre was, for her and a lot of other people, galvanizing.

The electricity in Turin was palpable. That first night of the conference, the New England delegates—Kingman, Eldredge, and local fisheries advocate Brett Tolley from the Northwest Atlantic Marine Alliance—met with fisheries scientist Seth Macinko over wine. Macinko told Eldredge where the money behind the alliance was coming from. "Then he built upon that with the background of the why, what's the motivating factor," she said. Before long he wasn't just talking about the alliance. He was talking about the conservation and philanthropic groups that had become catch-share proponents, and their growing global network, and its efforts to bring capital investment to the seas. A couple of days later, he gave a more structured presentation. It blew Eldredge's mind.

It's easy to imagine. The talk Macinko gave at Terre Madre is a version of the keynote he gave at the Sixth World Forum of Fisher Peoples in 2014, "Has the Leopard Changed Its Spots?" There's a

YouTube video of it that makes Macinko's appeal to small-scale fishers plain. He pulls from newspaper articles, studies, and NGO papers to define the worldwide push toward ocean privatization. He calls the promoters of catch shares the Privatizer Parish, and cites studies that scare the public into thinking privatization is their last hope to save fishing. Drawing from economic theory that dates the ideas back to the fifties, he reduces the arguments for privatization to a sales pitch for a takeover of seas. "The real problem here is there's a failure to distinguish a tool from an ideology," he says. Rights-based fishing policies like catch shares, and attendant privatization, have become inextricably linked to the notion of good stewardship of the seas. "It's reached the state now where the privatization model is *the* solution on offer all around the world."

This is especially true as EDF moves its catch-share programming overseas, eyeing fisheries in twelve nations for transition. And as the Walton Family Foundation makes investments in catch-share programs in Indonesia, Peru, Chile, and Mexico, all countries with some combination of four things: key trade relationships with the United States, a plethora of small-scale fisheries, fertile regulatory conditions for catch shares, and connections to the Walton family. With philanthropies like The Prince's Trust, Bloomberg, and the Rockefeller Foundation, plus the World Bank, all researching ways in which private investment can slip in, and with multinational investors interested, the pressure on small fishers around the world is great.

Which is why Macinko's talk has become a policy framework under which small-scale fishers now convene. Though he has no formal position with the World Forum of Fisher Peoples, a human-rights movement in small-scale fisheries, Macinko helps the movement analyze and interpret international socioeconomic trends on the oceans, an effort that informs the group's internal policy positions and the approach it takes when engaging with the United Nations and other global entities.

He is a logical thought leader in this world. A former commercial fishermen and a fixture on docks since the seventies, Macinko specializes in fisheries law and management at the University of Rhode Island's Department of Marine Affairs, and is a rare bird among academics in his ability to talk policy to fishermen and scientists alike. He is among a small community of researchers focused on rights-based fishing, but he doesn't take money from pro–catch-share funders, as some do. Instead, his work offers straight-ahead analysis of what he sees happening on the water. And what he sees is systemic privatization, with severe consequences for communities and people that fish, and no direct financial return to the public. The money claimed by ocean landlords, Macinko argues—if collected by the government instead, through programs that preassign catch but keep the rights to fish in public ownership—could support health care or education, perhaps. Or anything else that societies need.

Critics say Macinko has traded his academic cred for advocacy. That he is a lone figure to eschew catch shares is plain. Even NGO thinkers and policymakers who once lobbied against catch shares are acquiescers today, sobered by the inconvenience of protesting against the direction that conservation dollars flow. Academics are equally susceptible. So that in the small-scale-fishers community, experts who can hold the line against this policy, and articulate why, give people a lot of hope.

His analysis of the global march on small fisheries, combined with the union of so many small fishers for the first time, was like fairy dust on Terre Madre. The days that followed, Eldredge said, were life changing. Regardless of where they came from, all of the fishers had stories to tell about privatization, and how it had affected their lives, markets, and communities. They heard each other, and they started talking about solutions.

Their best ideas congealed around language about basic human rights, food security, and the power of fishing to alleviate poverty in coastal communities. As Eldredge describes it, their manifesto "really has a lot to do with the spirit of being a real human being on the ocean. Not a factory. Not an investment property. Not owned by people in some kind of trading house in an office. But the spirit of men and women that go out on the sea and fish." The FAO adopted a version of this document two years later with the intention of making it an international instrument to lift up small-scale fisheries and support them.

By then, the Global Partnership for the Oceans, the World Bank effort aimed at creating opportunities for investment capital on the seas—an opposite kind of proposition—disbanded. It was facing pressure from governments that had been besieged by small fishers pushing them to abandon the idea of commoditizing the oceans. The World Bank's fisheries team was also dismantled. And while the same ideas still live among the 150 partner organizations that convened them—governments, international organizations, civic groups, and private-sector interests—their position was wounded, if not dead.

Now small-scale fishers, in a rising tide linked worldwide through Slow Fish, have the global political footing to fight back. For a lot of people in little boats, it's a victory. Even though it's just one battle in what looks to be a long war with a well-armed opponent.

Around the world, there are enough examples of unhappy endings to stoke the fight. When the Australian abalone fishery in Tasmania moved to catch shares, for example, 60 percent of the access was quickly owned by one absentee American who controlled 85 percent of the value of the fishery. In Chile, as fisheries sought to privatize in 2013, public protest erupted over a plan that would have given that country's ocean resources to seven powerful families. And in Iceland, there's been huge public pushback over consolidation of fishing access among the rich. Voters approved a referendum to begin buying the rights to access fish back into public trust in 2012, though the country is still working to untangle them from the banks. Three years later, more than 20 percent of the country's voters signed a petition to block the privatization of lucrative mackerel. Turns out that two Progressive Party leaders who were personally invested in the fisheries stood to gain millions from it.

Despite talk about the tragedy of the commons, and how privatization can fix it, institutional economist Elinor Ostrom won a Nobel Prize in economics in 2009 because she showed that, entrusted with the care of a shared resource, people did indeed take care of it, proving that common properties can be successfully managed without privatization. Though it's often forgotten, as is the fact that the "tragedy of the commons" theory was partly retracted by its author in the nineties, Eldredge, a student of history, takes no lesson for granted. Blond ponytail streaming behind sunglasses, hand on the throttle, she is a rare enough sight on any water to make clear how much culture is still left to lose.

Back in Cape Cod, in the heart of the trap, Captain Ernie Eldredge cuts the motor. Kingman goes starboard, grabs the inside wall, and pulls the boat as close to it as he can. Father and daughter take up the port side, reaching gaffes into the water with arms forged of the same genetic code, and pull. The net they wrench from the seafloor is a beast, it's mesh like bubble wrap, a soggy little cage through which human fingers barely fit. They keep pulling, hand over hand. Slowly.

As the crew and captain pull the bottom net, they are corralling any fish inside it like a pile of balls on a parachute, working them into a small corner of the trap. The *Lester* floats along, towed beneath their bodies as they work the net with their arms. By the time they reach the opposite end of the trap, their catch will be swimming just off the port side, ready for a trip from the water to the boat in a dip net.

The telltale signs of a good haul aren't there today, though. The pogies are not jumping. There's no swirl in the water from the schooling mackerel. No deep funnel from a big school of black sea bass or bluefish. And there's no squid ink—nothing on the rim of the net to show that a squid's defense mechanism has been kicked up from the inside. Eldredge pulls the net harder, gripping the narrow mesh hand over hand so that the *Lester* edges right into the corner of the trap. With the net cinched up like a tea bag, the catch pinned in the corner, the prize turns out to be about fifteen pounds of squid. Bait fish, probably.

"Well, that's it," someone says. And so it is.

The *Lester*'s low-catch fate today is not unlike that of a lot of other fishermen on these waters. There's a history of overfishing in New England groundfish, and ocean warming has driven many species north. With cod stocks collapsed, there isn't a lot to catch. And the catch share has added costs, making fishing more difficult for boats on tight margins. Thus, many communities have been left reeling and clinging to $33 million in federal disaster aid up and down the North Atlantic coast.

Eldredge can put that aside, however. Holding the *Lester* steady with Kingman in the bow, she watches her father zip around them in a skiff, tightening the ropes on the weir to keep it fishing another day. Her father is resident handyman, engineer, meteorologist, biologist, mentor, and a host of other things. The consensus is that he knows the *Lester*'s engine well enough to patch it with a twist-tie from a sandwich bag. He is also the chief navigator of the *Lester*—the driving being trickier than it would seem, affected by everyday changes in the weather, the tide, the wind. Eldredge says she will be perpetually behind him as she chases him up the learning curve. She will chase him anyway.

And, meanwhile, she's got her own strengths. On the drive back, her phone lights up in a Ziploc bag inside her lunch cooler. Local people are already hailing her from shore, curious about the catch. These are her customers in a bare-bones, direct-to-consumer operation, its main advertisement on Cape Cod by word of mouth. There's no marketing scheme here, no administrators, no grant money. Between fifty and a hundred people connect with her just like this—on her phone—day after day. Most turn up at the dock after the boat comes in, some toting gifts, concoctions made from the last catch like the handcrafted bluefish pâté that she loves. Called Cape Cod Community

Supported Fishery, her family's direct-to-consumer business distributes around the tristate area and at a few local markets, too. Soon, the crew will start a small mussel farm on the family's two trap sites, using all recycled gear from the traps. In the future, if they succeed, who knows? Maybe scallops. Maybe oysters.

Eldredge isn't tempted by fishing anything other than these traps. Or to grow the business into some kind of commodities supplier. She loves the art of it all. Smoked bluefish on avocado toast with arugula. Fish stock made from scup. Squid manicotti and bonito seared sashimi style. She just wants to be here, pushing history forward. Her own piece of it, one monkfish, one scup at a time.

Since 2012 Terra Madre has settled in her bones like something that has always been there. It's made her a fisheries advocate in New England and internationally through Slow Fish. And it's given her a vocabulary for the things she already knew: that clean, small-scale fishing that concerns itself with human rights and gender and traceability and the quality of the supply chain is what her family has always done. And that she intends to stand for it, even while what is happening to her town and on her family's dock to make it harder is echoing all over the world.

Informed as she is by years of study, she already knows, very deeply, how policy has run its finger along the spine of her community since colonial times and even earlier. And she knows that policy, whatever it is, has always been dominated by industry heavies. Knowing it makes her feel less anxious, she says. Yet from Terra Madre, she also knows that she isn't alone. As the gaps between the common people and the big business of the sea grow wider, she aims not to count democracy as a casualty.

Gulf Wild

Tagged

FISH NUMBER 5089301 REALIZES THE dream. Jason De La Cruz ferries it, packed on ice, by truck from the hold of *Head Hunter 44* to the Wild Seafood dock. The thing is a gem. Caught by captain Dan MacMahon, a spearfishermen for more than forty years and a diving legend, all of the *Head Hunter*'s fish are beauties. So much so that even though De La Cruz has employees now, and pick-ups are rarely on his to-do list, he still makes the hour-and-a-half trip to collect them himself.

When he wheels the fish into Wild Seafood, biologist Lew Bullock is there. He's already set up a sampling table on the dock beneath the boardwalk on Madeira Bay, his long wooden ruler and knives at the ready. While a few thousand pounds of fish are coming out of the truck, Bullock hefts one—a gag grouper weighing nineteen pounds—and sets it down against the ruler. He measures it. Then makes the cut. Right there where the skin meets the skull, about a finger's width from the eyeball, he sinks the knife in, splitting the brain in half. He scrapes the otoliths loose as if scraping the inside of a pumpkin.

Usually, a crowd of gawkers looks on. It's the best thing about working in this place: the rows of tourists and shoppers dangling from the boardwalk a rough ten feet above, people relaxed and curious who just want to know what Bullock is up to. "I'm pulling otoliths," he tells them. And then gets out the clear case in his pocket with an otolith inside. Or the cardboard placard with the blown-up image of an oto-lith sliced and backlit under a microscope.

While the people above him look on, along with hungry pelicans, Bullock explains how otoliths help him tell this fish's story to science. How he checks the ovaries and the gonads to try to understand when and where the fish spawn. It's the audience biology rarely has. And now, there on the dock, he can talk straight to people who might even eat this fish in the next few days. He can tell them all about the work being done to make it one of the cleanest-caught and best-cared-for species of seafood in the world.

This particular fish is on the large side for a gag grouper, its lips fingerlike, the dorsal fin hilly, with leopard-like spots. Most people have probably eaten far more of these than they've seen whole. It's a novelty for them to see the tens of thousands of gag grouper unloaded here. Very few are driven in. Most take a ride down an aluminum slide from the boat to the dock and are sorted by hand, then repacked on ice. The spectacle is what gets people hanging around: the captains pulling fish after fish out of icy boat holds and De La Cruz buzzing all over the dock, separating one species from the next into plastic totes, al-ready plotting their journey through the fish market.

While people stand overhead and watch, they learn that thanks to the innovations at Gulf Wild, this fish is not lost in the crowd. Instead, it carries one of the first individually numbered fish tags in the world. Gulf Wild is among the only seafood products in America, and perhaps anywhere, to go straight from sea to table with a numerical marker that tells its consumer everything they might want to know, not just about this catch or this species, but about this particular fish.

The folks at Gulf Wild like to call it the fish's Social Security num-ber. Drop these digits into a tracking system on the Gulf Wild website and its story is all there: That the fish was examined by Bullock on the docks on behalf of the Florida Fish and Wildlife Research Insti-tute. That it was caught by MacMahon with a harpoon and brought to shore aboard the *Head Hunter*. A photo of the boat is there too, sidled up to a ramp with its twin outboard motors, a fleet little vessel that can ride a slick forty miles an hour. There's even an underwater video of the *Head Hunter* crew, eight minutes in all, making an identification of a sunken steamship somewhere amid crystal blue.

———

IN THE FEW years since the catch share began here, gag grouper has returned to the Gulf of Mexico in shocking abundance. Since 2010 it has been managed under a rebuilding plan that requires commercial fishermen to catch fewer fish through the catch share and also shortens the fishing season for recreational fishermen. What was just over six thousand metric tons of reproducing-age fish in 2006 nearly doubled by 2012.

Proponents of catch shares hail gag grouper and red grouper and red snapper as among the greatest commercial and environmental successes the programs have seen in America. The Environmental Defense Fund is proud enough of these fish that it is highlighting two during a 2016 campaign to get diners and ecologists addicted to American seafood. Red snapper and red grouper join the *Deadliest Catch*'s Alaskan snow crab in the mix. Pacific perch from the Gulf of Alaska is in there too. As is Pacific skate, lingcod, yellowtail rockfish, and chilipepper rockfish from the West Coast trawl program. Also included are Atlantic species like pollock, redfish, silver hake, and monkfish. Most are managed in catch shares. And successes like those in gag grouper underscore how hard caps on catch and sound science— whether brought about by catch shares or not—can and do revitalize fish species. And that when good science is the backbone of management, it can direct the conservation work that can recover fisheries.

EDF wants American consumers at this table, the one with the sustainable seafood on it. And that's not just because its leadership wants the oceans to be healthy. Or because they want fishermen who fish sustainably to be profitable. It's also because a constituency of satisfied fishermen is not enough to promote seafood policy. And the organization's leaders anticipate that its preferred policies will need more advocates. Consumers are big ones. So, too, are the retail chains that serve them, and that are now being pressured by efforts like those at EDF to do it without pillaging the oceans.

No one in EDF's Oceans Program was willing to speak on record for this book. But they are aware that catch shares have downsides. And that they've had a devastating impact on some communities and fishermen. People within the organization say they have spent a lot of time grappling with those issues and puzzling over ways to help mitigate them in new catch shares. The Walton Family Foundation has similarly set goals to buffer catch shares' pitfalls, aiming to retrain the people who lose out so they can work other jobs in the seafood supply chain or run businesses like Gulf Wild and Wild Seafood.

That's important while EDF increasingly moves its catch-share programming overseas, eyeing fisheries in twelve nations where between 62 and 70 percent of the world's fish are caught. All are slated to be managed under catch shares by 2020, per the organization's goals. In part, those efforts follow new Walton Family Foundation investments in catch-share programs in Indonesia, Peru, Chile, and Mexico.

"Our board and our foundation is very committed and really believes the only way this work can be successful and durable is if the livelihoods of the fishing communities improve along with the fisheries," says Teresa Ish, the marine program officer at Walton Family Foundation. "While we don't necessarily put in our grants, 'In order to be successful you must develop a catch share that looks like X,' it is well understood that our grantees are focused on good, fair equitable design that also leads to on-the-water improvements and financial improvements."

EDF is the chief steward of the catch-share work abroad, also being called rights-based work. Ish, who like most of the Walton

Family Foundation's marine policy staff has a background as a practitioner—in her case, of fishery science—said she expects development of these systems to address what it will mean if certain people or communities or buyers are left out. The ultimate goal, however, is success on the sea.

"Someone the other day asked me, 'Well, is Walton saying that the only way to get there is rights-based management?' And we don't think that," Ish says. But what she has seen is that catch shares are most successful at bringing good management, enforcement, and governance to fishing, and doing that through the market-based tools that the Walton Family Foundation advocates. As long as they produce these results best, catch shares will be a funding priority.

Catch-share designs are becoming more sophisticated. Community-based programs are placing a quota in control of regional nonprofits like the Cape Cod Commercial Fishermen's Alliance, which stumped for catch shares in New England, and the Oregon-based Ecotrust. These types of regional systems could be a design model for efforts overseas. The quota-based, tradable programs that are the main fare in the United States are not what Walton's grantees are expected to develop, Ish says. Such designs are not a good fit in the third world, where small-scale fisheries are more the norm and where more community-based approaches are favored.

But the investment scenarios first developed in the United States, and now exported abroad, are expected to drive this change regardless of design, raising the specter of related financial and social fallout. The theory behind the push for investment is that foreign governments will lack the financial infrastructure to transition fisheries on their own. Which means that if this initiative succeeds—and there are many millions of dollars at stake—fisheries all over the world will soon open their doors to investors big and small. To pay for boat buyouts. To fund innovations in the seafood supply chain. To fund enforcement strategies and technology and loans to people who buy in. And to seed the cooperatives that manage community fishing assets. What role those investors come to play in overseas markets is a story yet to unfold.

Within the Marine Fish Conservation Network, sentiment about these plans has not changed. And some members, like Angel Braestrup of tobacco-program fame, say the stakes are astronomically higher abroad, where forces like drug cartels can control assets and exert influence in places where government is not at its strongest.

Meanwhile, problems within established catch shares are becoming more entrenched. Researchers have found countries that were once considered leaders in managing catch-share systems are making changes to rein in their pitfalls. Those changes have been spurred by rural depopulation in places like Iceland, where consolidation caused seafood processors to shutter and eliminated jobs, and by lawsuits. Those lawsuits have not popped up just in the United States, but also in Canada, Iceland, Norway, and elsewhere.

Avoiding those kinds of outcomes will be a challenge. The odds against leaving all the stakeholders productive and happy are stacked. "Any time we think about how we improve fisheries, we have to be honest and recognize that there are going to be winners and losers," says Ish. The hard part is how to transition them equitably. How to create the resources for building new economies when catch shares cut people off from the old ones. But she's pointed about one thing: if we want to promote sustainable fishing on the oceans, and see the economic and social benefits that come with new management, it can't look like the same people, in the same number, fishing the same way.

Buddy Guindon agrees. He knows that ultimately the move to catch shares makes seafood more corporate. That someday it will be down to a small number of hardworking companies that are supported by a community that helps them thrive. But he believes that's necessary in order not to fish the ocean bare.

It's why he still supports the catch-share policy push. And why, in the wake of the Fukushima nuclear disaster, he joined EDF to promote catch shares in Tokyo, spending seven or eight days meeting with government and university scientists, fishermen, and industry groups to discuss whether catch shares could continue a trend now seen in fish in Japan. It turns out, however ironically, that fishery closures due to nuclear waste caused an intense rebound in fish populations in Japanese waters. The increasing fish size and their abundance convinced regulators that if their fish could be this healthy, radiation aside, perhaps the country should be doing something different to manage them.

"I look forward to going back and helping them work on their fishery stuff. They certainly have a mess. But it's a mess like any other mess," says Guindon. He says this lightly, in the unflappable tone in which he delivers most things. In this way, he is perfect for this work. Someone who's not afraid to say what he thinks, or to disagree with others. Still a poster boy, his image recently appeared in a TED-style talk in Stockholm by Kathryn Murdoch, the catch-share supporter and EDF trustee whose husband, James, is heir to the Murdoch media empire. Guindon was also filmed aboard his boat on a *Vice* episode that aired in 2015. And now stars in the new reality television show *Big Fish, Texas* on the National Geographic channel.

He plans to be at this work as long as he can. Guindon wants to leave his sons an ocean he is proud of, that the whole industry is proud of. He wishes he could have gotten more done when the politics were favorable: more reef fish in catch shares, laws to keep every fish caught on board, cameras on every boat to ensure it, and logbooks, too, and an auditor to check if they match. Those things are lost for now. To politics. To turnover at the U-shaped table. To squabbling and lawsuits with the recreational industry. Pressure from Congress—concerned about job loss and economic upheaval in coastal communities—has also caused the National Oceanic and Atmospheric Administration to slow its catch-share efforts.

Similarly, when new ideas for the seafood act started floating forward in Congress again in 2015, they were universally unpopular in conservation circles, aimed as they were at reducing ocean protections while conservatives held power in Congress. A House bill introduced by Alaska Representative Don Young, a Republican, called for a contentious amount of wiggle room when it came to tethering fishing rules to science. When it landed in the Senate, before Marco Rubio—the senator from Florida and then a Republican presidential hopeful chairing the Oceans, Atmosphere, Fisheries, and Coast Guard Subcommittee—he did not pick up this hot potato. Neither did conservation groups, which all recognized they already have a law they don't dare open up to a new round of legislating by Republicans. The year 2016 will likely pass without the scheduled reauthorization, leaving the seafood act as it is for now, and liberals in their stalemate over whether catch shares will ever be legislated or better funded.

Today among catch-share proponents, there is a sense that the movement has done what it can with US seafood—for a while. The high-value species left on the table are in New England. And New England is fighting catch shares hard. But proponents are proud of what catch shares have accomplished in America, especially in the Gulf. After years on the overfished list, red snapper and gag grouper are off the list and on their way to sustainable cred. They are also among a trio of fish from this region that are getting the "good alternative" nod from Monterey Bay Aquarium's Seafood Watch, along with red grouper. And both are undergoing extensive analysis by the Sustainable Fisheries Partnership to chart the path toward sustainability certification.

Consumers might not know about the rebound of these fish. But quite a number of them know the Gulf Wild brand. Today it is delivered to high-end retailers and distributors throughout the country. Though it has a small group of leaders at its core, Gulf Wild accounts for more than 10 percent of the reef fish landed on the American shores of the Gulf of Mexico. Guindon tagged just more than 2 million pounds of fish in 2015; De La Cruz tagged another 800,000 pounds—or about half a million fish in all. And those fish reach far—to ATB in Texas, to Wegmans grocery stores in Maryland and in Washington, DC, to the Heinen's grocery store in Cleveland, and to Seattle Fish Co. in Denver. Chefs like Rick Moonen at RM Seafood in Las Vegas, the most famous sustainable seafood restaurant in the country, are customers, too.

The grants from EDF ran out long ago, the goal always being for Gulf Wild to become an actual business. In the end, the period of support didn't last much longer than it did for most nonprofit-sponsored efforts that buoyed fishermen after the Deepwater Horizon spill. Now Gulf Wild's fish houses fund the management of the brand and its conservation work. They put fishermen to work on forty-one boats in 2015, all of them adhering to conservation standards that reduce accidental catch, boost scientific data collection, and meet goals intended to safeguard the health of the fish Gulf Wild targets.

———

"No GUTS, NO glory, right?" De La Cruz says. He's standing on the dock outside Wild Seafood. The sun is shining. The water is a postcard blue, the birds diving at his catch. Most of what he's ever imagined in business is right there at his feet now. He's got a new boathouse on the dock. And will soon have a new retail shop. Madeira Beach Seafood is still the biggest seafood fish house on the bay. But Wild Seafood is the second biggest now. And growing.

De La Cruz is pointed when he says that he could not have done it without catch shares. That it was this policy that propelled his business. Those hundreds of thousands of pounds of fish—the ones assigned to him through catch shares—they're probably worth more than his house now. And while the property rights that attend them are the chief drivers of problems now bedeviling EDF and the Walton Family Foundation, they also make it so that De La Cruz can go to the bank and borrow money. And only with financial support could he have helped to build one of the most innovative seafood products in the world.

It's a furiously hot day while he tells his story. De La Cruz and a troop of young workers are hustling back and forth between a boat—unloading his grouper—and a cooler brimming with ice water to drink. The handful of teens and twenty-somethings are rushing around, packing the fish on ice, while about as many women—wives and friends—are recording the weights of the catch one tote at a time on a digital scale. The tourists are hanging off the boardwalk again, watching the young captain, shirtless and in yellow oilskins, pull the grouper from the boat and flip each fish in a perfect arc down an aluminum slide.

De La Cruz sorts the fish as they fall, the workers scurrying to push totes brimming with them first to the scale, then to larger bins where yet more workers are shoveling ice. Each one of these bins weighs about as much as a cow. Inside, the fish are stacked neatly side by side, each with a Gulf Wild tag tethered to its flesh and commanding twenty-five cents, sometimes forty cents, more per pound than it once did at the docks, boosting pay for fishermen.

Gulf Wild has given consumers one of the most traceable seafood products they have ever seen. And made the Gulf more ecologically sound through conservation. But beyond all that, stories like this one, the story of how a regular, hardworking guy like Jason De La Cruz built Gulf Wild, continue to make the case for catch shares with consumers and fishermen alike.

De La Cruz is a long way from the bare rectangle across the water where he started as a bait-catching kid. Now, when word gets out he needs a captain, guys show up at his front door, two or three of them a day. Some fishermen—particularly those whom De La Cruz beat to permits in the days of the $500,000 gamble—don't sell to him. They hate him for having cooperated with environmentalists, for having played a game that so swiftly put many longtime fishermen out of business.

But to hear De La Cruz tell it, he just reacted to a world that was changing. The future knocked. He opened the door.

North Atlantic

A Rare Sight, and a Remedy

WHO OWNS THESE FISH?

It's a question Tim Rider doesn't ask himself. When he thinks of the open Atlantic that he loves, the blue sea rising and falling off the coast of Maine under rods and reels and his thirty-foot fiberglass boat, the *Finlander*, he knows the fish in this ocean are no more his than anyone else's. But when he thinks of his three-year-old son, he wonders what will be left of this life—the life of an American fisherman—by the time his boy is a man.

It is a life that seemed to find Rider. One cod at a time. One cask. One pollock. A wolf fish here and there. A whole lot of redfish. He doesn't remember exactly when the bug bit him. It was too early in life to note. But he remembers well how his mother indulged him. How when he was seemingly too young to know where his passion lay, she would call the school nurse and spring him under the guise of doctors' appointments, then take him charter fishing instead. The fare was mackerel. Somehow love and heart met sea and food and they got tangled up in him in a place they still live.

He wants that for his own child. He wants the boy's sea legs as sturdy as his own. That little face with the brown almond eyes, the one that stares at back at him from his cell phone while he is riding the sea, he wants it gazing at this water someday, and with the same affection.

"What's next? Are we going to lease recreational rights to my three-year-old so he can have an opportunity? . . . What's going to be there for that generation if everything has a price tag on it that's a natural resource?" When his son reaches his own age, which is thirty-eight, will he see the day when we carve up the Grand Canyon? What about the redwoods? Or the national forests? Rider says this somewhat facetiously. Yet fifty years ago, if anybody ever said the government was going to give away the rights to the fish in the ocean, would anyone have believed it? And was it worth this trade—public property for private market gain? For consumer choice made easier?

"I do not believe that we should be leasing our public resources like commodities trading, and that anyone should be sitting at home collecting a check for not going fishing, or that big companies should be able to purchase large amounts of the quota and sit back collecting checks. It's not a public resource if you do that," Rider says.

He says this on the back of the deck of the *Finlander*, a rod and reel in his hand. He's cast a line in the water and is jerking a jig along the ocean bottom, a triple deck of hooks with flashes of metal and brightly colored lure some 250 feet below. He's not really looking while he does this. Just pulling the line along, feeling it walk along the bottom of the water. While he talks, it is clear that he has been doing this—the thing with the jig—nearly as long as he's been talking.

Goateed with a day's stubble and wearing a sweatshirt proclaiming FISH IS GOOD, he's relaying something he saw at a meeting. Where one guy said, "Well, you know I bought a bunch of permits," and then talked about how renting fish is his retirement plan now. "It's not the fishes' responsibility to fund people's retirements," says Rider.

He has thrown all in on this belief. This is the maiden voyage of the *Finlander*. It's a boat that's deeply rooted in the Slow Fish movement, which, on the heels of catch shares, has seeded a growing presence in the United States. In March 2016 Slow Fish held its first international conference in the Western Hemisphere in New Orleans, convening fishers from all over the world, but importantly from all over America.

The conference focused on strategies for hanging on to ocean access, preserving fishing heritage, and still fostering transparency and sustainability and building value chains that benefit consumers. The future it proffers is an alternative to privately owned commodity brands like Gulf Wild. Slow Fish advocates instead for public ownership, for local control. And it's supporting Rider, helping to grow the New England Fish Mongers, the brand allied with the fishermen on this boat, through volunteers. The slogan that has sustained them, derived from Slow Fish advocates at the Northwest Atlantic Marine Alliance, is "Who Fishes Matters." Rider believes it does. That it is everything.

There are three crewmen on board this boat, each one fishing a corner. To fish by hand like this requires a lot of hands, so Rider likes teaching young fishermen and toting everyone from customers to policy advocates and chefs on his trips. While they fish he tells them why he fishes this way, with just one pole, one line at a time, wasting nothing. And he also tells them that catch shares could be the death of him, or at least of his tiny industry.

There are just a few commercial hook-and-line boats like this one left on the Atlantic coast—fishing rod and reel from a tiny pool of fish left in common ownership—which makes the *Finlander* one of the only day-boat operations left in New England. There is such a policy preference for catch shares here now that regulators have banished the common pool into a geographic area a whopping eighty miles from shore. This makes it tough for rod-and-reel boats—small boats are the pool's chief participants—to fish the pool safely anymore. The fuel it takes to chug those eighty miles also means slim profits for those that do.

It's a regulatory environment that makes what will happen tomorrow at a farmers' market in Saco, Maine, all the more amazing. That's where the fish landing on the *Finlander*'s deck will be sold whole to buyers, regular people browsing the wares from local farms in a grocery store parking lot. Such fresh day-boat catch, hawked next to a chalk sign and a burlap banner proudly proclaiming them the bounty of the New England Fish Mongers, is a rare sight in New England now. And getting rarer.

The *Finlander* is actually the second version of itself and Rider's third boat. There was another, smaller vessel by the same name on which Rider and his crew used to fish. It was replaced with this thirty-foot fiberglass vessel this summer because its predecessor had been pushed farther and harder on this rough water than any tiny boat should go. Building a new boat took more time and more money than anybody expected. By this morning, Rider and his crew were so antsy to hit the water that they left at 3:00 a.m. in a not-so-accommodating tide, so that the maiden voyage of the *Finlander* began with the spry vessel charging against the tide at twenty knots, or about twenty-three miles an hour, jogging over the waves like a horse determined to throw its passengers. Driving the boat, Rider could see nothing past the spray over the boat's nose, so he drove through his instruments instead.

That the exhaust pipe was off-gassing fumes in the wheelhouse was just an unwelcome bonus. Typically there is a blanket that covers the pipe as it runs from the bunks in the fo'c'sle through the wheelhouse to the roof, so that the heat inside the pipe just stays there. But the wrong blanket was ordered and didn't fit. And by then there was no amount of waiting that seemed worthwhile to anyone. Only at sea was it discovered that, sans blanket, the special resin that holds a kind of heatproof gauze over the exhaust pipe would smoke like burnt plastic. It smoked that way for the first few hours, until the whole crew got queasy. No one knows what's in this toxic perfume. It arrived in a blandly labeled can—*exhaust wrap paint*—with the name of a town, a phone number, and nothing more. The joke was that it shaved three years off everyone's life. And even that was not enough to keep the Mongers off the water.

For the hour before sunrise, Rider was telling everyone he was going to catch the first fish on this boat. He's been saying it for days, too, during the last tireless push to get the newly minted *Finlander* in the water. But once the fishing began it hardly mattered. Once the sun started to peek above the rolling blue waves to the east, he drove to a once-favorite spot and the Mongers did what they do: they hit the deck and started dropping lines. The sun shining now, it's Mitch Hartford, the fortyish goateed father of a young daughter, who reels the first fish in. A hefty pollock. A keeper.

Everyone checks it out. Rider turns from the portside stern. Karl Day, a retiree who met Rider working on a line crew for the phone company—a job Rider still has—leans in from behind the wheelhouse on the starboard side. And twenty-one-year-old Zach Wark, feet planted on the starboard side of the stern, casts a glance over his shoulder.

This is Wark's first day on the job. Sort of. He was hired about a month ago. At the time he was working at a local Goodwill warehouse and quit on the spot, a job fishing being his dream, or at least he thinks so far. He's been running errands for the *Finlander* ever since, collecting parts and being a general servant during a construction stint that turned out to last weeks. But he arrived at the docks at 2:30 this morning beaming. "This is a very good day for me," he said. He's standing in the stern in suspendered Grundéns and mirrored shades, catching what he can. He fishes like he has a hit list, he says. The stranger, the rarer, put it on the list.

He nearly adds one. Within an hour or two Wark is reeling in a cod, shoulders square and leaning back against the tug of the fish, when a poor beagle, another name for a mackerel shark, swipes the cod for itself, leaving nothing but lips on the line. "Damn!" he shouts. About six or seven feet long, the shark slides alongside the boat. Rider jumps portside with a gaffe to spear it. "If I stick him with this one you're gonna want to . . ." Hartford finishes, "gaffe with the other one?" "Yes," Rider says. "We need all gaffes ready." But the shark passes only once and too far away to reach.

The sun is high and the fish are biting some, at least. The crew has been so long on land that to find any fish and have a small offering for the market tomorrow is all that Rider really hopes for. Now he reaches into a plastic tote full of them and pops the gills, bleeding the fish one by one. There is not much blood. After the last of the fish gives its final flip or two, the blood drained out, Rider guts an entire tote in a few quick minutes with an expert slice from the tail to the head, or sometimes the other way around, and a quick two-finger scoop of the body cavity. He does this with the hose running, rinsing each fish before laying it whole on ice. When he's done, he gives the fiberglass deck a quick spray, the innards floating out the well-placed holes, called scuppers, in the stern. The seabirds know quite well that this moment is coming, flying fast from where they trail the boat for scraps.

The day passes like this. The sun shining and the blue ocean shimmering and tossing the *Finlander*, giving it that Maine ocean christening, the catch hand-caught one by one, cleaned, and put on ice. The Mongers drift for a while, fishing. Pollock and reds and porgies, a few keeper cod. Day even pulls in a triple—all pollock, all keepers. Then Rider kicks up the motor, finds another spot, and drifts again. He checks out old spots to see if they're still hot. Explores the grounds, trying to understand what the next season on this ocean brings.

When there are about 170 pounds on board, Rider calls for one more drift and then the ride home. It isn't a huge catch today. It won't get anybody paid. But it will get some fish to the market and let the customers know the Mongers are around. Rider has got a lot riding on those customers. He spent $160,000 on the *Finlander*. And the Mongers have to be successful selling direct to consumers for his investment in the boat to pencil. He can't get the prices he needs from bulk buyers otherwise. They tell him outright: "Your fish are diamonds, but I can just buy that shit over there for fifty cents." Which is why he's got to have customers who will pay eight dollars a pound and who will appreciate the fish were caught by hand the day before. Since most people aren't used to head-on gutted catch, Rider says, "We're using drug-dealer tactics selling fish. First one's free. Then it's gonna cost you."

————————

A LOT OF his success will depend on what happens at the U-shaped table. At issue lately is whether the New England Fishery Management Council, which presides over the fish in this region, will let fishermen like Rider fish closer to the shore, where he's more likely to survive both in life and in business, or continue to reserve that area for the boats in the catch share. Rider can join the catch share any time with the permit that he has and fish closer. But he doesn't want to add related fees to his lean operation, and the only other advantage is the opportunity to rent more catch at rates he can't afford. Somewhere along the way it became a point of pride to avoid it. And to be fairly public in his thoughts about what catch shares have wrought.

Lots of boats have gone out of business in the transition, mostly trawl boats while cod stocks are down. But as access consolidates fast among large boats while people sell out, "They are getting a stranglehold on the fishery," Rider says. Soon, the people at the U-shaped table will decide how much of a stranglehold, setting limits on how much groundfish one entity can own. With those limits proposed at 20 percent, Rider and other activists, united by the Northwest Atlantic Marine Alliance, have turned up at meetings in orange T-shirts bearing the slogan WHO FISHES MATTERS. They don't want to bless a scenario in which five entities could one day control an entire species of fish. At a meeting in September 2015, they stood up and walked out to make that point, an orange sea of anger followed by a bunch of college students—Slow Fish volunteers—and supporter Jarvis Green, the former NFL player who is also a shrimper.

There are alternatives to this kind of anger. And to the deep consolidation of small boats and the loss of family businesses that have hit

New England and other places so hard. A good place to see one is in Oregon, where the state has ordained the Oregon Albacore Commission to oversee the collective branding and support of the Oregon albacore fishery. Each year hundreds of small boats set sail from Oregon onto the Pacific in search of this migrating fish as it passes. Most of the boats are family businesses, crewed by generations. Captains armed with binoculars can spot the albacore while they feed, jumping on schools of anchovies. Like the *Finlander*, these boats hand-catch their fish using a combination of rods and reels. They also use troll poles— a pole towing lines.

Oregon albacore doesn't belong to anybody. Instead, fishermen and the seafood industry pay fees to buy and sell it, and that money is used to advertise Oregon albacore to consumers. It's also been used to garner sustainability certification—underpinned by science—and to fund scholarships for students. Albacore buyers have developed pouch and canned products to supply grocers and delis. And Oregonians with a taste for this stunning fish—its loins make for a phenomenal sashimi— can find places to buy it fresh through the commission's website. Oftentimes those places are just boats tied up in Oregon ports. Consumers are encouraged to walk the docks and find them, buying direct from fishermen and bridging the gap between ocean and dinner plate on their own. It's a program that supported 351 small boats in 2015. All sustainable. Environmentally. Economically. And socially too.

Absent such thinking in New England, it's unclear whether protest from activists and fishermen like Tim Rider will have influence. But what happens in the United States now matters around the world, as catch shares are expected to be replicated in communities abroad. When she talks about this, Michèle Mesmain, the convener of the international Slow Fish movement, says the stakes are not small. Fisheries are being privatized in places so impoverished that fishers who can't afford to take a bus to give their opinion at a meeting could be left without a voice. Where fish is bartered for vegetables and for potatoes, people cut off from the seas face starvation. And in some parts of the world, whole communities have disappeared while people migrate away when fishing ends, or those communities adopt tourism until they are unrecognizable.

While Mesmain makes no distinction between the alphabet soup of catch-share programs—ITQs, IFQs, and the privatized kind of TURFs (which stands for territorial use rights for fishing)—all of them, she says, take a public resource and put it in the hands of an authority that is not a public agency. With conservation groups simplifying the message around catch shares, "It's very hard now to tell people, 'Hey, the story of fisheries is not what it seems,'" she says.

She believes strongly that the government has a role to play in saving the oceans, and talks about things like renewing trust, convening local boards with more accountability and transparency, and fairness as being essential to leadership. She says fixing fisheries should mean including everyone in new plans for the oceans. And that means making sure people participate at the meetings, are listened to, and that the process concerns itself with whether some of them could end up maligned by the ocean-grabbing interests that creep in. She doesn't like the idea of people growing up mad at the government, because their fathers were mad at the government, and raising children who are still mad at the government. It's happening in the United States. And even big players on the seas in Alaska, successful players, live alongside those hardest hit and feel, in spite of their own good fortune, that their community has lost.

Healthy social fabric will not just come to these places. People will have to work to bring towns like Gloucester back again. And in order to truly design fisheries that are fair and equitable, sustainable for everyone, Mesmain says, you need all voices, no matter how small.

What the Slow Fish movement proffers is that nobody has to own the seas. There are lots of ways to manage fish. And other ways of preassigning catches—like assigning them to particular fishermen, then letting them revert to the government or a common pool after a term—would fix firm catch limits on the sea just as well as catch shares. Such programs would offer the same safety and ecological benefits that catch shares have brought, and fuel price increases too, without the private property rights that have caused so much social inequity and upended jobs and businesses and whole towns. The fact that some people come to Slow Fish with a belief that catch shares saved their communities is beside the point to Mesmain. "Whether it's sufficient or not, I feel it violates the public trust. You can preassign catch without turning that into a property right." The ocean is a common resource. And any form of privatizing it or claiming it is closing the commons.

Such preassigned catch may not lead to individually traceable fish. And it won't make it easy to fund businesses like Wild Seafood that can innovate the fish market. Or build the kind of labeling and social media tools into brands that give consumers the most insight into what they're eating, as Gulf Wild has done. But it can look like Oregon albacore—community-branded fisheries that support both ocean health and equitable access for everyone.

———

RIDER IS LUCKY in one way. Slow Fish has his back, even if fishery managers do not. Two local volunteers—chiefly Amanda Parks and, at times, her partner Spencer Montgomery—have provided enormous support while he builds New England Fish Mongers. They handle the marketing and help hawk the fish at the farmers' market on Saturday, among the fresh fruit and the farm-raised vegetables, the artisanal jams and dills and soaps and creams. When people turn up at the Shaw's parking lot, they are not just staring at a few fish in a cooler and a burlap banner and a chalkboard. They are talking to people who understand the value of hand-caught catch and can explain to shoppers what that means—and how to cook it.

Rider needs all the help he can get. By day, he still works a line crew for the phone company—he has to while the Monger business builds—and in his off time parents a three-year-old with a wife who probably would like to see more of him. He used to be a marathoner, so he sees the long game. But on the drive back to shore he makes cracks about his health and says that he is a walking advertisement for Red Bull. In two days, he has not slept longer than an hour or two in naps, mostly in the bow. Lately, he says the hardest part about falling asleep is knowing how soon he has to be up again. He works tomorrow at 5:00 a.m. It's 7:00 p.m. as the boat pulls into Portsmouth, New Hampshire, where it will moor for the summer. And before morning Rider needs to buy a second cooler for the market and a folding table too. Hartford takes pity on him and takes the Grundéns home to clean.

After the boat is settled in its new slip, there's a brief but somewhat celebratory pit stop. Ironically, it's at a McDonald's. Everyone is tired and hungry and the food is fast. They line up in salty jeans and Carhartts, sweatshirts and baseball caps, and wait in the glaring light. The Filet-O-Fish stares back from the menu, slathered in tartar sauce and cheese. It's wild caught. Certified sustainable. And as fast food goes, it isn't even all that bad for you. But this crew of day-boat fishermen knows that none of the pollock in those sandwiches came from their waters. There's no room for Atlantic pollock in this industrial supply from Alaska. No room for local catch in that relentless churn of private supply and big demand. They order burgers and fries, strawberry creme pies and sodas. They eat talking about the politics at the U-shaped table, their next trip on the water, and whether the New England Fish Mongers can hold out against the gentrification of the sea.

Meanwhile, in the parking lot, in the bed of the truck, are the coolers of whole fish that will sell tomorrow. There are redfish and cod. Cask and wolf fish. And whole Atlantic pollock. Lots of it. All on ice, all fresh caught. To consider just one pollock, it's a beauty. Its scales are a patchwork of shining silver, its belly white, its gills still red and fresh. The pupils of its eyes are clear and black, the kind of clear that says its life ended only hours ago. The iris around it is a blue-green mirror of the waters from which it came.

A person who knows the water in which this fish lived can hold it in their hands and feel that place, where the waves are choppy, where the water can turn quick and mean, and sometimes only whales break the vast expanse of rolling, welcoming, unforgiving blue. They can smell the ocean where the sea meets the air, and later, they can taste it. After this fish is stuffed with herbs and lemon, brushed with olive oil and grilled, it brings the sea into their mouth. The salty North Atlantic alive in that white, flaky meat that looks so much like the soul of an animal and nothing, nothing at all like the cubes of protein falling off conveyor belts on the Bering Sea.

Not every wild fish can be taken this way. And the world is a bigger place with more people in it than will allow everyone to eat wild fish that are hand caught. But every wild fish that gives its life to the dinner plate comes with a question now: should it give its value to the hand of the harvester or to a new generation of ocean landlords?

Timeline of Catch-Share Programs

PACIFIC

2001
Sablefish Permit Stacking

2011
Groundfish Trawl Rationalization

NORTH PACIFIC

1992 Western Alaska Community Development Quota

1995 Alaska Halibut and Sablefish IFQ

1999 American Fisheries Act (AFA) Pollock Cooperatives

2005 Bering Sea and Aleutian Islands (BSAI) Crab Rationalization Program

2007 Central Gulf of Alaska Rockfish Cooperatives*

2008 Non-Pollock Trawl Catcher/Processor Groundfish Cooperatives (Amendment 80)

*Began as a pilot program in 2007 and was formally implemented in 2012.

1996–2002
Congressional Moratorium
on Establishment of
New IFQ Programs

NEW ENGLAND
2010
General Category Atlantic
Sea Scallop IFQ

Northeast Multispecies Sectors

ATLANTIC
2016
Highly Migratory Species
Individual Bluefin Quota
Program**
** Program implemented in 2015, but
quota allocated in 2016 and represents
Year 1.

MID-ATLANTIC
1990
Surfclam and Ocean
Quahog ITQ
2009
Golden Tilefish IFQ

GULF OF MEXICO
2007
Red Snapper IFQ
2010
Grouper-Tilefish IFQ

SOUTH ATLANTIC
1992
Wreckfish ITQ

Timeline courtesy of NOAA, edited to fit page.

ACKNOWLEDGMENTS

To the men and women who fish our oceans, whose work feeds us all, and who welcomed me onto their docks, their boats, and into their story, I owe a debt I can't repay.

I am especially grateful to those who suffered me aboard their vessels and as their bunkmate: Shannon and Ernie Eldredge, Russell Kingman, Tim Rider, Mitch Hartford, Karl Day, Zach Wark, Vern Crane, Kasper Harvey, Bob Baldwin, Justin Sutherland, Aaron Longton, Mark McClelland, and Rocket.

I benefitted greatly from Buddy Guindon's patience. His efforts to explain his industry, his values, and his story—down to the width of the monofilament—took hours. That he took this time with me knowing we didn't always agree says much about his character. Such honest intellect is a rare quality, and essential in someone whose mission is to facilitate holistic change. I can think of few people as well suited to his purpose. His commitment to it was my gain.

The guts and business acumen that is the daily stuff of Jason De La Cruz makes for a very long to-do list that only ever gets longer. I appreciated any place on that list, and he always seemed to find it, even in ten-minute increments that he often stretched. Watching his success and the growth of his business was a joy. I am enormously thankful to Jason for sharing his story and his experience with me, and for helping me to understand the business case for catch shares.

This work would not have been possible without the generous support of the Fund for Investigative Journalism. My thanks are due to the board, and especially to Sandy Bergo, for seeing the value of this reporting many years ago and for continuing to support it along the way to this book. Similarly, the judges of the Alicia Patterson Foundation Fellowship selected this work for a 2013 fellowship that enabled me to travel to catch shares around the nation. Without this journey, I could not have found the circumstances and the people that would ultimately tell this story. Margaret Engel was an especially big help along the way.

These funders foster much of the good work coming from independent journalists in America, and I cannot stress enough how critical their support is to me and to many others. Harder still to find the right words to express my deep gratitude to the people who decided I would receive these limited funds. Reporting of this depth is otherwise often prohibitively expensive, and such assistance has given me enormous opportunities.

My agent Jessica Papin at Dystel Goderich saw this mountain of reporting in an early stage and believed it could tell a powerful story. Her careful attention and advice helped me to turn it into a book proposal and then a book. She is astrologer, advocate, and psychiatrist all in one. Good thing for that.

My editor Elisabeth Dyssegaard at St. Martin's helped me to see the line between writing and actually saying something. I am most appreciative of her thoughtful feedback. And for Laura Apperson at St. Martin's, who was a wealth of tiny details that made the difference between being guided through the publishing world and fumbling through it. I am lucky for her prompt attention to most everything. My production team—Stephen Wagley and Alan Bradshaw, especially—was superb.

I am also profoundly, sincerely grateful to my colleagues at InvestigateWest, not only for providing support for my early catch-share reporting, but for suffering my constant travel these last years and never complaining about it. Working with someone who is always on the lam cannot be easy, and InvestigateWest is populated by the kind of people whose only comment on the matter was always encouragement. Jason Alcorn, Carol Smith, Kim Drury, and Heather Kosaka: thank you. My gratitude to Robert McClure in particular is boundless. His support for my grants and fellowship, his excitement and insights about my first catch-share stories, and his unwavering support throughout the reporting and writing of this book was tireless. Hard to say which is his strongest billing: his sharp nose for news or his heart for it.

It was Rick Lyman, then a national editor at *The New York Times*, who said a thing that probably seemed simple but made much of this work successful: "People don't care about fish or fishing. They care about seafood." Turns out he was right. His simple remark reshaped my work at an early stage, and to my advantage.

As I pursued this project, many people shared deep knowledge of this subject with me. My phone, my email, and often my dinner table have been populated by gurus, cheerleaders, and upbraiders all. Every journalist should be so lucky as to be surrounded by people who will point you in the right direction and also call you on your baloney. I am better for all of them—even the ones who are critical of my work—and I hope they know how welcome they always are.

My world is also a wealth of very talented writers. I am so glad. My pitch club has been a great touchstone and a brainstorming venue for some of the more challenging aspects of writing this book. Some of its members read drafts of its initial proposal, and David Wolman retooled it into something that landed an agent. Bill Lascher made us agent twins by introducing me to Jessica. And Linda Wojtowick, Zack Beyman, and Hanna Neuschwander read sample chapters in those early days.

It was Jon Ross who read early drafts of chapters when I couldn't see them any longer. He helped me to see them through fresh eyes. Toby Van Fleet, Rebecca Clarren, Linda, and my husband, Bjorn van der Voo, all endured the entire first draft, a momentous job, and provided critical insight on pacing, lyricism, fairness, and the quality of the reporting. In addition to those kindnesses, Becca coached my application and interview for the Alicia Patterson Foundation Fellowship. And Linda inspired and researched the epigraph at the front of this book. AmyJo Sanders and Alandra Johnson read portions of the final draft for clarity, as did Bjorn. And journalist Max Towle assisted from New Zealand, as did translator Ani Kartikasari. It is Oakley Brooks to whom I owe the beer.

Every book should also have a dog. My dog Onyx can hunker down and write with the best of them. I had her sanity-inducing company on many a marathon, and I am blessed with it for as long as she'll have me.

I also had the support of my family. The whole lot of them are full of optimism and couches and are nice enough to me to tell me when to take breaks. Time with my family was a nice outgrowth of such frequent travel these last four years. Those hard-earned rests will be well remembered, especially the seafood. My mother makes the best home-cooked stuffed clams I've ever had. My stepfather, Dave, digs them. It was Dave who instilled in me a love of fishing, boating, and the oceans. Between the two of them, they tied culture to water for me and made this book worth writing.

Not least, my husband, Bjorn, who has outsized faith in me and walks this path alongside me, has my love and thanks until the end. It is one thing to tell a person you believe they can do a thing. It is quite another to ferry them macaroni and cheese while they do it. He is always up for the latter, proof that I won the husband lottery.

NOTES ON SOURCES

All quotations in this book are derived from interviews with the author unless otherwise noted in the text. Those interviews were conducted between May 2012 and April 2016. For brevity's sake, only interviews to which information can be directly attributed are listed in the chapter notes below. Hundreds of interviews were conducted for the book, however, and all the insights gleaned from those conversations guided years of travel, the author's thinking, and the development of the book's chapters.

CHAPTER 1

Details of life aboard a pollock trawler stem from interviews with Dave Wagenheim, a former marine biologist, and Liz Mitchell, who is a member of the board of the Association of Professional Observers, in Eugene, Oregon. Additional information was taken from the article "What You Need to Know about Working on an At-Sea Processor" on the At-Sea Processors Association website. The scene depicted aboard the factory processor was crafted from Wagenheim's descriptions, federal fisheries biologists' log forms, and Wagenheim's YouTube video "Pollock Fishing in the Bering Sea, Alaska," filmed aboard the *Highland Light*.

Information about the content of fish sandwiches derives from nutritional information and sustainability reports from McDonald's, Subway, Burger King, and Long John Silver's, found online. Other pollock product descriptions, as well as the figure for the annual harvest amount of pollock from the Bering Sea, comes from the Genuine Alaska Pollock website, specifically the articles "A Worldwide Favorite" and "The World's Largest Sustainable Fishery." Child-friendly recipes involving fish sticks were found on the Gorton's Seafood website.

Data on accidental catch came from the National Oceanic and Atmospheric Administration's *Bering Sea Chinook Salmon Bycatch Report* and the North Pacific Fishery Management Council's *Report to the North Pacific Fishery Management Council on the 2013 Bering Sea Pollock Intercooperative Salmon Avoidance Agreement* by Karl Haflinger and John Gruver. It also comes from the North Pacific Fishery Management Council report *Revise Bering Sea/Aleutian Islands Prohibited Species Catch Limits*.

Injury statistics come from Oregon State University and the National Institute for Occupational Safety and Health report *Work-Related Traumatic Injuries Onboard Freezer-Trawlers and Freezer-Longliners Operating in Alaskan Waters during 2001–2012* by Lucas, Kincl, Bovbjerg, Lincoln, and Branscum. Historical information about the Alaska Fisheries Act Pollock Cooperatives was sourced from the NOAA report *The Economic Performance of U.S. Catch Share Programs* by Ayeisha A. Brinson and Eric M. Thunberg and from Michael Webber's book *From Abundance to Scarcity: A History of U.S. Marine Fisheries Policy*.

The scene aboard the *Taty Z* was conveyed in recorded phone interviews with Pat Pletnikoff between April 2013 and April 2016, as was the history of St. George. Additional historical details came from the article "St. George" on the Aleutian Pribilof Islands Association website, as did facts about island wildlife. Other wildlife facts came from the article "Pribilof Islands Land Mammals" in NOAA's document library online. The passage regarding the decline of halibut draws from the author's 2015 reporting for *Slate* and for *InvestigateWest*.

CHAPTER 2

Source material for chapter 2 came from numerous interviews with Jason De La Cruz between May 2013 and April 2016, as well as with Matt Joswig in January 2016. Details of the Environmental Defense Fund's early position on catch shares were sourced from an interview in February 2016 with Doug Hopkins, who led the organization's first oceans program. Additional detail for the scene at the Holiday Inn in Corpus Christi, Texas, on October 22, 2009, derives from meeting minutes of the Gulf of Mexico Fishery Management Council and on-line photos available on the Holiday Inn's website.

Details about the overfished status of grouper in 2007 were taken from the National Oceanic and Atmospheric Administration Fisheries Service report *Fish Stock Sustainability Index*, published in March 2007, from its *Gulf of Mexico and Tilefish IFQ: Catch Share Spotlight No. 14*, last updated in November 2009, and from the Southeast Data, Assessment, and Review report *Gulf of Mexico Gag Stock Assessment Report* from March 2014. The reference to Atlantic salmon comes from Paul Greenberg's *Four Fish: The Future of the Last Wild Food*. The figure for the value of US Seafood comes from the NOAA's report *Performance of US Catch Share Programs*, accessed online.

CHAPTER 3

Chapter 3 was researched on location in Kodiak, Alaska. Descriptive scenes were the observations of the author, save for those aboard the

Time Bandit. The *Time Bandit* scenes derive from season 2, episodes 9 through 12 of *Deadliest Catch*, filmed in 2005 while Tom Miller was a crewman aboard the vessel.

Information about job loss in Kodiak, data on the crab lease/rental economy, and data about the degree of vessel loss and consolidation in the crab fishery were sourced from the work of Gunnar Knapp at the Institute of Social and Economic Research at the University of Alaska in Anchorage, in particular his report *Economic Impacts of BSAI Crab Rationalization on Kodiak Fishing Employment and Earnings and Kodiak Businesses*. General census and economic data about the Kodiak Island Borough comes from the borough itself.

Statistics related to fishing deaths both nationally and among crabbers were supplied by the US Department of Labor, Bureau of Labor Statistics, specifically its report *Fatal Occupational Injuries by Selected Characteristics*. The author's understanding of the history of the US Fishery Management Councils was informed by Michael Webber and his book *From Abundance to Scarcity: A History of U.S. Marine Fisheries Policy*.

Information about the geography and climate of the Bering Sea is derived from *World Atlas* and from www.beringclimate.noaa.gov, a website maintained by the National Oceanic and Atmospheric Administration.

Other NOAA research was used to understand the condition of the crab fishery both before and after catch shares, and economic outcomes related to the program, specifically the reports *Stock Assessment and Fishery Evaluation Report For King and Tanner Crab Fisheries of the Bering Sea and Aleutian Island Regions: Economic Status of the BSAI Crab Fisheries* by Brian Garber-Yonts and Jean Lee; *Catch Share Spotlight No. 4 Bering Sea & Aleutian Islands (BSAI) Crab (King & Tanner) Rationalization Program*; *National Overview/United States Summary*; and the website "Crab Rationalization" at www.npfmc.org /crabrationalization.

Additional interviews with background sources and with Bob Mc-Garry in May 2012 informed the author's understanding of the pre–catch-share crab fishery. Details of the costumes and chants at the Washington, DC, protest come from an interview with former Kodiak resident Rhonda Maker, also in May 2012, who attended it.

CHAPTER 4

This chapter was developed through a series of interviews with Buddy Guindon that began in Galveston, Texas, in May 2013 and continued by phone through April 2016. Information about the historical regulation of the red snapper fishery was derived from the Gulf of Mexico Fishery Management Council's data partner, SEDAR Southeast Data, Assessment and Review, *Stock Assessment of SEDAR 7 Gulf of Mexico Red Snapper. SEDAR7 Assessment Report 1.*

CHAPTER 5

The narrative underpinning chapter 5 was developed onboard the *Viking Spirit* in October 2015. All the scenes depicted are the observations of the author. Details of the economics of the voyage, as well as the circumstances of the crew and of Bob Baldwin's ocean holdings, derive from interviews recorded with all aboard the vessel over four days. The trip was documented in photographs, which were later used to identify apparel and the slogan on Kasper Harvey's sweatshirt. The Warm Springs description is courtesy of Baldwin, and was checked against the Wikipedia entry for "Baranof Warm Springs, Alaska."

Two reports from the National Oceanic and Atmospheric Administration, National Marine Fisheries Service, were relied on for fishery details: Information about the declining number of halibut owners was found in *Transfer Report—Changes Under Alaska's Halibut IFQ*

Program, 1995–2014. Information about similar declines in sablefish ownership, as well as the geographic distribution of both halibut and sablefish owners and the portion of the catch delivered by renters, was taken from *Fishing Year 2012 Pacific Halibut-Sablefish IFQ Report*.

CHAPTER 6

Chapter 6 relied on interviews with Richard Garcia and Jared Auerbach in Boston in January 2013 and phone interviews with Buddy Guindon, Michael Clayton, Jason De La Cruz, and Chris Brown between May 2013 and January 2016. More than a dozen interviews were conducted on and around the docks in Gloucester and in Hyannis Port, Massachusetts, and in Portsmouth, New Hampshire, in 2013 to inform this chapter. Those interviews underpin the remark that Red's Best was keeping a lot of fishermen in business during the groundfish collapse.

Details of the sinking of the *Elizabeth Helen* are sourced from US Coast Guard reports obtained under the Freedom of Information Act. Chris Brown added additional information about the effect of the boat's sinking on Trace and Trust, and the logistical challenges that resulted from the small number of boats during the program's pilot.

Facts about the Deepwater Horizon oil spill come from the documentary *BP and the Oil Spill*, directed by Volker Barth for Anthro Media, as well as from timelines developed by Fox News, specifically *Disaster in the Gulf: 107 Days and Counting*, published on the Fox news website. General facts about the Gulf of Mexico come from GulfBase.org.

CHAPTER 7

Scenes from aboard the *Golden Eye* were reported aboard the vessel. The quotations derive from interviews with Aaron Longton, both aboard the vessel and in a follow-up conversation in January 2016.

Information about the history of the port at Port Orford was taken from the article "History of the Port of Port Orford Dock" on the Port of Port Orford website and from questions submitted via email to Steve Courtier, the port's manager. Population figures and other economic data can be found in the article "Stats on Port Orford" on the City of Port Orford's website.

Background information about the West Coast groundfish fishery comes from *Responses to the West Coast Groundfish Disaster: Lessons Learned for Communities and Decision Makers*, a report by Wesley Shaw and Flaxen Conway at Oregon State University, and from the National Oceanic and Atmospheric Administration reports *2015 Update for the West Coast Catch Shares Program* and *Economic Data Collection Program* by Steiner, Pfeiffer, Harley, Guldin, and Lee. Michael Milstein, public affairs officer for NOAA in the West Coast Region, was instrumental in translating the bycatch and lease data found within and providing landing data for Pacific whiting for 2015.

Information about industry sustainability was found on the Marine Stewardship Council's website and in the organization's press release "U.S. West Coast Groundfish Achieves MSC Certification."

An interview with chef Kali Fieger in October 2015 informed the passage about the quality distinction between trawl-caught and line-caught sablefish. Leesa Cobb, executive director of the Port Orford Ocean Resource Team, also provided details about the rockfish conservation area and early program implementation. Details about hardships affecting groundfish trawlers in the catch-share program are drawn from the author's 2014 reporting for *Oregon Business Magazine* for which the author interviewed dozens of fishermen and community leaders in Newport, Oregon.

A federal judge's remarks on the program, in dismissing the lawsuit that sought to disband it, come from "Order Granting Federal Defendants' Motion for Summary Judgment and Denying Plaintiffs' Motion for Summary Judgment" in the case of *Pacific Coast Federation of Fisher-*

men's Association, et al. v. Gary Locke, et al. in the United States District Court for the Northern District of Columbia.

CHAPTER 8

The Walton family's visit to Galveston, Texas, was described by Buddy Guindon in an interview with the author there in 2013. Details were clarified in subsequent phone interviews through 2016. Photographs of Guindon from the in-person interview were used to recall his outfit. Figures estimating the size of the Walton fortune are from the "America's Richest Families" 2015 rankings by *Forbes* and from the *Politifact* article "Just How Wealthy Is the Wal-Mart Walton Family?" by Tom Kertscher.

The Walton Family Foundation's support for catch shares was quantified by using the foundation's own grants and financial reports, listed on its website. Support for catch shares from the Gordon and Betty Moore Foundation was similarly quantified using that foundation's online reports. Quotes from Teresa Ish, the Walton Family Foundation's marine program officer, derive from an interview with her in December 2015. Google Maps and related street views were used to describe the Bentonville offices. The purpose of the Bentonville office of the Environmental Defense Fund is detailed on its website.

Specifics of the conservation measures at Gulf Wild derive from the Guindon interviews and the YouTube video "SeaWeb's Ocean Voices TJ Tate of Gulf Wild." The video features T. J. Tate, Gulf Wild's sustainability director, describing those efforts in 2014.

Interviews in January 2016 with Lee Crockett, the former executive director of the Marine Fish Conservation Network who is now the US director of oceans at Pew Charitable Trusts, informed the section about the rift between the network and the Environmental Defense Fund in 2000. Interviews in December 2015 with Mark Spalding, president of the Ocean Foundation, and Phil Kline, now a senior oceans campaigner at Greenpeace, augmented the section, as did an interview with Angel Braestrup, executive director of the Curtis & Edith Munson Foundation, in December 2015. Braestrup provided critical background on the US tobacco quota program. Details of its dissolution come from the article "Tobacco Quota Buyout" by Kelly Tiller at the Agricultural Policy Analysis Center in Knoxville, Tennessee.

The analysis of early funding provided to the EDF in support of catch shares comes from the report *A New England Dilemma: Thinking Sectors Through* by Seth Macinko and William Whitmore from the Department of Marine Affairs at the University of Rhode Island.

David Festa's work history was sourced from his LinkedIn page and from biographical information found in the EDF's web archives and past web posts regarding Festa, located on the Way Back Machine. Science in support of catch shares comes from the EDF, specifically the report *Catch Shares Benefit Fishermen and the Environment: A Scientific Compendium*. Timothy Essington at the University of Washington clarified the role of catch shares in improving the nation's fisheries in his study *Catch Shares Improve Consistency, Not Health, of Fisheries*. An overview of the study in the Lenfest Ocean Program Research Series in December 2009 was helpful in accessing the work.

Social science on catch shares noted in this chapter can be found in the study *Fisheries Privatization and the Remaking of Fishery Systems* by Courtney Carothers and Catherine Chambers at the School of Fisheries and Marine Science at the University of Alaska and in the study *Creeping Enclosure, Cumulative Effects and the Marine Commons of New Jersey* by Murray, Johnson, McCay, Danko, Martin, and Takahasi. Information about how the 2006 Magnuson-Stevens Act Reauthorization affected conservation was taken from the report *Magnuson-Stevens Fishery Conservation and Management Reauthorization Act of 2006: An*

Overview by the National Oceanic and Atmospheric Administration, Fisheries Service.

The EDF's Catch Share Design Center is today called the Fishery Solutions Center. Information about the facility came from its website and from an interview with Kate Bonzon, its senior director, in August 2013. Background on Jane Lubchenco came from the Oregon State University website, the article "Our Board of Trustees" on the EDF's website, and an interview with Lubchenco in March 2014. The catch-share policy she spearheaded is available on the National Marine Fisheries Service website.

Opposition to catch shares in the European Union was led by Client Earth. Materials from its campaign are available on the Client Earth website, specifically the article "Reforming the European Common Fisheries Policy." Food and Water Watch has produced several studies examining the effect of catch shares, available on its website, that clarify the organization's position. The Ocean Foundation's article "Catch Shares Not the Silver Bullet They Hoped For" is on its website and explains that organization's position on catch shares, along with accompanying reference materials.

CHAPTER 9

This chapter was substantially informed by the author's 2013 reporting on the halibut industry for both *High Country News* and *Seattle Weekly*. Scenes from Kake and Petersburg, Alaska, derive from visits to both towns in May 2012 and a return trip to Kake in June 2015. Geographical detail comes from nautical maps developed by the National Oceanic and Atmospheric Administration's Office of Coast Survey.

Summaries of the marine services offered in Kake and Petersburg come from the author's observations; the Petersburg, Alaska, Economic

Development Council; interviews with officials at and/or the websites for Icicle Seafoods, Trident Seafoods, and Ocean Beauty in Petersburg; and interviews with the former administrator of the Kake cold storage facility.

General information about the Tlingit clans and moieties was sourced from the Tlingit People website at http://thetlingitpeople.weebly .com/index.html and from the essay "Alaskan Tlingit and Tsimshian" by Jay Miller, which was found in the University of Washington Libraries' digital collection online. More specific details about the subsistence diet, annual harvest, and recipes of Tlingit people come from Pauline Duncan's book *Tlingit Recipes of Today and Long Ago* and from the United States Forest Service report *Haa Atxaayi Haa Kusteeyix Sitee, Our Food Is Our Tlingit Way of Life: Excerpts from Oral Interviews* by Richard Newton with Madonna Moss. Hunting and subsistence traditions were also described to the author by Adam Davis, community and economic development specialist for the Organized Village of Kake, and Rudy Bean, Kake's city administrator, in interviews in June 2015.

Longtime Kake resident Marvin Kadake also provided historical detail about the community of Kake in an interview in June 2015. Additional historical detail comes from the State of Alaska's Community Database, assembled by its Department of Commerce, Community, and Economic Development in its Division of Regional Affairs. Other facts come from the University of Alaska publication *Kake Day Keezx Yakyeeyi* by Pulu, Jackson, Jackson, Gordon, Dominicks, Strang, and Copsey, available through the university's Materials Development Center, Rural Education section. This latter document was made available to the author at the Kettleson Memorial Library in Sitka, Alaska. Bob Mills, president and CEO of the Kake Tribal Corporation, provided additional historical detail about Kake's fishing industry in interviews in June 2015 and again in January

2016. Historical information about the Kake Cannery comes from a National Park Service National Historic Landmark Survey in March 1998.

Adam Davis also provided important insight into the Kake community's cultural loss and the revitalization of its subsistence culture. Bob Mills provided details of Kake's projected economic rebound and related planning.

All data on the loss of halibut quota ownership among native communities in rural Alaska was sourced from NOAA's Fisheries Service *Report on Holdings of Individual Fishing Quota (IFQ) by Residents of Selected Gulf of Alaska Fishing Communities 1995–2014.*

CHAPTER 10

Jason De La Cruz's story came from De La Cruz himself through a series of interviews that began in person in Madeira Beach in May 2013 and continued by phone until April 2016. Buddy Guindon added details about the seafood supply chain, as did Michael Clayton, the consultant and CEO of Trace and Trust, in an interview in January 2016. The Oceana study dubbed *Oceana Study Reveals Seafood Fraud Nationwide* was sourced to highlight problems in the seafood supply chain.

Details of David Festa's presentation to the Milken Institute came from a transcript of the talk, called "Innovative Funding for Sustainable Fisheries and Oceans," available through the Federal News Service, and the accompanying presentation slides. The description of the hotel was taken from event photos and from the "Meetings and Events" brochure offered by the Beverly Hilton in Los Angeles. Attendees and testimonials for the Milken Institute Global Conference 2009 are available on the Milken Institute website. The timing of the talk, as it relates to Festa's service on the Obama transition team, is sourced from his LinkedIn page. Larry Band's biographical information is sourced from SeaWeb's speaker bios from its 2006 Seafood Choices Alliance event in Boston.

The scenes from Intrafish were reported on location at the Roosevelt Hotel in New York on May 28, 2015. The panel discussion featuring Glenn Cooke was called "How, Where and Why?" Facts about the dire state of protein production were verified in the United Nations Environment Programme report *Assessing Global Land Use: Balancing Consumption with Sustainable Supply*. Seafood deals leading up to the event were sourced from Dow Jones & Company, specifically the articles "Bregal Partners Backs Recap for American Seafoods to Reduce Debt" by Laura Kreutzer; "Tuna Brands Could Merge After Thai Union Deal" by Ben Pietro; and the staff report "Paine & Partners Is More than Halfway to Fund IV's $850M Goal."

Information about the 50in10 initiative came from an interview with Megan Arneson, its acting executive director, in December 2015 and from the 50in10 website. Additional detail was sourced from Hal Hamilton's article "50% in 10 Years: A New Global Collaboration to Restore Fisheries" in *The Guardian* and from the World Bank presentation "What Is the Global Partnership for Oceans and Why and How Can the Fisheries Stakeholders Be Engaged" by James L. Anderson and Michael Arbuckle. The Global Partnership for Ocean's blueprint for financing the worldwide transition to catch shares is detailed the report *Towards Investment in Sustainable Fisheries. A Framework for Financing the Transition*, compiled for the Environmental Defense Fund, the Prince of Wales's International Sustainability Unit, and 50in10 by Larry Band and Justin Mundy.

Work in Belize is detailed in the article "Case Study: Collective Impact of Managed Access Program Puts Belize Fisheries on Path to Recovery" on the 50in10 website, and was verified with Megan Arneson. The EDF describes its work in that country, and in others, on its website in the article "How to Turn around the Overfishing Crisis."

Information about countries targeted by the Walton Family Foundation comes from an interview with Teresa Ish, its marine program officer, in December 2015. The Bloomberg Philanthropies' article "Investing in Sustainable Global Fisheries: Going from Theory to Practice" describes that organization's catch-share work in Chile, Brazil, and the Philippines in partnership with the Rockefeller Foundation.

CHAPTER 11

The narrative in chapter 11 was derived from police records containing synopses of translated DVD interviews with forty-four surviving crewmen and officers of the *Oyang 70*. The records were submitted to the Coroner's Court at Wellington, New Zealand, for an inquiry into the deaths of three people aboard. They were obtained by the author through the Official Information Act of New Zealand with the assistance of Max Towle, a New Zealand journalist. Translator Ani Kartikasari helped to develop pseudonyms for the crewmen to protect their confidentiality and safety.

Assembling these documents into a uniform narrative of the boat's sinking was a labor-intensive endeavor that was undertaken the following way: Each synopsis was accompanied by a series of diagrammed ship maps detailing each crewman's activities during the ship's sinking. The maps were used to divide the events of the *Oyang 70*'s sinking into decks, and then into areas of those decks. Once a narrative emerged from each area of the boat, those stories were organized along a uniform timeline by matching key events across all decks, specifically: the slide of the boat to port, the infiltration of water into the engine room, the final failure of the engine, the failing of the lights, the intercom announcement calling the crew to the deck, and the evacuation itself. The resulting tale focuses on Parmin because of where he was standing. His post on the deck during the *Oyang 70*'s sinking provided him with a vantage point that no other crewman or officer shared. Because all the firsthand detail related to the boat's sinking derived from summaries of translations, no quotes were used. In addition to the narrative these documents provided, they also revealed key insights into the working conditions and upkeep of the *Oyang 70*, as well as the temperament of its captain, the ship's divisive racial culture, and its food supplies.

Details about the boat's location at the time of its sinking, the size of the haul in its net, the function of the water pumps aboard the boat, the weight of its load and balance of that weight, crew training, and the height of the water on the factory deck when its workers abandoned it were developed by experts for the coroner's inquest. These details were sourced from the inquest report *In the Matter of an Inquiry into the Death of Yuniarto, Heru; Samsuri and Taefur*, which was compiled for hearings that began April 16, 2012, in the Coroner's Court at Wellington.

The age of those who died in the accident is known through exhibit 1 to the coroner's inquest, which was a crew list of the *Oyang 70* that was compiled before the ship left Port Chalmers. It, too, was obtained through the Official Information Act of New Zealand with the assistance of Max Towle. The ages of the surviving crewmen and officers were redacted. Additional photo exhibits were used to describe the *Oyang 70*, the rescue operation, and the area where the rescue occurred.

Information about how crews aboard the *Oyang 70* were hired and paid, by whom and from where, as well as the treatment of those crews aboard foreign-flagged vessels and of their families comes from the research article "Not in New Zealand's Waters, Surely? Linking Labour Issues to GPNs" by Stringer, Simmons, Coulston, and Whittaker. The research provided significant detail on past desertions from foreign-flagged vessels in New Zealand and some detail of previous efforts to address working conditions aboard foreign-flagged ships. Christina Stringer provided additional facts about those efforts, and about the marketplace that drove such conditions aboard the ships, in a Skype interview with the author in September 2015.

A subsequent inquiry into foreign-flagged ships in New Zealand by the New Zealand Ministry of Agriculture and Fishery was summarized in the document *Report of the Ministerial Inquiry into the Use and Operation of Foreign Charter Vessels*. The report was used to source detail about the size of the southern blue whiting harvest, the number of owners in the program, the number of corporations leasing access, the number of boats, how many of them were foreign flagged, the age of the *Oyang 70*, export data, and recommendations for change. Additional fishery data for southern blue whiting comes from the Ministry for Primary Industries website.

Detail on US imports comes from the *Fisheries of the United States 2010* report by the National Marine Fisheries Service. Facts about the southern blue whiting's sustainability certification come from the Marine Stewardship Council website. The press releases announcing certification came from the Deepwater Group website. The news was reported by *The Fish Site* and *Seafood New Zealand*.

Information about the legal aftermath of the *Oyang 70*'s sinking, as well as the implementation of reforms, comes from a November 2015 Skype interview with Craig Tuck, an attorney and the founder of Slave Free Seas, and subsequent email correspondence. Additional detail comes from email correspondence with Karen Harding, attorney for the *Oyang 70* crew, beginning in January 2016, and with Christina Stringer. Reporting by Michael Field, specifically the article "Fishing Company Faked Documents," published on the New Zealand news website Stuff, and the *Radio New Zealand* article "Former Oyang Crew in Legal Battle," were also used to describe the incident's aftermath.

CHAPTER 12

Chapter 12 was reported on location in Madeira Beach, Florida, in 2013, during the period in which Wild Seafood was becoming stiff competition for the area's fish houses. Subsequent phone interviews with Jason

De La Cruz informed the writing. In addition to the sources quoted within the chapter, reportage derived from interviews conducted on the docks and at fish houses and restaurants between Cortez and Tarpon Springs, Florida, in May 2013. The comparison between industrial agriculture and catch-share programs comes from the Food & Water Watch report *Fish, Inc.: The Privatization of U.S. Fisheries through Catch Share Programs*. Demographic data for Madeira Beach, Florida, was sourced from the website USA City Facts.

CHAPTER 13

The narrative inside the Sea Watch processing facility in New Bedford, Massachusetts, was compiled on location. No cameras were allowed, so details of the facility's processes and interior come from audio recordings of John Miller, Sea Watch's vice president in charge of operations, as he describes them and from drawings sketched by the author while inside in June 2015.

New Bedford's status as the scallop capital of the nation is a regular refrain, and was confirmed using Neil Ramsden's article "Scallop Industry Awaits Price Impact of US Catch Quota Cut" in *Undercurrent News*. Information about the product markets for surf clams and quahogs, and the number of companies processing the mollusks, came from interviews with Tom Alspach, an attorney for Sea Watch International, between December 2013 and April 2016, from John Miller, and from a Mid-Atlantic Fishery Management Council memorandum detailing those facts dated May 27, 2015. The figure for how much was paid to purchase clams and quahogs in 2014, as well as slumping harvests and competition from imports, also derives from the memo. Alspach provided details about the industry's history of consolidation and Sea Watch International's holdings and lease arrangements.

Similar information for Snow's was provided by Chris Lischewski, CEO of Bumble Bee Seafoods, in an email exchange with the author beginning in December 2013. Lischewski also provided information about his own US citizenship and that of the company's board of directors. Details of the Snow's facility, product information, quahog holdings, and year of acquisition by Bumble Bee Seafoods comes from the company's website. Additional historical detail about the industry was sourced from the report *Recommendations for Excessive-Share Limits in the Surfclam and Ocean Quahog Fisheries* for Compass Lexecon by Mitchell, Peterson, and Willig.

Facts about the deal in which Lion Capital and Centre Partners acquired Bumble Bee Seafoods came from the Centre Partners press release "Centre Partners Completes $980 Million Sale of Bumble Bee Foods to Lion Capital" and the Bumble Bee press release "Bumble Bee Seafoods Announces Completion of Acquisition by Lion Capital."

Data on ownership of surf clams and quahogs came from the Greater Atlantic Region of the National Marine Fisheries Service, specifically the datasets *2015 Initial Surf Clam Allocations* and *2015 Initial Quahog Allocations*.

The author's understanding of data collection methods on ownership by the Greater Atlantic Region of the National Marine Fisheries Service came from interviews with council staff Jessica Coakley in December 2015 and José L. Montañez in December 2013; and from the National Marine Fisheries Service, Greater Atlantic Region Greater Atlantic Region Bulletin *Atlantic Surfclam and Ocean Quahog Information Collection Program Requirements*. Context for these regulations was clarified by Lee Anderson, vice chair of the Mid-Atlantic Fishery Management Council, in interviews in December 2013. The US General Accounting Office report on foreign ownership of US seafood, *Individual Fishing Quotas Better Information Could Improve Program Management*, included detail about data collection on ownership.

Susanne Rust's article for the Center for Investigative Reporting, "System Turns US Fishing Rights into Commodity, Squeezes Small

Fishermen," supplied information about Maruha Nichiro and Nippon Suisan Kaisha ownership of Bering Sea Crab. The 2009 golden tilefish rules are spelled out in the Environmental Defense Fund report *Catch Shares in Action—United States Mid-Atlantic Golden Tilefish Individual Fishing Quota Program* by Sarah E. Poon with José L. Montañez.

Facts about the Sea Watch clam cook-off come from staff reporting at *Undercurrent News*, specifically the article "Sea Watch Names Winner of Creative Clam Challenge" and James Wright's article "Gould Wins Sea Watch International's Creative Clam Challenge" for *Seafood Source*.

Information about lobbying for 20 percent ownership caps in New England groundfish came from the Northwest Atlantic Marine Alliance and specifically from the press releases "Fishermen Walk Out and Tell Policy-Makers: The System Is Broken" and "New England's Community-Based Fishermen and Supporters to Demonstrate against Corporate Consolidation and Inaction by Fisheries Policy Makers" by Brett Tolley and Leigh Belanger. Jason Smith's article "Pacific Seafood Sues Government Calling Fishery Quota Restrictions Illegal" for *Undercurrent News* provided details about the lawsuit to bust West Coast groundfish caps.

CHAPTER 14

The description of RM Seafood, its food, and the articles outside the bathroom wall were reported on location in January 2014. Rick Moonen was interviewed the following month and provided information about his background, sustainable seafood philosophy, belief in catch shares, seafood sourcing preferences, and activities on Capitol Hill. Additional biographical information about Moonen was sourced from the RM Seafood website and from the James Beard Foundation website.

The dates of Harry Reid's tenure as majority leader came from the

US Senate website, specifically the article "Majority and Minority Leaders and Party Whips." Details of the Magnuson Stevens Reauthorization activities come from the National Oceanic and Atmospheric Administration Fisheries website, specifically the section "Magnuson-Stevens Act—Ongoing Reauthorization Activities." Facts about Slade Gorton come from the *Biographical Directory of the United States Congress*. Similar biographical information about Bruce Babbitt comes from the article "Bruce Babbitt, Interior Secretary" in the online archives of *The Washington Post*. Biographical facts about Jane Lubchenco were sourced from the Oregon State University website, the David Steves article "Jane Lubchenco's Teachable Moment as NOAA Head" for *Oregon Public Broadcasting*, and her research with colleagues, specifically the journal articles "Science in Support of the Deepwater Horizon Response" and "Predicting and Managing Extreme Weather Events." Her resignation announcement was reported on by Emily Yehle and Allison Winter in the article "Lubchenco Announces Resignation, Spurs Talk about Who'll Replace Her" for *Greenwire*.

The author's understanding of the political climate on Capitol Hill in 2013 derives from interviews with Rick Marks, a lobbyist for the Southern Offshore Fishing Association, in March 2013; Bob Vanasse, the executive director of *Saving Seafood*, in January 2016; chef Richard Garcia in 2013; Buddy Guindon between May 2013 and April 2016; the 2014 interview with Moonen; and from background interviews. Phil Kline, a senior oceans campaigner for Greenpeace, provided insights into the Marine Fish Conservation Network's position on the Magnuson-Stevens Act in 2013 through interviews with the author that began in December 2015. Details on the provisions of the act came from reading it. Information about spending on lobbying activities during this time came from querying the Lobbying Disclosure Act Database.

Facts about NOAA's approach to catch shares come from the *NOAA Catch Share Policy Executive Summary* and a version of the map *Catch Share Programs by Region,* which shows that the agency was once targeting thirty-two additional catch-share programs. The PowerPoint presentations "NOAA Catch Share Policy: Next Steps" from May 2010; "Council Coordination Committee Meeting" by Gary Reisner, CFO/CAO, in May 2011; and "FY2011 Status: A Briefing to MAFAC" by Reisner in October 2010 provided some financial detail about requests and awards for catch-share implementation funds. Katherine Brogan, media relations specialist at NOAA, provided the remaining catch-share funding figures in an email to the author in February 2016.

Details about the congressional reception featuring Moonen's cooking in February 2013 come from the Environmental Defense Fund flyer titled "Please Join Top Chef Masters Finalist Rick Moonen," available on its website. They also come from the press release "Fishermen and Chefs Unify over Sustainable Fishing" by Matt Smelser and from the follow-up article "Fishermen and Chefs United: Keep Catch Shares on the Table" by Matt Rand, both on the EDF website.

Information about Buddy Guindon's lawsuit against the federal government comes from the case *Guindon v. Pritzker* filed in the District of Columbia. Details about fishermen's request for catch shares in the South Atlantic comes from the article "Catch Shares Schemes Rise from the Dead in South Atlantic" on the Coastal Conservation Association website. Facts about the Gulf of Alaska (GOA) Rockfish Program come from the North Pacific Fishery Management Council's website.

CHAPTER 15

The narrative in chapter 15 was reported aboard the *Lester F. Eldredge* in June 2015 and through interviews with Shannon Eldredge aboard the vessel and in subsequent email correspondence. An initial interview with Eldredge was conducted in Chatham, Massachusetts, in June 2013.

Historical facts about weir fishing come from Allen Lutins's master's thesis, "Prehistoric Fishweirs in Eastern North America," available on his website. The statistics on catch shares come from the Environmental Defense Fund map "Catch Shares around the World," which the Property and Environment Research Center has on its website.

The scene at Terra Madre was reported through interviews with Eldredge, a September 2015 interview with Brett Tolley, a community organizer for the Northwest Atlantic Marine Alliance, and a December 2015 interview with Michele Mesmain, who was the convener of fishers at the conference. Details of Seth Macinko's talk were reported from the YouTube video of a similar speech, called "Seth Macinko—Challenges Facing Small-Scale Fisheries" and posted by the World Forum of Fisher Peoples.

The Environmental Defense Fund describes its work abroad on its website in the article "How to Turn around the Overfishing Crisis." Information about countries targeted by the Walton Family Foundation comes from an interview with Teresa Ish, its marine program officer, in December 2015. The Bloomberg Philanthropies' article "Investing in Sustainable Global Fisheries: Going from Theory to Practice" describes that organization's catch-share work abroad in partnership with the Rockefeller Foundation. Additional facts about the World Bank's Global Partnership for the Oceans comes from the World Bank Presentation by James L. Anderson and Michael Arbuckle, "What Is the Global Partnership for Oceans and Why and How Can the Fisheries Stakeholders Be Engaged." Details of the status of those efforts come from an interview with Megan Arneson, acting executive director of the 50in10 initiative, in December 2015.

Ownership data on the abalone fishery comes from the research of Seth Macinko, specifically comments that he made during meetings about renewing Community Fishing Policy in the European Union at the Danish Parliament building in August 2013. The comments were reported in *Fishermen's Voice*, in the article "Shifts of Fishing Access Criticized at Danish Conference." Information about Chilean protests over privatization of that country's fisheries comes from David Dougherty's news report *The Privatization of Chile's Sea* on the Real News Network. The description of issues in Icelandic fisheries is sourced from the reporting of Paul Fontaine in the *Reykjavik Grapevine*, specifically the article "Iceland Struggles to Settle the Fishing Quota Dispute," and from the article "Controversial Tax on Fisheries Profits in Iceland: An Improvement to the Fisheries Management System?" on the *Normer* website.

Facts about Elinor Ostrom come from the Nobel Prize website and from a post-mortem article highlighting her achievements in *The Economist*, titled "Elinor Ostrom, Defender of the Commons, Died on June 12, Aged 78." The amount of fisheries assistance given to New England fishers during the cod crash comes from a February 2014 press release from David Cicilline, the Rhode Island congressman, titled "New England Fishermen to Receive Nearly $33 Million in Federal Disaster Assistance."

CHAPTER 16

The scene at the dock is a composite of the author's own observation on location in May 2013 and of biologist Lew Bullock's work, observed via FaceTime, in January 2016. Those observations were combined with interviews and email correspondence with Bullock between January 2016 and April 2016 and with Jason De La Cruz between May 2013 and April 2016. The scene was written as a composite to accommodate fish number 5089301, which set the design standard for the Gulf Wild tracking system. The number still works in the Track Your Fish feature on the Gulf Wild website.

Details of the Environmental Defense Fund's 2016 seafood campaign come from the article "12 Fish You've Probably Never Heard Of but Should Eat" on the organization's website. EDF provides next steps in its catch-share campaign, including information about the twelve countries it now targets, on its website, specifically in the articles "How to Turn around the Overfishing Crisis" and "A Sustainable, Global Food Supply Is Within Reach. Here's Why." Information about the Walton Family Foundation's efforts to remake ocean policy around the world comes from a December 2015 interview with Teresa Ish, the foundation's marine program officer.

Facts about catch-share–related lawsuits around the world, and the decision by some countries to retool catch-share programs to mitigate downsides, come from the University of Alaska study *Fisheries Privatization and the Remaking of Fishery Systems* by Courtney Carothers and Catherine Chambers.

Buddy Guindon's next steps as an advocate come from Guindon himself, via the interviews listed. His media and appearances were in Episode 25 of the HBO show *Vice* and on the show *Big Fish Texas* on the National Geographic Channel. Use of his image by Kathryn Murdoch can be seen in the YouTube video "Kathryn Murdoch Speaks at the First Annual EAT Stockholm Food Forum." Murdoch's own status as an EDF trustee is available on the Eat Forum website. Guindon also provided information about legislative efforts for catch shares and about Gulf Wild distribution and tagging numbers, as did De La Cruz.

Information about the recovered state of the grouper and red snapper fisheries was taken from the article "Are Our Fisheries Laws Working? Just Ask about Gag Grouper," on the National Oceanic and Atmospheric Administration Fisheries website, and from the red snapper or grouper listings on the Monterey Bay Aquarium's Seafood Watch website. Detail about the Sustainable Fisheries Partnership analysis was sourced from the partnership's website, specifically the timeline found under the heading "GOM Reef Fish."

Lee Crockett, director of US Oceans at Pew Charitable Trusts, provided important perspective on the Magnuson-Stevens Act reauthorization in an interview in January 2016. Information about legislation introduced and its progress in the House and Senate was also tracked on the NOAA Fisheries website on the page "Magnuson-Stevens Act—Ongoing Reauthorization Activities."

CHAPTER 17

Scenes aboard the *Finlander* were reported on location in June 2015 and in subsequent interviews with Tim Rider. The trip was documented in photographs, which were later used to identify clothing. The author was on location at the Saco farmers' market the following day and interviewed Slow Fish advocate Spencer Montgomery for information about the relationship between those advocates and the New England Fish Mongers.

Details about Slow Fish come from an interview with its convener, Michèle Mesmain, in December 2015. Additional information about the Slow Fish conference in New Orleans was found on the Slow Fish 2016 website.

Information about the "Who Fishes Matters" campaign comes from the Northwest Atlantic Marine Alliance, and specifically from the press releases "Fishermen Walk Out and Tell Policy-Makers: The System Is Broken" and "New England's Community-Based Fishermen and Supporters to Demonstrate against Corporate Consolidation and Inaction by Fisheries Policy Makers" by Brett Tolley and Leigh Belanger. Additional detail was provided in interviews and correspondence with Tolley that began in October 2013.

Facts about the Oregon albacore fishery come from the *Annual*

Oregon Albacore Tuna (Thunnus alalunga) Report, 2015 by Christian Heath at the Oregon Department of Fish and Wildlife, from the Oregon Albacore Commission website, and from an April 2016 interview with its executive director Nancy Fitzpatrick.

INDEX